PUNJAB DIVIDED

Politics of the Muslim League and Partition
1935-1947

Punjab Divided

Politics of the Muslim League and Partition 1935-1947

AMARJIT SINGH

KANISHKA PUBLISHERS, DISTRIBUTORS

NEW DELHI-110 002

KANISHKA PUBLISHERS, DISTRIBUTORS
4697/5-21 A, Ansari Road, Daryaganj
New Delhi-110 002
Phones: 327 0497, 328 8285
Fax: 011-328 8285

First Published 2001

ISBN 81-7391-413-3

PRINTED IN INDIA

Published by Madan Sachdeva for Kanishka Publishers, Distributors, 4697/5-21 A, Ansari Road, Daryaganj, New Delhi 110 002; Lasertypeset by Heart Data Processing, Delhi, and Printed at Nice Printing Press, Delhi.

Preface

This book is based on my doctoral thesis; The Muslim League and Punjab Politics: 1935-1947, submitted to the Kurukshetra University, Kurukshetra in 1998. This is an attempt to explore the role of Muslim League in Punjab politics, how it influenced and shaped the provincial politics in its most turbulent years through its transformation from a narrowly based, essentially an urban party to mass based instrument of political mobilization and realization of specific political goals. By all accounts, it was a remarkable achievement for very few political formations could achieve so much in such a short period of time. Moreover efforts have been made in this work to apportion the responsibility for the partition on the role played by Muslim League in the Punjab i.e. in the heartland of future Pakistan.

The partition of Punjab and the creation of Pakistan was not only a significant event in the historiography of Indian freedom movement against the British Raj but it also added an important chapter in the annals of modern history. Although the Punjab was a Muslim majority province but for a long time its politics was controlled by and dominated by the Unionist party which had maintained an inter-communal character. The Unionist party had occupied a large political space so much so that it articulated even the partisan Muslim interests under a centralist secular umbrella organization. This marginalized the Muslim League, for a long time, in the provincial politics since it had not much role left under such a dispensation. As a result, during the 1930s, the Punjab Muslim League had little political stature and virtually no following nor any organizational structure.

In the provincial Legislative elections of 1937, the Punjab Muslim League bagged only two seats in a house of 175 in comparison to the 95 seats of the Unionist party. This marked the beginning of the adoption of new strategies, techniques and programmes by the Punjab Muslim League in order to establish its dominance in the provincial politics. The politics of the province during the decade which preceded partition, in fact, saw a fierce struggle between the Unionist party and the Muslim League in order to establish their respective hegemony in the provincial politics. However, as late as till 1940 the Muslim league and Muhammad Ali Jinnah, the Sole spokesman of the Muslim India, remained a non-entity in the provincial politics.

The Pakistan Resolution of March 1940 adopted by the All India Muslim League at its Lahore session provided fresh lights to the activities of the Punjab Muslim League. However, it was only after 1942 that the Muslim League began to emerge as a mass based party. By the year 1946 the League positioned itself in the province as the sole champion of Muslim interests and in the provincial Legislative elections of the 1946 the League begged seventy-five seats. Thus, the League was now within a striking distance of achieving its grand goal of Pakistan. What brings about this turn around in the League's fortunes in such a short span of time has been the focus of this study.

A chronological account of political development is central to its historical reconstruction. However, history is not merely a collection of events but, more importantly, a study of interaction between dominant political ideologies and given power structures at a given point of time and space. In this work, the interplay of these elements is articulated, in order to account for political developments of the province between 1935-47. A systematically constructed account of significant events discloses the dominant ideologies of the different political parties. This work also examine the social bases of provincial politics and mobilization strategies applied by the Muslim League and other political parties. The Government of India Act of 1935, provided an essential politico-administrative framework within which the Muslim League and other political parties organized themselves to pursue their respective ends.

History cannot be studied in isolation. Therefore, an attempt has been made, in this work, to know something about the politics of other provincial political parties *vis-a-vis* Muslim League. The elements of national politics which affected the provincial politics have also been studied in detail. Reference has also been made of those international events which profoundly influenced the provincial politics. The attitude of the British Raj and the relationship which existed between the Raj and the Muslim League which in turn affected the politics of the province has also been dwelt in.

A great deal of work has been done on the subject by various scholars. Penderel Moon, *Divide and Quit*; C.H. Philips and M.D. Wainwright (ed.) *The Partition of India: Policies and Perspectives 1935-47*; Peter Hardy, *The Muslims of British India*; M.N. Das, *Partition and Independence of India*; Stanley Wolpert, *Jinnah of Pakistan*; Ayesha Jalal, *The Sole Spokesman: Jinnah, the Muslim League and the Demand for Pakistan*; Raj Mohan Gandhi, *Understanding the Muslim Mind*; Anita Inder Singh, *The Origins of the Partition of India 1936-1947*; Farzana Shaikh, *Community and Consensus in Islam* and Mushirul Hasan (ed.), *India's Partition: Process, Strategy and Mobilization* are some important works which have discussed at length the growth of Muslim League in Indian politics and the interplay of British, Congress and the Muslim League strategies which culminated in the partition of India. Paul Brass, *Language, Religion and Politics in North India*; Imran Ali, *Punjab Politics in the Decade before Partition*; Prem Choudhary, *Punjab Politics: The Role of Sir Chhotu Ram*; Ian Talbot, *Punjab and the Raj 1849-1947*; David Gilmartin, *Empire and Islam: Punjab and the Making of Pakistan* and Ian Talbot, *Khizar Tiwana: The Punjab Unionist Party and the Partition of India* are some important works which deal with the politics of the Punjab during the decade which preceded partition and growth of the Muslim League in North India and Punjab.

Penderel Moon has held accidents of history responsible for the turn that the provincial politics took. He suggests that the sudden death of Sir Fazl-i-Hussain in 1936 provided a chance to Jinnah to win over the Muslims of Punjab in favour of Muslim League. Peter Hardy argues that Muslim League succeeded in the Punjab by overshadowing the well entrenched

Unionist politicians through more stringent primordial appeals. David Gilmartin suggests that the Muslim League succeeded because of its ability to exploit the factional divisions within the Unionist Party after the death of Sir Sikander Hayat Khan in 1942. He further explains that the *Pirs* and *Sajjada-Nashins*, the erstwhile collaborators of the Unionist in rural Punjab shifted their allegiance to Muslim League since they found its religious appeal closer to their likings which subsequently turned the tide of Punjab politics in favour of the Muslim League. Ian Talbot, on the other hand, argues that the Raj deserted its collaborators, the Unionists, by the close of the Second World War. This, in turn, gave unprecedented impetus to the Muslim League. Prem Choudhary argues that the war time unpopular policies of the Unionist Government and the miseries of the people shifted the balance of Punjab politics towards the Congress and the Muslim League in the south-eastern and western Punjab respectively. Paul Brass suggests that the growth of the Muslim separatism in North India was determined and manipulated by an elite whose interests such politics were designed to serve and whose propaganda based on communal identification was responded to by the Muslims of the North India.

The scope and scholarship of the above mentioned works cannot be faulted. However, there are still some aspects which have escaped the scholarly scrutiny. For example, firstly, the role played by the Punjab Muslim Students Federation for the cause of the Muslim League and Pakistan has not been fully mapped. Secondly, why the rural Muslim elite, hitherto the backbone of the Unionists, defected to the Muslim League, has not been adequately commented upon. Thirdly, the causes of the *Pirs* and *Sajjada-Nashins* shifting their allegiance to the League, has not been properly understood. Fourthly, the impact of the international events, particularly the Second World War and how it contributed to change relationship between the three principal actors in the province i.e. the Raj, the Unionists and the Muslim League, have not been adequately covered. Lastly, the impact of the national politics, particularly the interplay of the Raj, Muslim League and Congress, have not been examined in detail.

The present work is a humble attempt to dwell on the above mentioned aspects and plug these gaps. Efforts have been made to study and critically examine all the available historigraphy on the subject. And, then every attempt has been made to fill up the gaps in our knowledge in the study of this subject on the basis of above mentioned critical scrutiny. Moreover, this work attempts to explain how the Muslim League reached down to the every voter and to an average Punjabi Muslim who held the key to the creation of Pakistan.

This work is based upon mainly primary sources, secondary sources have also been exhaustively dealt upon. Syed Shamsul Hasan collection, S.S. Pirzada's Documents, Punjab Muslim Students Federation's Documents, speeches and writings of M.A. Jinnah and his correspondence with the leaders of the Provincial Muslim League have been studied thoroughly. Other primary sources include government records, Linlithgow Papers, Mountbatten Papers, Private Papers of Indian leaders, Proceedings of the Punjab Legislative Assembly, published Documents of the Muslim League, National and regional newspapers, periodicals and journals. Autobiographies and biographies of contemporary leaders and the twelve volumes of Transfer of Power have also been consulted.

While doing this work I have incurred the debt and gratitude of many people. At the outset I am especially thankful to my supervisor Professor S.C. Mittal, for his helpful guidance, critical suggestions and moreover he helped me to say what I wanted to say. I take this opportunity to express my gratitude to late Professor R.C. Jauhri who has initiated me into the field of research in history and made valuable suggestions on this subject. I owe much to Professor K.C. Yadav for providing me valuable source material on Muslim League and for his useful suggestions on the subject. I am beholden to Professor J.S. Grewal, Professor A.C. Bose, Professor Pardaman Singh, Professor I.H. Siddiqui and Professor Hari Om for giving me an opportunity to discuss my work with them and benefited from their views. I owe thanks to Dr. R.S. Sangwan, my colleague in the department, who read the manuscript of the book and also made useful suggestions. My thanks are due to Sh. Madan Gopal, a contemporary of Sir Khizar Hayat Khan Tiwana, the Premier of Punjab, for sharing his rich experiences of those times with me. I am thankful to my father, Sh. L.D. Girdhar, who has done a great deal of translation work for me which has immensely benefited my research work. I do not have the words to express my gratitude to my friend Sh. Bhupesh Katyal, who has rendered his valuable help at every stage of my work. I am also thankful to Sh. Parveen Kaushik, who drew the maps.

I gratefully acknowledge the help rendered by the staff of the following institutions: The National Archives of India, New Delhi; The Nehru Memorial Museum and Library, New Delhi; The Haryana State Archives, Panchkula; The Punjab State Archives, Patiala; Civil Secretariat Library, Chandigarh; Panjab University Library, Chandigarh; Kurukshetra University Library, Kurukshetra and Department of History Library, Kurukshetra University, Kurukshetra.

I owe thanks to my brother Dr. Samarjeet Singh and my wife Anamika for their cooperation and constant encouragement. I am also thankful to Sh. Madan Sachdeva for the publication of this work.

Kurukshetra
February, 2001

AMARJIT SINGH

Contents

1

Socio-Economic Profile of Punjab

The Punjab of early twentieth century was a great deal bigger than the present day Punjab.[1] It approximately comprised, besides the present Punjab, the Punjab of Pakistan and also two other Indian provinces of Haryana and Himachal Pradesh. It sprawled across 3,54,736.76 sq. kms. and had a population of 2,84,90,857.[2] The Punjab was a landlocked region in the North-West corner of India. Situated between 27°37' and 34°2' N latitude and 69°23' and 74°2'E longitude[3], it had its clearly defined natural boundaries. Along the northern borders of the province, the Himalayan ranges divided it from Tibet and Kashmir. Between these ranges and the Indus, the Hazara district of the North-West Frontier Province completed the northern boundary. On the west, it was separated from the North-West Frontier Province by the Indus. To its south lay Sind, Rajasthan and Mathura districts of United province, while on the east the river Yamuna divided it from the United province and on the north-east the mighty Himalayan range separated it from the Chinese territory.[4] Geophysically, the province was divided into four divisions,[5] namely:

(*i*) The Himalayan Region;
(*ii*) The Sub-Himalayan Region;
(*iii*) The Indo-Gangetic Plains; and
(*iv*) The North-West Dry Area.

The Himalayan Region covered an area of some 55,980

sq. kms,[6] much of which was uninhabited. A few people, who lived here, were settled in tiny hamlets perched on the hill sides, each surrounded by small patches of terraced fields, irrigated by the streams, which ran down every gulley, or by the abundant rainfall of the hills. The nature of the area prevented the growth of large towns. Trade was confined to the little towns situated on the roads that crossed the high passes, which led into Tibet. The chief means of the economy were the yields of the fields and the produces of numerous blocks of sheep and goats.[7]

The sub-Himalayan Region, measuring about 23,310 sq.kms.[8], had by and large, ample rainfall.[9] However, irrigation was almost unknown in this tract.[10] The mountainous tracts of the Murree and Kahuta tehsils of the Rawalpindi district of this tract were approximately close in characteristics to the Himalayan tract, this tràct also include the outlying range of the Shivaliks. The region comprised some of the densely populated portions of the province, like district of Sialkot. The chief means of economy in this region was agricultural and pastoral products,[11] trade and commerce was insignificant.

Then came the Indo-Gangetic plains, the most important region, comprising the western plains, eastern plains, Malwa region and the south-eastern tract known as Hariana. The western and eastern plains were traversed throughout their length by great rivers—the Sutlej, Beas, Ravi and Chenab. Inundation canals had been carried from these rivers, for irrigation purposes. Irrigation from wells was also easily available in these plains, as such, the plains were good in fertility, security of produce and populousness.[12] Trade and commerce was significant in these plains and it had some important and prosperous cities like Gujaranwala, Sheikhupura, Amritsar, Lahore and Jullundur. The central portion of the tract which included the district of Ludhiana was, commonly known as Malwa. It had an average fertility. The rainfall was generally highest and the soil was suitable for the productivity. Well irrigation was practised along the Sutlej and northern border. The opening of the Sirhind canal had greatly altered the agricultural conditions of this part of the province.[13] Later on, the Satluj Valley Project further increases the irrigated area.[14]

Along the southern borders of the eastern plains lay the tract known as Hariana which constituted the most unfertile portion of the area under consideration. A large part of this tract skirted the Rajasthan desert; the soil was inferior; the rainfall scanty and precarious, irrigation was unknown in this part except in the south-eastern corner, where well could be profitably worked.[15] The region had suffered most severely in famine years, but much of it was later protected by the construction of the Sirhind canal and the Sirsa branch of the Western Yamuna Canal.[16]

The fourth region, i.e. the North-West Dry area, comprised the districts of Shahpur, Mianwali, Montegomery, Lyalpur, Jhang, Multan, Muzzafargarh and Dera Ghazi Khan. Earlier, it was mostly a vast expanse of arid waste and the haunt of pastoral people, but after the coming of the canals, it claims to be one of the biggest granaries of the world.[17] The average rainfall for the region was 22.86 cms.[18] Trade, commerce and manufacturing was significant in this region. To carry the surplus produce of the region to the port for export three of railway lines had been constructed and so great was the traffic that from their point of convergence in the west a double track to Karanchi was provided.[19] The region was the most wealthy and populous portion of the province.

In the early twentieth century, administratively, the province was divided into five divisions, 29 districts, 106 tehsils, 177 towns and 34,630 villages[20] as Table 1.1 shows. Each division was under the charge of a commissioner, each district was administered by a deputy commissioner, who was aided by upto five extra assistant commissioners.[21] Beneath the district were *tehsils* which were under the charge of *tehsildars* and *naib-tehsildars* who held revenue and judicial powers. Then came the *zails*, each comprising 10 to 30 villages and under the control of a *zaildar*.[22] The institution of the *zaildar* was in fact unique to the Punjab's local administration. It reflected the importance which the British attached to securing the support of the rural notables. The *zaildar* supervised the village headmen (lambardars) and acted as an honorary police officer incharge of the village police. The natural division and district-wise boundary of the Punjab, 1931 is shown in Map 1.1.

Map 1.1: Natural Divisions, Punjab, 1931

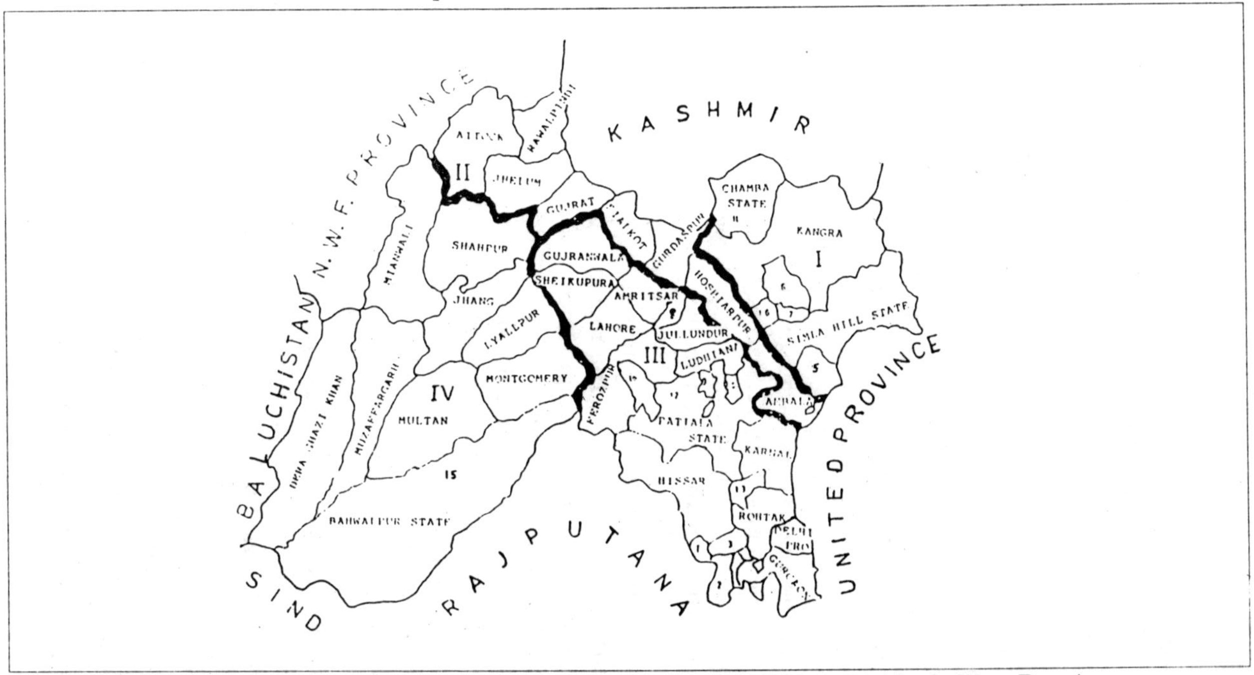

I. Himalayan Region, II. Sub Himalayan Region, III. Indo Gangetic Plains, IV. North West Dry Area
Punjab States are Indicated by Arabic Numbers.
Source: The Census of India, Punjab, 1931, Vol. XVII, Part-I, 1931, Lahore, 1933, p. 2.

Table 1.1
Administrative Divisions, Area Population[23]

Division/ District	*Area Sq. Kms.*	*Number of Towns*	*Number of Village*	*Population*	*Tehsil*
1	2	3	4	5	6
Ambala Division					
Hisar	13,502	6	963	8,99,479	Hisar,Hansi,Bhiwani, Fatehabad, Sirsa
Rohtak	6,400	7	722	8,05,621	Rohtak,Gohana, Jhajhar, Sonepat
Gurgaon	5,861	8	1,358	7,40,163	Gurgaon, Nuh Ferozpur-Jhirka, Ballabhgarh,Palwal
Karnal	8,094	6	1,380	8,52,614	Karnal,Panipat Kaithal,Thanesar
Ambala	4,874	8	1,723	7,42,902	Ambala,Kharar, Jagadhari,Ropar, Naraingarh
Simla	261	5	202	36,786	Simla, Kotkhai
Total	38,922	40	6,348	40,77,565	
Jullundur Division					
Kangra	25,838	1	713	8,01,312	Kangra, Kullu, Nurpur,Hamirpur Palampur
Hoshiarpur	5,820	6	2,099	10,32,187	Hoshiarpur, Dasuya, Una,Garh Shankar
Jullundur	3,707	8	1,210	9,43,721	Jullundur, Nawanshahar, Phillaur,Nakodar
Ludhiana	3,761	4	851	6,72,494	Ludhiana,Jagraon, Samrala
Ferozepur	11,111	10	1,507	11,56,732	Firozepur, Zira, Moga, Muktsar. Fazilka
Total	50,236	29	6,380	46,06,446	

1	2	3	4	5	6
Lahore Division					
Lahore	6,946	8	1,121	13,78,570	Lahore, Kasur, Chunian
Amritsar	4,126	5	1,036	11,17,120	Amritsar, Taran Taran, Ajnala
Gurdaspur	4,983	9	2,243	9,70,898	Gurdaspur, Batala, Pathankot, Shankargarh
Sialkot	4,087	6	2,066	9,79,617	Sialkot,Darka Pasrur,Narowal
Gujaranwala	5,980	7	1,219	7,36,138	Gujranwala, Wazirabad, Hafizabad
Sheikhupura	5,968	5	1,031	6,96,732	Sheikhupura, Nankana Sahib, Shahadra
Total	31,994	40	8,716	58,79,075	
Rawalpindi Division					
Gujrat	5,826	5	1,440	9,22,427	Gujrat,Phalia, Khariam
Shahpur	12,404	13	973	8,21,490	Shahpur,Khushab, Bhalwal, Sargodha
Jhelum	7,182	4	884	5,41,076	Jhelum,Pindadan, Khan,Chakwal
Rawalpindi	5,776	2	1,170	6,34,357	Rawalpindi, Gujjarkhan, Murree,Kahuta
Attock	10,663	7	615	5,38,960	Attock,Pindigheb, Talagang, Fatehganj
Mianwali	1,397	4	398	4,11,539	Mianwali, Bhakkar, Isa-Khel
Total	21,347	35	5,480	39,14,849	

1	2	3	4	5	6
Multan Division					
Montgomery	11,702	4	1,958	9,99,772	Montegomery, Okara,Dipalpur, Pakpattan
Lyallpur	8,350	6	1,241	11,51,351	Lyallpur,Samundri Toba Tek Singh, Jaranwala
Multan	15,260	3	1,916	11,74,900	Multan,Shujabad, Lodhran,Mailsi, Khanewal, Kabirwala
Jhang	8,941	5	981	6,64,833	Jhang,Chiniot, Shorkot
Muzafargarh	15,764	6	862	5,91,375	Muzaffargarh, Alipur,Kot, Adu, Leiah
Dera Ghazi Khan	13,792	9	739	4,91,044	Dera Ghazi Khan, Jamb, Sanghar, Rajanpur
Bilochtrans Frontier Tract	6,698	—	9	29,642	Bilock Trans-Frontier Track
Total	80,467	33	7,706	51,02,917	
Grand Total	2,56,928	177	34,630	2,55,80,852	

The above discussion indicates that nature was very kind to Punjab. Its vast fertile plains, rich alluvial soil, perennial rivers, other resources and modern canal system created by the British helped to have rich productions.[24] The rich geo-economic conditions of the province and the well maintained administrative system further added to the population of the province. Hence, the density of the population was also high. The high density of the population in Punjab, with regional variations, is shown in Table 1.2.

Table 1.2

Density of Population in 1931[25]

Division	*Area in Sq.Kms.*	*Population*	*Density per sq.km.*
Ambala	38,884	40,77,565	105
Jullundur	48,801	46,06,446	94
Lahore	31,642	58,79,075	188
Rawalpindi	55,395	39,14,849	71
Multan	82,375	51,02,917	62
Total	2,57,100	2,35,80,852	420

This density was made up of several densities, varying in 1931 from below 100 in the Kangra district to more than 500 in the district of Amritsar. Generally it varies everywhere in accordance with agricultural resources. The district of Lyallpur affords an important and most striking instance in this respect. In that district only 15 persons per square mile were found in 1891, but with the extension of the canal irrigation, cultivators flocked to it from other parts of the province, raising the density to 368 in 1931.[26] Apart from these, other important factors, which exercised any considerable influence on the density, were the climate, the growth of industrial and trading centres, the facility of means of transportation and marketing.[27] For example, Mianwali, Dera Ghazi Khan and Kangra had a small population, because of the lack of the resources.[28]

The preponderant position of agriculture in the economic life of the people is reflected in the distribution of the

Table 1.3

Percentage of Rural/Urban Population[29]

Year	*Urban*	*Rural*
1891	10.7	89.3
1901	10.6	89.4
1911	9.8	90.2
1921	10.3	89.7
1931	12.4	87.6

population between the urban and rural areas as the occupation of the people determind their habitat. Table 1.3 shows the proportion of urban and rural population at the various censuses.

This excessive uneven distribution as between the towns and country side indirectly shows the economic backwardness of the population. In provinces like Bombay and Madras the development of organized industries resulted in a phenomenal rapid growth of the towns' population, in marked contrast with the almost stationary character of the urban population in Punjab.[30] The Britishers did not build up any industrial base in Punjab, hence, there was no large scale migrations towards the town.[31] The decrease during the decade 1901-1911 in the urban population was owing to the outbreak of the epidemics which took an extraordinarily heavy toll of life in the towns.

The population in Punjab, unlike other provinces, was divided into three major religions and several minor one, as is shown in the Table 1.4.

Table 1.4

Population of Punjab by Religions[32]

Year	*Hindus*	*Sikhs*	*Muslims*
1891	1,02,37,700	18,70,481	1,29,15,645
1901	1,04,78,721	21,30,987	1,41,41,122
1911	87,73,621	28,83,729	1,22,75,477
1921	87,79,651	31,10,060	1,29,55,341
1931	81,25,202	45,38,220	1,33,32,460

According to the census of 1931, the proportion of the major communities per 10,000 of the population was: 5340 Muslims, 3018 Hindus and 1429 Sikhs i.e. 54.40 per cent Muslims, 30.18 per cent Hindus and 14.30 per cent Sikhs. It is evident that the Muslims formed the majority in the province. The Muslims predominated in the districts of Gurdaspur, Sialkot, Gujaranwala, Sheikhupura, Gujrat, Shahpur, Jhelum, Rawalpindi, Attock, Mianwali, Montgomery, Lyallpur, Muzzaffargarh, Jhang, Multan, Lahore and Dera Ghazi Khan.[33] Their proportion varying from 91 per cent of the total population in Attock district to 51 per cent in Gurdaspur district, while in the districts of Jullundur, Ferozpur, Amritsar, Ludhiana and Eastern Punjab their population varies from 45 per cent to 15 per cent.[34]

Muslims were not only in majority in numbers but economically they were also strong. They controlled over 95 per cent of the land in these districts such as Gujrat, Jhang, Jhelum and Attock.[35] Even in the eastern districts where the Hindu and Sikh land owning position was much stronger, Muslims still owned substantial amounts of land. In the Gurgaon district they owned over 30 per cent of the land,[36] whilst in Amritsar they possessed over 25 per cent of land.[37]

Generally, the Muslim society was organized on a tribal and kinship basis. Leadership to the Muslim society was provided either by the *Biradari* leaders or by the *Pirs*, popularly known as the *Sajjada Nashins* (Custodian of the *dargah* and literally who sits on the prayer carpet). The *Pirs* of Punjab possessed great authority in the eyes of Muslim tribesmen. Apart from their spiritual influence they were also large landowners, and were thus ideally placed to play a leading role in the rural politics.[38]

It was believed that the *Pirs* had inherited *baraka* (Charisma) from their ancestors who from the eleventh century onwards had played a major role in Punjab's conversion to Islam. *Baraka* was also believed to have been transmitted to the tomb (*dargah*) of the saint itself. A large number of people flocked to the shrines (*dargah*), particularly at the time of the *Urs* celebration. They came in the hope of receiving spiritual and more frequently material blessings.[39]

The *Sajjada-Nashin's* role as a mediator was formalized by the *piri-muridi* tie between him and the shrine's worshipper. The latter took an oath of obedience (*Byayat*) to the *Pir* and thereafter become his *murid* (disciple). In return for the *murid's* regular offerings, the *pir* provided him with access to *baraka*. The *murid* was expected to be absolutely obedient to his *Pir* and the relationship between them was likened to that between the Prophet and his companions.[40] The leading *Pirs* had thousands of *murids*. Pir Fazalshah of Jalalpur in the Jhelum district alone claimed over 2,00,000 disciples.[41] The size of such followings gave the *Pirs* great political influence. Their profound economic conditions further added to their political influence.[42]

After the Muslims came the Hindus, who were largely dispersed in the central and southern parts of the province. They were in majority in the districts of Hisar, Gurgaon, Rohtak, Karnal, Simla and Kangra, while in the districts of Ambala and Hoshiarpur their numerical strength was greater than that of any other community. In the western districts their population was less than 20 per cent.[43] However, the variation in Hindu population between 1901 to 1941 was quite unhealthy, as is shown in the Table 1.5.

Table 1.5

Decrease in Hindu Population in Punjab[44]

Year	*Population in Every 10,000*
1901	4,127
1911	3,579
1921	3,506
1931	3,018
1941	2,911

The censuses reports of 1921 and 1931 carefully examine the causes for the decrease in the number of the Hindus. The first cause of diminution among the Hindus was the changed instructions issued in the 1911 census about the definition of Sikhism. Prior to that year only those persons were recorded as Sikhs who, strictly followed the tenets of the tenth Guru, Gobind Singh, but since then any one was recorded as Sikh who returned himself as such whether or not he practised those tenets.[45] The second cause was the absorption of the many members of low castes, who adopted Sikhism in order to escape the inferiority complex.[46] Apart from the lowest classes a large number of conversions to Sikhism were taken place from amongst the Hindu agricultural castes. Thus the Hindu Jats decreased from 15,39,574 in 1901 to 9,92,309 in 1931, while the Sikh Jats increased from 13,88,877 to 21,33,152 during the same period.[47] Conversion to Sikhism among the Hindu Rajput and Saini castes were also heavy.[48]

On the social plane, the Hindus were faring reasonably well. However, they were divided into a number of sects, such as, *Bairagis, Udasis, Sanyasis, Gorak Panthis, Dadu Panthis, Kabir Panthis, Kalu Panthis, Ram Dasias, Arya Samajis* and *Sanatan Dharmis.*[49] Economically the Hindus were better off. In Upper Punjab, though they were in the minority, they dominated the economic life in urban areas. They held sway over the realms of industry, trade and commerce.[50] In Lahore, for instance, the Hindus owned 60 per cent of the registered factories and paid eight times as such sales tax as the Muslim traders.[51] The majority of the banks, shops and commercial institutions, belonged to them throughout Punjab.[52] The Hindus owned substantial amount of land in the eastern Punjab.[53]

Under the impact of modernization, the Hindus of the Punjab organized themselves effectively, specially under the banner of Arya Samaj.[54] Arya Samaj became very popular in Punjab and it raised the social status of the depressed classes among the Hindus and also prevented them from joining other religious denominations.[55] The leaders of the Arya Samaj, like Lala Lajpat Rai and Lala Lal Chand, made it a less devotional and more secular organization, which remained closer to the Hindus as a community and as a people. These leaders, led the way towards political action, first in the Indian National Congress and then in the Punjab Hindu Sabha. They, like the Jewish intellectuals who founded Zionism, or the anglicized Muslims who dreamed of Pakistan, sought political solutions to the problems that faced the Hindu community.[56] These efforts, subsequently, prepared the urban Hindus to play a prominent role in the politics of the province. The enlightened rich urban Hindus, like Lala Harikrishan, Sir Manohar Lal and Raja Narendra Nath, who had their followings among the urban Hindus, provided leadership to this community.

The Sikhs were the third largest community in the province. The Sikh community was concentrated in the Jullundur and Lahore Divisions and Montgomery and Lyallpur districts of the Multan Division. However, the Sikhs did not have a clear majority in any district except in Ludhiana, where they were more numerous than either the Hindus or the Muslims.[57] In the Ambala Division, the Sikhs were mainly concentrated in the Hissar and Ambala districts. They formed

18.46 per cent of the total population of the Ambala district and 6.03 per cent of the Hissar district.[58] The Sikhs formed 24.5 per cent of the total population of the Jullundur Division and 19.98 per cent of the total population of the Lahore Division.[59] In the Rawalpindi Division, they were 4.98 per cent of the total population and in the Multan Division, the Sikhs were 18.82 per cent in the Lyallpur district, 13.17 per cent in the Montegomery district and 4.4 per cent in Multan district.[60] From 1891 to 1931 the Sikh population, in fact, marked a rapid increase, as is shown in Table 1.6.

Table 1.6

Increase in Sikh Population in Punjab[61]

Census	*Actual Number of Sikhs*
1891	18,70,481
1901	21,30,987
1911	28,83,729
1921	31,10,060
1931	45,38,220

This big rise in the Sikh population from 1891 to 1931 was not due to natural increase alone. The fundamental reason for this rapid increase was the mass conversion to Sikhism among the lowest classes Hindu Jats and Rajputs.[62] Between 1891 to 1901 the Sikh increased at the rate of 13.9 per cent as compared with 2.4 per cent among the Hindus.[63] For example, there were 6,360 Sikhs in 1911 in Amritsar, in 1921 there were 14,125.[64] It is not possible to give an adequate explanation of this movement except that Sikhism was often accepted for economic reasons, the expenses at social ceremonies and rites among the Sikhs being less than those of the Hindus.

The Sikhs were, primarily, divided into two categories i.e. *Keshdharis* and *Sehajdharis*. Those Sikhs who followed the rules laid down by Guru Gobind Singh and had been baptized were known as *Keshdharis*, and the remaining were called *Sehajdharis*. Further, the Sikhs were divided into a number of sects, as is shown in Table 1.7.

Table 1.7

Sects Among Sikhs[65]

Keshdharis	*Sehajdharis*
Hazuri	Hazuri
Mazhabi	Nanak Panthi
Nihang	Radha Swami
Nanak Panthi	Ram Dasia
Ram Dasia	Ram Rai
Ram Rai	Udasi
Udasi	Sarwaria

With their growing number, the Sikhs gradually strengthened themselves. They acquired large amount of lands, entered into professional and administrative services and also joined the armed forces in large number. Moreover, from the opening decade of the 20th century till the 1940s, members of the Sikh aristocracy and later on the Sikh middle class remained important in the realm of politics. The landed aristocratic families such as Majithias, Ramgarhias and Ahluwalias and later on the urban middle class such as Master Tara Singh and Giani Sher Singh provided leadership to the Sikhs of the province.

In the later half of the 19th century, because of certain reasons, the communal tendencies had its emergence in the province. Its first reason was the activities of the Christian missionaries. In the later half of the 19th century a good number of Christian missionaries entered into the Punjab and converted the people to their faith.[66] The census of 1881 enumerated 13,912 Christians in Punjab, but that of the year 1891 raised the figures to 19,750, a 40 per cent increase in ten years, which caused a stir.[67] Different communities led by their respective leaders took steps to check onslaughts on their religions. As a result, religious societies and institutions functioning on communal lines came up. To begin with, they maintained defensive posture, but later on became offensive because of their growing economic and political interests.[68] Secondly, the political leaders of different communities, in course of time, provided new colour to the idea of communalism, thus, they increased the gulf between the communities.[69]

Thirdly, the new middle classes who were in keen competition in the new field of activities, especially economic, clashed on different levels in different fields elsewhere and further added to the communal tendencies And lastely, modernization was another factor that encouraged communalism.[70] The Punjab government instead of checking this growing communal tendencies or educating the people for healthy living encouraged communal strife according to its policy of 'divide and rule'. The result was communal disharmony, discord and mutual suspicion, in the minds and hearts of different communities for each other.[71]

The press and printed media, which were both modern phenomena also contributed to the growth of communalism and separatism.[72] In 1921, there were 276 newspapers and periodicals in Panjab. Out of these 178 were in Urdu, 58 in English, 26 in Gurumukhi, 10 in Hindi and 3 in different languages. Amritsar, Lahore, Rawalpindi, Lyallpur and Sialkot were major centres of publications.[73]

Most of these periodicals and newspapers served as the aggressive mouth piece of revivalist movements. The *Arya Samaj* published 30 newspapers, Sikh views were expressed in 10 newspapers, the *Anjuman-i-Himayat-i-Islam* ran its own monthly magazine.[74] Apart from such specialist papers, most of the ordinary papers devoted considerable coverage to the discussion of religious and communal affairs. The communal propaganda carried out by the press and media, in later years became one of the important cause of the outbreak of serious communal riots in the province.

Now, a word about the economy. Agriculture was the chief means of economy of Punjab, about 60 per cent of the total population depended upon it.[75] Agricultural production provided all the foodgrains consumed within the province and yielded large quantities of raw materials like cotton and oilseeds, on which not only trade and commerce but also the principal manufacturing industries in the province were based. The fertile soil of the province, facilities of irrigation afforded by the canals, abundance of labour and great inherited agricultural skill, simply failed to make the province, an agricultural advance region. Even, the living conditions of the average peasantry was far from satisfactory. One of the basic cause responsible for the backwardness of agriculture and the improvishment of the cultivator was the endless sub-division and fragmentation of the land. The sub-division of holding means the small size of the total area held or cultivated. In 1924 H. Calvert have studied this aspect of the agricultural problems and the results of his inquiry were published in 1925, as explained in Table 1.8.

Table 1.8

Land Holdings in Pubjab[76]

Size of Holding	*Percentage of Owners*	*Percentage of Land*
Below 1 acre	17.9	1.0
Between 1-3 acres	22.5	4.4
" 3-5 acres	14.9	6.6
" 5-10 acres	18.0	15.1
" 10-15 acres	8.2	11.5
" 15-20 acres	4.3	8.4
" 20-25 acres	2.7	6.8
" 25-30 acres	4.8	20.4
" 50 acres and above	3.3	25.7

For the province as a whole the average size of owner's holding was between 7 and 8 acres. The larger holdings were found in the *barani* tracts and in the newly settled canal irrigated areas of the province, where the population had not yet reached the stage constituting a high pressure on the soil. Conversely the densely populated tracts in the old settled sub-mountainous areas with good rainfall were naturally broken into smaller holdings.[77]

The average area of the holding was not only small but also it was scattered in a number of fragments or plots.[78] Fragmentation of owners' lands was a normal accompaniment of division of property according to the laws of inheritance, so that very few of the holdings were in one compact block.

There were fields which were sometimes over half a mile long but a few yards wide, while in certain cases fragmentation has been carried so far as to prevent all attempts at cultivation.[79]

To meet the problem of small holdings and fragmentation, the Co-operative Societies under the auspices of Co-operative Department began the task of consolidation of the holdings since 1920-21.[80] Punjab Government passed Punjab Consolidation of Holding Act in 1936.[81] During 1937-39, about 87 thousands acres were consolidated with the help of this act.[82] These measures did bring some relief but this relief did not cure the ill itself.

Another important cause of the improvishment of the peasantry was the existence of dreaded debt. The presence of a huge volume of agricultural indebtedness, which was unfortunately for the most part unproductive, checked improvement in all directions and constituted one of the most serious problems of agricultural economy in Punjab. According to an inquiry made into this matter by M.L. Darling, the total debt for Punjab was Rs. 90 crores in 1921.[83] The enquiry further revealed that in Punjab the debt averaged Rs. 31 per cultivated acre and Rs. 76 per head of the agriculturist population and that it was atleast nineteen times of land revenue demand.[84] Another enquiry made into this matter by the Punjab provincial Banking Enquiry Committee, put the total agricultural debt of Punjab at Rs. 135 crores in 1929, thus showing an increase of 50 per cent on estimate for 1921.[85]

The poor economic conditions of the average peasantry compelled it to borrow money from the money-lenders, who used to charge exorbitant rates of interest.[86] By 1900 the indebtedness became a dangerous phenomenon.[87] The farmers had nothing to pay their debts except their valuable land. As

Table 1.9

Transfer of Land From Cultivator to Money-Lender[88]

Year	*Transfer by Sale (In acres)*	*Transfer by Mortgage (In acres)*
1892	6,52,500	3,16,000
1900	1,19,000	2,90,000

a result, land began to pass to money-lenders on an alarming scale, either through sale or mortgage system, as it is shown in Table 1.9.

In the beginning, the Government welcomed the transfer of land from poor to rich, because it thought that the facility of transfer would place the land at the disposal of those who would bring capital. The new owner, however, did not invest any capital in improvement of the land, and contended themselves with the highest rent. As a result, the situation became worse.[89] Some civil officials warned of the possible danger of unrest, as a result of the large scale transfers. The warnings took a sense of urgency when S.S. Thourburn, Deputy Commissioner, Dera Ghazi Khan, published his book, *Musalmans and Moneylenders in the Punjab*.[90] To check it from growing into a monster the government passed the Punjab Alienation of Land Act, 1901.[91] Under this Act, non-agriculturist classes were not allowed to buy land from a member of an agricultural tribe nor to take it in mortgage for more than twenty years.[92] The Act, was hailed by the agricultural classes as the magna carta of their freedom.[93]

But after the passing of this Act, difficulties were found in its working. It had, therefore, to be amended as many as ten times till 1940. The main difficulty in the working of the Act, was that it had provided against the expropriation of the agriculturist by a non-agriculturist or by an agriculturist of different tribe or group, but nothing was provided in the Act, against the expropriation by the same tribe or tribe of the same group. This was, however, remedied by the Punjab Act V of 1938, section 3, which provided that no alienation of land could be made by a member of the agriculturist tribe to a member of the same tribe or of a tribe in the same group.[94] After the provision of this clause there was little complaint on this account.

Agriculture, it is obvious, was the chief means of economy of Punjab, hence, the majority of its population lived in villages. Like other provinces, Punjab was ill-equipped financially and technically for the task of industrial development. There were only 152 factories in Punjab in 1901-1902 and their number rose to 673 in 1932-33.[95] Multan, Lahore, Sialkot, Rawalpindi, Lyallpur, Ludhiana, Gurdaspur, Amritsar and Ambala were the centres where some organized industries were in existence.[96] However, the overall industrial position in the province was far from being satisfactory. Trade and commerce in the province was fairly good. The main trade of the Punjab was carried on by rail and river with other parts of India or with foreign countries through the ports of Karachi, Bombay and Calcutta.[97] Multan, Lahore, Lyallpur, Amritsar, Fazilka, Ludhiana, Kaithal and Sirsa were the important trading centres for the internal trade.[98] The colonial rule, however, with its essential feature of the economic exploitation had an adverse effect on the natural growth of the economy of the province.

It is obvious from the above discussions that the Punjab, in the early twentieth century, had rich social composition and was also a land of rich resources. Socially, the population of the province was divided into three major communities i.e. Muslims, Hindus and Sikhs. The Muslims formed majority in the province. The western, central and eastern parts of the Punjab were dominated, in terms of socio-economic status, by the Muslim landlords, Sikh landlords—urban Hindu notables and Hindu peasant proprietors, respectively. Agriculture was the chief means of the economy of Punjab, however, the distribution of land was quite uneven. Industrially the province was much backward, however, trade and commerce was quite fair.

The socio-economic conditions of the people of Punjab had profound impact on the politics of the province. The Muslim landlords of the western Punjab, Sikh aristocracy, enlightened and rich urban Hindus of the central Punjab and caste conscious Jat Hindus of eastern Punjab played a prominent part in the politics of the province.

Foot Notes

1. The term 'Punjab' literally means the 'Five Rivers' and by implication the land of five rivers. However, not withstanding the literal meaning of the term it did not refer to any well-defined geographical region until the British converted it into a big province after the uprising of 1857. For details see J.S. Grewal, 'Historical Geography of the Punjab', *Journal of Regional History*, Vol. I, 1980, pp. 1-14; also Khushwant Singh, *History of the Sikhs*, Vol. I, 1469-1839, Princeton, 1963, p. 5.

2. The Province was, then, divided into two parts, the 'British Territory', and 'Punjab States'. The former had an area of 2,57,096.35 sq.kms. of 72.5 per cent of the total area of the province and enumerated population of 2,35,80,852 or 82.5 per cent of the total population. In the present work we are concerned with that part only. The 'Punjab States' had an area of 97,640 sq. kms. and a population of 49,10,005 or 27.5 per cent of the total area and 17.2 per cent of the total population. For details see *The Census of India, Punjab, 1931*, Vol. XVII, Part I, Lahore, 1933, pp. 1-11.
3. *The Report of the Administration of Punjab*, 1911, Lahore, 1913, p. 1.
4. *Ibid.*, pp. 1-2.
5. *The Census of India, Punjab, 1921*, Part-I, p. 5.
6. The region comprised the district of Simla and Kangra, for details see, K.S. Narang and Hari Ram Gupta, *History of the Punjab 1469-1857*, 1961, pp. 6-7.
7. A. Branford, "Management of Sheep in the Punjab", *Journal of the Central Bureau of Animal Husbandry and Dairing in India*, I, 1927-28, pp. 56-59.
8. *The Census of India, Punjab, 1931*, Vol. XVII, Part-I, Lahore 1933, pp. 3-4.
9. It comprised the districts of Ambala, Hoshiarpur, Sialkot, Jhelum, Rawalpindi and Attock. The ten years average rainfall for this region was 78.53 cms, see *The Census of India, Punjab, 1931*, Lahore, Vol. XVII, Part I, pp. 34-40.
10. A.G. Ashgar and C.L. Dewan, "Quality of Drain, River and Canal Waters of the Punjab", *Indian Journal of Agricultural Sciences*, 11.6.1947, pp. 377-88.
11. A. Branford, *op.cit.*, pp. 156-59.
12. C.P.K. Fazal, 'Environmental Influence on Punjab Economic Life', *Punjab Geographical Review*: 2:1 (1947), pp. 44-46.
13. *The Imperial Gazetter of India, Punjab*, 1908, Vol. I, pp. 65-66.
14. *Administrative Report of the Canals in the Punjab*, 1928-29, pp. 6-7.
15. See K.C. Yadav, *Haryana: The Land and People*, 1966, pp. 1-65.
16. Sohan Lal, 'Development of Irrigation in Punjab', *Pakistan Quarterly* 1:5 (1950), pp. 71-75.
17. See, K.S. Ahmad, "Agricultural Region of the Punjab", *Punjab Geographical Review*, Vol. I, 1942, pp. 21-27.
18. See, *The Census of India, Punjab, 1931*, Vol. XVII, Part-I, Lahore, 1933, pp. 4-5.
19. *The Report of Administration of Punjab*, 1911, p. 13.
20. *The Census of India, Punjab, 1931*, Vol. XVII, Part II, Lahore, 1933, p. 99.

21. For details of district administrative system, see S.K. Sharma, 'Evolution of District Administration in Punjab from 1850-1919', *Punjab History Conference Proceedings*, Seventh Session, Sept. 1972, pp. 173-88.
22. *The Report of the Administration of Punjab*, 1911, p. 11.
23. *The Census of India, Punjab, 1931*, Vol. XVII, Part-II, Lahore, 1933, pp. 6-11.
24. For details see C.P.K. Fazal, 'Environmental Influence of Punjab', *Economic Review*, Vol. I, 1447, pp. 44-46.
25. *The Census of India, Punjab, 1931*, Vol. XVII, Part-I, p. 85.
26. *Ibid.*, pp. 84-85.
27. *Census of India, Punjab, 1911*, Vol. XIV, Part-I, p. 65.
28. *Census of India, Punjab, 1931*, Vol. XVII, Part-I, pp. 71-80.
29. *Ibid.*, pp. 89-90.
30. *Ibid.*, p. 44.
31. H. Calvert, *Wealth and Welfare of the Punjab*, Lahore, 1936, pp. 56-57.
32. *The Census of India, Punjab, 1891*, p. 93, *Census of India, Punjab, 1901*, p. 169, *Census of India, Punjab, 1911*, p. 97, *Census of India, Punjab, 1921*, pp. 34-42, *Census of India, Punjab, 1931*, p. 317.
33. *Census of India, Punjab, 1931*, Vol. XVII, Part-I, p. 289.
34. *Ibid.*
35. Ian Talbot, *Punjab and the Raj 1849-1947*, 1988, p. 20.
36. A. Husain, *Final Settlement Report of the Gurgaon District 1938-43*, Lahore, 1944, p. 9.
37. H.D. Craik, *Final Report of the 4th Regular Settlement of the Amritsar District 1910-1914*, Lahore, 1914, p. 3.
38. For details see, Ian Talbot, *op.cit.*, pp. 20-25.
39. *Ibid.*
40. M. Milson, *A. Sufi Rule for Novices*, Cambridge, 1978, p. 46.
41. Ian Talbot, *op.cit.*, p. 22.
42. For example, *Pir* of Jhanian Shah owned 7,000 acres of land and the Shrine of Bahu-ud-din Zakariya in Multan possessed 5,000 acres of land. See, G.L. Chopra, *Chiefs and Families of Note in the Punjab*, Vol. 2, Lahore, 1940, p. 242.
43. *The Census of India, Punjab, 1931*, Vol. XVII, Part-I, p. 300.
44. *The Census of India, Punjab, 1941*, Vol. VI, pp. 46-47.
45. *Census of India, Punjab, 1921*, Vol. XV, p. 114.
46. *Census of India, Punjab, 1931*, Vol. XVII, p. 308.
47. *Ibid.*
48. *Ibid.*
49. *The Census of India, Punjab, 1921*, Part-I, pp. 180-82.
50. *The Census of India, Punjab, 1931*, Vol. XVII, Part-I, p. 328.
51. *Ibid.*, pp. 525-27.

52. K.C. Yadav (ed.), *Rural Haryana in the 19th Century,* Kurukshetra, 1981, pp. 40-45.
53. For details, see Ian Talbot, *op.cit.*, p. 28.
54. For details, see K.W. Jones, *Arya Dharm: Hindu Consciousness in 19th-Century Punjab,* Delhi, 1989.
55. Lajpat Rai, *Arya Samaj,* pp. 220-33.
56. K.W. Jones, *op.cit.*, p. 315.
57. *The Census of India, Punjab, 1931,* Vol. XVII, Part-I, p. 289.
58. Kirpal Singh (ed.), *Select Documents on Partition of Punjab 1947: India and Pakistan,* Delhi, 1991, pp. 236-37.
59. *Ibid.*
60. *Ibid.*
61. *The Census of India, Punjab, 1931,* Vol. XVII, Part-I, p. 317.
62. *Ibid.*, p. 308.
63. *The Census of India, Punjab, 1901,* Vol. XVII, p. 122.
64. *The Census of India, Punjab, 1921,* Part-I, p. 311.
65. *Ibid.*, p. 183.
66. J.C. Archer, *The Sikhs,* Princeton, 1946, pp. 260-64.
67. *The Census of India, Punjab Report, 1891,* Vol. VII, p. 97.
68. For details see K.C. Yadav, 'Partition of India: A Study of the Muslim Politics in the Punjab', *Punjab Past and Present,* Vol. XVI-I, 1983, p. 107.
69. See *Report of the Administration of the Punjab 1931-1932,* Lahore, 1934, pp. 6-8, and Gulshan Rai, 'Communal Conflict in the Punjab', *Civil and Military Gazette,* April 16, 1937.
70. For the growth of Communalism, See, Ashok Mehta and A. Patwardhan, *Communal Triangle,* Allahabad, 1942, Paul Brass, *Language, Religion and Politics in North India,* Cambridge, 1974 and Bipin Chandra, *Communalims in Modern India,* Delhi, 1978.
71. K.C. Yadav, 'Partition of India: A study of the Muslim Politics in the Punjab, *Punjab Past and Present,* Vol. XVI-I, 1983, p. 8.
72. Ian Talbot, *op.cit.*, p. 77.
73. *The Report of the Administration of Punjab,* 1922, p. 146.
74. *Ibid.*
75. For details see M. Afzal Hussain, 'Agriculture in Punjab', *Punjab Past and Present,* 1939, pp. 141 to 171.
76. H. Calvert, *The Size and Distribution of Agricultural Holdings in the Punjab,* 1925, p. 3.
77. Punjab Government, *Bulletin of the Joint Development Board,* 1930, p. 13.
78. H. Calvert, *op.cit.*, pp. 14-15.

79. M.L. Darling, *The Punjab Peasant in Prosperity and Debt*, pp. 29-30.
80. *Report of the Working of Co-operative Societies in the Punjab*, 1921, p. 26.
81. *Punjab Gazette Extraordinary*, November 24, 1936.
82. *Reports on the Operations of the Department of Land Records*, 1939, p. 15.
83. M.L. Darling, *op.cit.*, p. 17.
84. *Ibid.*, pp. 16, 19, 20.
85. *Report of the Punjab Provincial Banking Enquiry Committee*, 1929-30, I. p. 222. The total agricultural indebtedness of the British Indian Provinces in 1929 was estimated at Rs. 900 crores. *Report of Indian Central Banking Enquiry Committee*, 1931, I, Part II, p. 77.
86. Khushwant Singh, *History of the Sikhs*, II, 1966, p. 152.
87. S.S. Thorburn, *Punjab in Peace and War*, 1904, pp. 352-53.
88. *Board of Economic Inquiry, Agricultural Statistics*, 1901-02, Publication No. 52, p. 6.
89. H. Calvert, *op.cit.*, pp. 7-9.
90. S.S. Thorburn, *Musalmans and Money Lenders in the Punjab*, London, 1886, pp. 252-53.
91. *The Report of the Administration of the Punjab*, 1901-02, Lahore, 1904, p. 31.
92. D. Gilmartin, 'Religious Leadership and the Pakistan Movement in the Punjab', *Modern Asian Studies*, Vol. XIII, No. 3, 1979, p. 493.
93. M.L. Darling, *op.cit.*, p. 259.
94. *Punjab Act V of 1938*, Section-3.
95. *Reports on the Working of the Indian Factories Act in the Punjab.*
96. B.S. Saini, *op.cit.*, pp. 261-76.
97. Punjab Government, *Reports of the External Land Trade of the Punjab, 1907-08*, pp. 2-4.
98. *Reports of the Punjab Provincial Banking Enquiry Committee, 1929-30*, pp. 71-74.

2

Early Politics and Elections of 1936-37

Dalhousie, the Governor-General of India, annexed Punjab to the Empire of Her Majesty, the Queen of England on 29 March, 1849.[1] The new acquisition was a valuable possession for the British, since it had great natural resources.[2] Dalhousie argues that the annexation of Punjab was necessary to safeguard the interests and security of British India,[3] and he called the new possession, a bright Jewel in the Crown of the Her Majesty.[4] Dalhousie and his successors exploited their new possession, to a great extent. To begin with Dalhousie established a 'Board of Administration' in Punjab in order to consolidate the British hold in the newly conquered territory.[5]

After the events of 1857, the British decided to use the region's native aristocracy as a great bulwork for the state.[6] The landed aristocracy was prepared to cooperate closely with the colonial regime in return for its patronage and access to its decision-making process. In this way they hoped to increase their standing amongst their rural followers.[7] The British made great efforts to identify every important family in each locality and compiled and recorded their history in the District Gazetteers. In the West Punjab, the Britishers turned to the leading Muslim landlord families to form an important pillar of their rule. Many of them had fought on the British side during the Sikh wars of 1848-49 and during the uprising of 1857. The Tiwanas of Shahpur, Hayats of Attock and Ghebas of Kot Fateh Khan were the most striking example of this kind.[8] The Legharis, Noons, Khans of Kasur, Gilanis, Qureshis, Maliks and Daultanas were some other prominent Muslim chieftains of the west Punjab who offered their allegiance to the Raj.[9] These powerful chiefs were given *Jagirs*, and later on were invested with magisterial powers in their respective estates.

Collaboration was also established with the leading *sufi pirs* of the region. The *sufi* shrines were the major centres of rural religious devotion and played an important part in the economic life of their surrounding areas. The British treated them in the same way as the large landowners and clan leaders, taking their encumbered estates under the court of wards wing, awarding them position of authority in the local administration and granting them lands in the canal colonies. The British, thus, established a unity of political interests between the landlords and the *Pirs*.[10]

The British drew the Sikh men of local influence to their support in the same way. Cash, land grants and honorary titles were all freely offered in exchange for pledges of loyalty. Ramgarhias, Sindhanwalis, Ahluwalias and Majithas were some important Sikh families who closely collaborated with the British.[11] In the eastern districts of Punjab the powers of landlords were considerably weaker. These areas were predominantly cultivated by the peasant proprietors. The British reached down to the villages of these areas with the help of revenue, irrigation and police officials. The British also maintained good relations with the peasant proprietors of the region and in general collaborated with the dominant caste of Hindu Jat peasants of these districts.[12]

The Punjabi chiefs' loyalty to their British masters made them the most powerful pressure group both in provincial politics and administration.[13] Equipped with this wherewithal, they quarantined the province against the nationalist and peasant movements from making in roads and gained further benefits accruing from a dependency relationship.[14] The lack of educational and political institutions, along with the peasants' total dependence upon the landlords, proved a lasting hindrance in the evolution of political consciousness among the ordinary

Punjabis. Even the small-town economy did not offer any extra political acumen.

To control in the cities the British focused initially on the same type of structures they used to establish control in the rural areas. In the cities control depended largely on intermediaries. Just as they tried to identify *biradri* leaders in the countryside, the British sought to find 'natural leaders' in the cities.[15] These urban notables or natural leaders, usually owned considerable urban residential property, commanded credit and controlled broad urban factions. Just as the population of Punjab's cities were religiously heterogeneous, these urban notables also came from all the three major religions of Punjab.[16] The Britishers increasingly incorporated, these urban notables, into municipal committees and district boards, as key figures in British urban administration.[17] Thus, for long the British rule checked the growth of political consciousness among the urban Punjabis by controlling these urban notables.

However, the mediation in the cities differed from that in the countryside. The urban notables were often less stable than their rural counterparts, making control through these urban notables was difficult and often limited. Moreover, by the end of the nineteenth century factors such as, growth of the education, urbanization, growth of the press and development of the middle classes subsequently led to the growth of political awareness in the region.[18] The evolution of political consciouness and nationalistic awareness began to change the situation for the better.[19] Initially, the middle class leaders raised their voice for the betterment of their fate. However, their impact was of little consequence. Subsequently, more efforts were made which led to the emergence of political parties,[20] as given in Table 2.1

To begin with, the political parties worked and concentrated on the interests of the urbanities, since these parties had their origin in cities and towns.[22] Lahore branch of Indian Association organized by S.N. Banerjee was first political organization of importance in Punjab. The activities of the Indian National Congress, founded in 1886, did not amount to anything more than annual gatherings in which a few interested in movement participated.[23] The Indian National

Table 2.1

Emergence of Political Parties in Punjab [21]

Political Party	*Year of Founding*
Lahore Branch of Indian Association by S.N. Banerjee	1877
Indian National Congress branch opened in Punjab	1886
Chief Khalsa Diwan	1902
Muslim Leage by Fazl-i-Husain	1906
Muslim Association by Mohammad Shafi	1907
All India Muslim League Branch (merger of Fazl-i-Husain and Mohammad Shafi's Parties)	1907
Punjab Hindu Sabha	1907
Central Sikh League	1920
Muhmmadan Rural Party by Fazl-i-Husain	1921
Punjab Unionist Party	1923

Congress during its formative phase was viewed as nothing but a gathering of a few holiday makers out for intellectual entertainment.[24] Some prominent Muslims of Punjab, like Fazl-i-Husain, Mohammad Shafi, Mohammad Shah-din and Maulvi Mahbub Alam also participated in the activities of the Indian National Congress. However, in February 1906, Sir Fazl-i-Husain founded the Muslim League at Lahore. Sheikh Umar Baksh became the President and Fazl-i-Husain himself Secretary of the new organization.[25]

In November 1907 at a conference of leading Muslims of Punjab held in Lahore, it was decided to establish a Muslim League in connection with the All India Muslim League. Mohammad Shah-din and Mohammad Shafi were elected as President and Secretary of the new Punjab Muslim League. Fazl-i-Husain's Muslim League was merged into this new organization and he was elected as the Joint Secretary of the new organization. Abdul Aziz (Editor, *Observer*) and Mahbub Alam (Editor, *Paisa Akhbar*) were other prominent members of the League.[26] Sir Mohammad Shafi a conservative Muslim leader, was the moving spirit of this organization, he remained its Secretary from 1907 to 1916.[27] Aims of the Muslim League were as following:

1. To safeguard and advance the political interests of the Muslims of Punjab and to infuse into them a spirit of enlightened patriotism.
2. To develop the idea of Muslim brotherhood among the Muslims of Punjab and to infuse the spirit of communal-harmony among the different religious sections of Punjab.
3. To work in coalition with the All India Muslim League for the overall betterment of the Muslims of Punjab.
4. To infuse a spirit of loyalty to the British Rule among the Muslims of Punjab.[28]

Muslim League made a rapid growth at the urban level. By the end of 1909, besides Lahore, district Muslim Leagues were established at Ambala, Ludhiana, Jullundur, Hoshiarpur, Firozepur, Multan, Muzzafargarh, Jhang, Attock, Rawalpindi, Gujrat, Gujranwala, Gurdaspur, Amritsar and Lyallpur.[29] During the years 1907-1917, the Muslim League vigorously struggled to have more Muslim representatives in the Municipal Committees, District Boards, Punjab Provincial Council and Imperial Council.[30] Sir Mohammad Shafi argued that the separate representation at all stages is the only effective method of safeguarding the Muslim interests.[31] During these years the activities of the Muslim League were dominated by the urban elite with the possible exception of Umar Hayat Khan Tiwana.[32]

Dissenting with the All India Muslim League's decision to cooperate with the Indian National Congress under the Lucknow Pact of 1916, Mohammad Shafi resigned from the Muslim League.[33] Sir Fazl-i-Husain became the Secretary of Punjab Muslim League and continued to hold that office till 1920.[34] Mian Shafi left Punjab in 1919 to serve on the Executive Council of the Viceroy and thereafter remained busy in Indian Politics.[35]

The Government of India Act. 1919, usually known as the Montague-Chelmsford Reforms, introduced major changes in the administration of the provinces of British India. Now a majority of the members of the Provincial Legislative Council would be elected.[36] The territorial constituencies were divided in two manners; first, seats were assigned to various communities in a system of separate electorates in accordance with the Lucknow Pact between the Muslim League and the Congress in 1916; and secondly, within the communal allotments, seats were assigned to urban and rural electorates.[37] In Punjab a total of 64 members of the Council were to be elected from territorial constituencies and seven more from special constituencies, as is shown in Table 2.2.

Table 2.2

Constituencies in Punjab Legislative Council, 1920[38]

Name of the Constituency	*Urban*	*Rural*	*Total*
Mohammandans	5	27	32
Non-Mohammandans	7	13	2
Sikhs	1	11	12
Special	—	—	7
Grand Total			71

The seven special constituencies included four for landlords (one for each major community plus a separate seat for the Baluch), one for university graduates and two to represent commercial and industrial groups.[39] The British and their rural allies did not want to see the more sophisticated and organized urban elites take advantage of the spread of representative politics into the province. The Punjab Government thus ensured that the franchise and distribution of seats for the new Legislative Council created by the Government of India Act of 1919 favoured the rural population. Separate electorates were created for the Punjab's rural and urban areas on the basis of total number of seats proportionate to their population. This meant that a mere four of the 34 Muslims elected to the Council would come from the towns.[40] Moreover, despite the widening of the franchise under the new reforms, the number of eligible voters in the general constituencies was only 3.4 per cent of the total population, in accordance with the census of 1921.[41]

Elections for the first Punjab Legislative Council were held in November 1920 and this election was a political development of great importance. Sir Fazl-i-Hussain was an important member of the newly formed Punjab Legislative Council and it was to him that other Muslim members looked for leadership.[42] Fazl-i-Hussain's special concern for the rural people led him to think in terms of organizing a new party and in the year 1921, with the support of the other rural members, he organized the Rural Party.[43] The Rural Party was open to all communities and its guiding principles were to work for the uplift of the backward rural areas and to sponsor programmes and measures to protect the backward people of Punjab.[44] In 1923, Sir Fazl-i-Hussain with the help of Hindu Jat leader Sir Chhotu Ram organized the Punjab National Unionist Party.[45] The guiding principle for the Unionist Party were, to improve the existing conditions of the peasantry, backward classes and backward communities living in the rural Punjab.[46] The Unionist Party contested the elections of 1923, 1926 and 1930 and secured a great success.[47]

The Muslim League, during 1920-1935, when the Punjab was governed in accordance with the Indian Council Act of 1919, failed to make its presence felt in the politics of the province. Sir Fazl-i-Hussain, the most powerful Muslim leader of the province, in fact, saw the Unionist Party, as a better vehicle for the interests of the Muslims of Punjab.[48] Moreover, the urban politics of the Muslim League, despite the efforts of its leader, remained peripheral to the ideological structure of the imperial state. Although the cities were administrative centres of Punjab's political system, however, the cities were politically subordinate to the rural areas, where the power and the ideological roots of the colonial state were based.[49] Thus, the urban politics of Sir Muhammad Shafi, Sir Muhammad Iqbal, Sir Abdul Qadir and Malik Barkat Ali was bound to remain subordinate to the rural politics of Punjab.

In 1924 an agitation was started by the Hindus against separate electrorate. In Punjab the agitation assumed alarming proportions and it was said to have been aggravated by the policy followed by Fazl-i-Husain with regard to communal representation in services, local bodies and educational institutions. In order to prevent the Muslims from being overwhelmed by the agitation, the All India Muslim League held its annual session at Lahore in May 1924 under the chairmanship of M.A. Jinnah.[50] Thus the activities of the Punjab

Muslim League were revived. However, this annual session was dominated by the Muslim Unionists and it helped more the activities of the Unionists rather than the Muslim League. In fact, Fazl-i-Husain, himself invited Jinnah to hold the annual session of the Muslim League at Lahore.[51]

In accordance with the 'Delhi Proposals' of 1928, the All India Muslim League had expressed its willingness to forego Muslim's right to separate electorate, provided their demands for the separation of Sind, introduction of reforms in North-West Frontier Province and Baluchistan, reservation of Muslim seats in Punjab and Bengal on the basis of population and one-third seats in the Central Legislative Assembly were accepted by the Congress and the British Rule. The leaders of Punjab Muslim League adhered to this scheme of the All India Muslim League. However, Sir Fazl-i-Husain rejected this scheme. Although, the protection of the Muslim interests was a major goal for Fazl-i-Husain, too, but he identified the Muslim interests with those of the Muslims of Punjab.[52] For him the right of separate electorate was more important than any other demand. Hence, in 1929, he organized the All India Muslim Conference in order to oppose the scheme of the all India Muslim League and to cooperate with the British Rule.[53] In fact, the All India Muslim Conference was dominated by the Muslim Unionists from Punjab. And, this conference had considerable influence on the Government of India's decisions concerning separate electrorates and the communal award.[54] Thus, the activities and ideology of the Muslim League were eclipsed by the activities of the All India Muslim conference.

Frustrated with the politics of the Unionist Party and the political atmosphere prevailing in Punjab, many of the Punjab's Muslim Leaguers, during the late 1920s and early 1930s, stepped outside the structure of State politics altogether to express a direct commitment to the ideal of a political order defined by Islam. Urban leaders in politics identified themselves with these symbols and established a public presence in Punjabi politics. A leader of stature, like Sir Muhammad Iqbal,[55] while defining the cultural alternative to the state's authority said in 1930:

> I would like to see the Punjab, North-West Frontier Province, Sind and Baluchistan amalgamated into a single

> state.... possessing full opportunity of developing within the body politics of India... There were two pitfalls into which Muslim political leaders fell. The first was the repudiated Lucknow pact which originated in a false view of Indian Nationalism and deprived the Muslims of India from chances of acquiring any political power in India. The second is the narrow visioned sacrifice of Islamic solidarity in the interests of what may be the Punjab ruralism, resulting in a proposal which virtually reduced the Punjab Muslims to a position of minority. It is the duty of the League to condemn both the pact and proposal. The pact was a dead mouse but the proposal was a living 'monster' which could be killed by the formation of the proposed state. Minus Ambala Division and perhaps—some districts where non-Muslims predominate.[56]

The idea of Muslim National and a political order based on Islamic symbols of Sir Muhammad Iqbal did not attract much attention of the Muslims of Punjab specially of the rural Punjab. In fact, the ability of urban leaders to express effectively the commitment of Muslims to an Islamic political order was circumscribed by the strength of patronage networks within the cities themselves, and also by the problems of effective political expression and action in rural and provincial politics.[57] Hence, the Unionist remained unchallenged.

In August 1932, the British Prime Minister announced the Communal Award. It conceded the right of separate electrorate and maintained the principle of weightage with some modifications in Muslim-minority provinces. In spite of Muslims' proportion of 56 per cent in the total population of Punjab, they were given only 86 seats out of the total number of 175 seats which was, according to Sir Fazl-i-Husain, a willingness to forego for the time being 6 per cent of their heritage.[58] The acceptance of this 'Award' by the Muslim League was another example of the subordination of League's politics to that of the Unionists.[59]

In 1935 the Muslims of Punjab were astir over the Shahidganj Issue.[60] The Muslim League seized this opportunity and endeavoured to launch a movement based on direct popular identification with religious symbols. However, the passive attitude of the Unionists, under the leadership of Sir

Fazl-i-Husain, sidelined this issue of Shahidganj because he considered the religious identity to be important in politics only to the degree that it helped to define Muslim claims to political power within the large structure of the British imperial order.[61] It was one more setback to the Muslim League.

In the year 1935 the British Parliament took an important step for the constitutional development in India and passed the Government of India Act of 1935. This Act was divided into two parts—one proposing a Federation of Indian States and British Indian Provinces and the other conferring autonomy on the provinces. Diarchy was abolished and Indians were now to be associated with decision making in virtually every department of provincial government[62]. By granting provincial autonomy the British planned to give autonomy to their friends and collaborators, and to retain control at the top. The Govt. of India Act of 1935 was the first constitutional measure introduced by the British in India which envisaged that the parties winning a majority of seats in the legislatures would form ministries which would function on the basis of joint and collective responsibility.[63]

The new Act revolutionized the electoral process, an electorate of some 36 million, as compared to an electorate of 7 million in 1920, and representing 30 per cent of the adult population was enfranchised.[64] Accordingly, 24 per cent of the adult population of Punjab was enfranchised, which was about 12 per cent of the total population of Punjab.[65] The Punjab Legislative Council was renamed as the Punjab Legislative Assembly and its strength was increased from 71 to 175 as shown in Table 2.3.

Table 2.3

Punjab Legislative Assembly Constituencies, 1937[66]

Constituency	*Urban*	*Rural*	*Total*
General	8	34	42
Muhammandans	9	75	84
Sikhs	2	29	31
Special	—	—	18
Grand Total	19	138	175

The special seats were distributed as—four seats were allocated to women, two to Muslims and one each to Hindu and Sikh. Indian Christians were to have two seats; European and Anglo-Indians, one each. One seat was allotted for University graduates, one for Commerce and Industry, three for labours and five for landholders (including one for the Baluch Tumandars).[67] Muslims were thus guaranteed 87 seats (84 in territorial constituencies, two women seats and the Tumandars seat as all electors in that seat were Muslim) which was one seat short of a majority. In practice they could also expect additional seats from landholders and labour constituencies. Out of the general constituencies, eight were reserved for the scheduled castes as per proposals of the Poona Pact (24 September, 1932).[68] On an average each of Punjab constituencies had a voting strength of 16,000 as compared to 33,000 in Madras, 18,600 in Bombay, 33,000 in United Provinces, 3,200 in Bengal, 20,000 in Bihar, 10,400 in Assam and 18,600 in Central Province.[69]

The provincial elections on the basis of the Government of India Act of 1935 were held in late 1936 and early 1937. For Punjab, the Poll notification was issued by the Chief Secretary, Government of Punjab on 6th November, 1936.[70] The Poll notification led to hectic political activities in the province. Although, both the Congress and the Muslim League were dissatisfied with the Act of 1935 and held that it did not go for enough to satisfy the political aspirations of Indians. The Congress stand was uncompromisingly opposed to the Act. Nehru had said, "There was going to be provincial autonomy but the Governor would be a benevolent and all powerful dictator keeping us in order. And high above all would sit the All Highest, the Supreme Dictator, the Viceroy, with complete powers to do what he will and check when he desires".[71] The All India Muslim League at its session held in April 1936 at Bombay passed a resolution against the Act. The resolution reads, "The act is anti-democratic, it will strengthen all the most reactionary elements in the country, and, instead of keeping as to develop on progressive lines, it will enchain and crush the forces working for democracy and freedom. The Muslim classes and Muslim masses will suffer from the new scheme as much as any other section of the Indian people".[72]

However, in spite of their opposition to the Act both Congress and the League decided to contest the elections, if only to make use of election campaign to spread their respective message to the electorate.[73]

The Hindu Mahasabha at its session held in April, 1935 at Kanpur also opposed the Government of India Bill 1935. The Mahasabha realised that the British had not maintained a balance between the urban Hindus and rural Muslims and hence the Act had become quite irrelevant.[74] The Akalis, too, exhibited a great deal of displeasure. Sardar Mangal Singh said that the Act cannot be regarded as an agreed constitution but as a constitution which has been forced upon unwilling and helpless people.[75] However, in spite of their opposition both Hindu Mahasabha and Akalis, like Congress and Muslim League decided to contest the elections.[76] The Unionist Party, unlike the other political parties, warmly greeted the Act, since it fulfilled many of its desires and principles and hence it began preparations for the forthcoming elections.[77]

The Unionist Party, Muslim League, Congress, the Hindu Electoral Board, Khalsa National Party, Shiromani Akali Dal, Itihad-i-Millat, Congress Nationalist Party, the Ahrars and Socialist Party contested the provincial elections.

Fazl-i-Husain, the supremo of the Unionist Party began preparations even in 1935. He began the task of organising the party to wage an electoral battle. In order to end the factional alignments in the party he persuaded Sir Firoz Khan Noon to leave Punjab to become Indian High Commissioner in London in early 1936.[78] At this juncture, however, differences cropped up between Sir Fazli Husain and Sir Sikander over the question of the leadership of the party.[79] Although Sir Sikander, at that time, was off in Bombay as Deputy Governor of the Reserve Bank of India but his friends like Nawab Muzaffar Khan, Mir Maqbool Mahmud and Ahmad Yar Khan Daultana, were active on his behalf.[80] In this move Sir Sikander was even supported by some of the Hindus and Sikhs like Raja Narender Nath and Sir Sunder Singh Majithia.[81] Since Punjab was bound to have a Muslim Premier and between Fazli and Sikander, the latter was a weaker man, hence was more acceptable to the Hindus and Sikhs. It was reported that Sikander Hyat, even, wanted to establish a party of his own to lead the next provincial cabinet.[82]

However, some prominent and influential Muslims like Sir Agha Khan and Chaudhary Shahbuddin supported the leadership of Fazl-i-Husain.[83] Many non-Muslims Unionists like Sir Chhotu Ram also remained very close and faithful to Fazl-i-Husain.[84] Some newspapers also wanted him to lead the Unionists.[85] Opposition to Sir Husain was, thus, short-lived and he was the ultimate choice to lead the Unionist Party.

In February 1936, Sir Husain formally began the task of reconstituting and reorganizing the party.[86] He prepared an elaborate blue print for this purpose which gave details relating to the organizational structure, functioning aims and objectives of the party.[87] The following five tier system was adopted at the organizational level.[88]

Central
Committee
|
District
Committee
|
Tehsil
Committee
|

Zail Committee	Town Committee (population of 7,000 to 30,000)	City Committee (population more than 30,000)
	Village Committee	

In April 1936, the office of the Central Committee of the Unionist Party was set up at No. 14-C Davis Road, Lahore under the Chairmanship of Ahmad Yar Khan Daultana who was General-Secretary of the Unionist Party. Sir Chhotu Ram was appointed as Vice-president of the party, while Sardar

Habibullah, Ghulam Muhy-ud-din, Syed Afzal Ali Hashi were appointed organising secretaries. Nawab Shah Nawaz of Mamdot become the treasurer, Amir-ud-din was appointed Private Secretary to the leader of the Party and Maqbool Mahmood was designated its Propaganda Secretary.[89] Fazl-i-Husain, the President of the party, had successfully held together different elements and did all the necessary spadework for giving the Unionist Party a good start under the new constitution. The Manifesto of the party, prepared by its President, reads as under:[90]

1. Attainment of dominion status through constitutional means, at an early date.
2. Provincial autonomy at the provincial level.
3. Secular basis of Politics.
4. Equal opportunities to all especially to the backwards living in the rural area.
5. Economic development with thrust on agriculture.
6. Industrial development.
7. Development of trade and commerce.
8. Provision of employment especially to the ruralists.
9. To check the menace of usury.
10. Promotion of education especially in the rural areas.
11. Against Social discrimination.
12. Justice cheap and without fear and favour at the earliest possible especially for the ruralities.

The offices of the District Committees, Tehsil Committees, Zail Committees, Town and City Committees were established at their respective administrative headquarters. Any person above 21 years of age, having faith in the aims and objectives of the party, provided, he would pay some nominal fee towards the party funds regularly, could become its member.[91] These members would elect their office bearers like President, Vice-President, Secretary and Treasurer. However, because of the short of time, office bearers could not be elected and ad-hoc committees were formed at all the hierarchical levels.[92] Election offices were opened at different levels and propaganda committees were set up at the constituency levels.[93] Some newspapers like *The Eastern Times* (Lahore) were commissioned for propagating the idea, aims and objectives of the party.[94] A sum of Rs. 50,000 was collected for the party work.[95] Some influencial *Pirs* of the region were contacted to issue statement on behalf of the Unionist Party.[96]

Unfortunately, the leader of the party, Fazl-i-Husain died on 9 July, 1936.[97] The central committee of the Unionist Party appointed Sir Sikander Hayat as the new party chief. With Noon in England and with the support of the factional organization led by his close associates, Sir Sikander without any challenge became the leader of the Unionist Party and carried on the work of Fazl-i-Husain.

The All India Muslim League as well as the Punjab Muslim League remained more or less a defunct body during 1930-35.[98] M.A. Jinnah in 1935 initiated the slow process of transforming this small fragmented party into a mass movement with district branch volunteers throughout the country, who could nominate candidates and spread the League's message in every Muslim town and village.[99] Punjab Muslim League was also revived under the presidentship of Sir Muhammad Iqbal. Malik Barkat Ali and Khalifa Shuja-ud-din were appointed as Vice-Presidents and Ghulam Rasul Khan was appointed as Secretary.[100]

In October 1935, Jinnah, infact, began the task of preparing Muslim League for the task of elections that would bring a fresh cadre of representatives to British India's provinces. To strengthen the League, bolster its bargaining position, and keep prepare it for contesting elections, Jinnah decided to appoint a new central Parliamentary Board and affiliate new provincial parliamentary boards. These boards, similar to those earlier established by the Congress, were to become Jinnah's organizational arms in extending his power over the entire Muslim Community. He asked the provincial Leagues to built the organizational structure of their respective provinces.[101]

The Punjab Muslim League, however, had little political structure and virtually no following, nor any opportunity to build an organizational structure. A close associate and right hand of Jinnah, Ispahani, remarked that, "In those days the League had not of course fifty coppers in its coffers. There was no office of the Party—the President and the Secretary, both honorary, carried their offices in their respective portmanteaus".[102] In order to strengthen the base of Muslim

League in Punjab, Jinnah approached Sir Fazl-i-Husain who was the most powerful leader of the Muslims of Punjab and also of the Muslim India. Jinnah offered him the Presidentship of the All India Muslim League at the Bombay session of January 1936, saying:

> I feel that at this moment no one can give better lead to the Musalmans of India than yourself.... we want a man of your calibre and experience, and nobody can well, at this critical moment, as far I can see, perform that duty and render that service to the community as your would be able to do. Your refusal will be the greatest misfortune and terrible disappointment.[103]

However, Fazl-i-Husain refused to accept the invitation of Jinnah.[104] Fazli did not want to align himself with a communal party. He was also against the wish of Jinnah that Muslims all over India should contest the elections on a common League platform. Husain believed that strong provincial parties could best tackle the peculiar conditions and problems in each province and thus did not want League participation in the provincial elections.[105]

M.A. Jinnah visited Punjab in April 1936 and once again tried to influence Fazl-i-Husain and asked him to join the Muslim League Parliamentary Board. Jinnah suggested that the Muslim Unionists should contest the provincial election on Muslim League tickets, he was, even, willing to allow them to cooperate with non-Muslim parties in the Assembly.[106] This time Jinnah received crushing rebuff from Sir Husain and Sir Sikander and he was warned:

> To keep his finger out of the Punjab pie, his meddling would simply encourage vociferous tendencies among some Muslims, we cannot possibly allow provincial autonomy to be tampered with in any sphere, and by any body, be he a nominee of the powers who have given this autonomy or a President of the Muslim League or any other association or body.[107]

Husain's decision not to support the Muslim League was also guided by the reality of the Act of 1935. According to the Act the Muslims will not have an overall majority in the

Assembly, this would make a coalition necessary, but for a communal party this would be difficult to attain. Whereas, the Unionist Party, which had maintained inter-communal character, would very easily have coalition with the other communities on the bases of protection of landed interests. However, this adamant attitude of Fazl-i-Husain annoyed Jinnah who remarked, "Fazli thinks he carries the Punjab in his pocket. I am going to smash Fazli."[108] But the Unionist Supremo was too strong to be smashed.

Frustrated in his efforts to gain influence over the Muslim landed elite, Jinnah had electoral alliances with the *Majlis-i-Ahrar* and *Majlis-i-Ittehad-i-Millat*, representing the urban middle classes.[109] In May 1936, Jinnah formed the Muslim League Central Parliamentary Board.[110] Out of its 56 members 11 were taken from Punjab, *Majlis-i-Ahrar* and *Majlis-i-Ittehad-i-Millat* were given due representation in the Central Parliamentary Board.[111] The members from Punjab were: Sir Muhammad Iqbal, Maulana Mohammad Ishaq Khan, Gazi Abdur Rahman, Mian Abdul Aziz, Pir Zain-ul-Abdin, Raja Ghajnafar Ali Khan, Rahim Bakhsh Ghaznavi, Mian Abdul Qadir, Chaudhary Afzal Haq, Chaudhary Abdul Aziz and Khawaja Ghulam Husain. In June 1936, the Central Parliamentary Board issued an election manifesto which reads as under:[112]

(i) To protect religious rights of the Musalmans. Due weightage shall be given to the opinion of the *Jamiat-ul-Ulema-i-Hind*.

(ii) To make every effort to secure the repeal of all repressive laws.

(iii) To resist all measures which encroach upon the fundamental liberties of the people and lead to economic exploitation of the country.

(iv) To reduce heavy cost of administrative machinery and allocate substantial funds for nation-building departments.

(v) To Nationalize the Indian Army and reduce the military expenditure.

(vi) To encourage development of industries, including cottage industries.

(vii) To regulate currency, exchange and prices.

(viii) To stand for the social, educational and economic uplift of the rural population.

(ix) To sponsor measures for the relief of agricultural indebtedness.

(x) To make elementary education free and compulsory.

(xi) To protect and promote Urdu language and script.

(xii) To devise measures for the amelioration of the general conditions of the Muslims.

Muslim League alliance with the *Ahrars* and *Ittehad-i-Millat* was not a consolidated one. In June 1936, the Millat withdrew on the grounds that the League was not demanding complete independence and decided to contest the elections on the *Shahidganj* issue.[113] The Ahrars withdrew in September 1936, as their hopes that the League had been promised vast sums of money for the elections by Bombay traders and Oudh *talukdars* turn out to be without foundation.[114] Thus, Jinnah was back where he had started with his support limited to a small group of urbanities under the leadership of Sir Muhammad Iqbal. The Muslim League also made a futile attempt to win over the support of some of the leading *Pirs* of the region.[115]

Jinnah formally inaugurated the election campaign of Punjab Muslim League on 12 October, 1936. Four subcommittees were created for this purpose and steps were taken to organise district committees throughout the province. Maulana Shaukat Ali, who had played a leading role in the Khilafat agitation, toured Punjab on behalf of the Muslim League.[116]

Indian National Congress was not in good condition in those days.[117] It had its branches throughout the province, however, these branches were not functioning well. The factional rivalry between Gopi Chand Bhargava and Dr. Satyapal further weakened the position of the Congress.[118] Although, the Civil Disobedience Movement had expanded the base of the Congress among all the three communities but the Communal Award had made Muslims to side with the Unionists.[119] Even the Urban Hindus were opposing the Congress under the banner of Hindu Election Board of Raja Narendra Nath.[120] The visit of some national leaders like Jawaharlal Nehru, Sarat Chander Bose and Vallabhbhai Patel somewhat improved the position of the Congress.[121] The election manifesto of the Congress primarily stood for complete independence and equal opportunity for all.[122]

The Sikhs, in the elections of 1937, were divided into two political camps i.e. Shiromani Akali Dal and Khalsa National Party.[123] The Khalsa National Party under the leadership of Sir Sunder Singh Majithia[124] and Sardar Jogender Singh extended its support to the Unionist Party.[125] It was the party of moderate and aristocratic Sikhs whose landed interests coincided with the interests of the Unionist Party.[126] Whereas the Shiromani Akali Dal, under the leadership of Master Tara Singh, Giani Kartar Singh and Jathedar Udham Singh, cooperated with the Congress party. According to an agreement Akali Dal decided to contest 14 seats and 10 seats were left for the Congressite Sikhs.[127] Both the political parties, Shiromani Akali Dal and Khalsa National Party in their respective manifesto promised to work for the abolition of the Communal Award.[128]

The Hindu Electoral Board (Hindu Mahasabha), essentially an organisation of the rich urban Hindu collaborators, took keen interest in the election of 1937.[129] Although, the leadership to the party was provided by the rich Hindu urbanites, but the party had its wide base among the rural and urban Hindus.[130] It did not have any well defined organisational structure, party programmes and any election manifesto.[131] Moreover, it was divided into two factions, one headed by Raja Narendra Nath and the second was headed by Gokul Chand Narang[132], some of its members even made a futile attempt to had alliance with the Congress.[133]

All the political parties, major and small ones, took part in the struggle. In all 459 candidates contested the elections of 1937.[134] The party—wise break-up is given in Table 2.4.

All the parties did their best to attract the voters. Leaders of different political parties toured throughout the province and propagated the ideals, aims and programmes of their respective parties. Sikander Hyat Khan and Sir Chhotu Ram were the chief spokesmen of the Unionist Party. Muslim League and the Congress even took the help of their national level leaders like M.A.Jinnah, Maulana Shaukat Ali, Jawaharlal Nehru, Vallabhbhai Patel, Sarat Chander Bose and Sarojini Naidu.[136] The ideals of the *Majlis-i-Ahrar*, which was contesting the election on the issue of Sahidganj, were propagated by Mir

Table 2.4

Party-wise Break-up of Candidates Contesting Election in 1937[135]

Parties	*Muslims*			*General*			*Sikhs*			*Others*	*Total*
	U	*R*	*O*	*U*	*R*	*O*	*U*	*R*	*O*		
1. Unionist Party	7	75	1	-	15	-	-	1	-	8	107
2. Hindu Electoral Board	-	-	-	5	12	1	-	-	-	2	20
3. Indian National Congress	1	6	1	7	26	1	1	12	1	2	58
4. Muslim League	4	44	2	-	-	-	-	-	-	1	51
5. Akali Dal	-	-	-	-	-	-	2	21	1	-	24
6. Khalsa National Party	-	-	-	-	-	-	2	18	1	-	21
7. Majlis-i-Ahrar	4	-	-	-	-	-	-	-	-	-	4
8. Ittihad-i-Millat	2	5	1	-	-	-	-	-	-	-	8
9. Congress National Party	-	-	-	3	3	1	-	-	-	-	7
10. Socialist Party	-	-	-	-	-	-	-	1	-	-	1
11. Independents	8	62	1	11	42	2	1	19	1	11	157
Total	26	192	6	26	100	4	6	72	3	24	459

Symbols: U—Urban, R—Rural, O—Other (Women, labourers).

Abdul Qayyam, Maulana Mazhar Ali and Khawaja Gulam Hussain.[137] *Ittihad-i-Millat* was represented by Sheikh Muhammad Alam and Khalid Latif Gauba.[138] Sir Sunder Singh Majithia and Master Tara Singh did it for the Khalsa National Party and Akali Dal, respectively.

The Unionist Party, contrary to their rivals, did not engage itself actively in the process of electioneering. The Unionist believed, that the natural leadership of the landlords and *Pirs* in the countryside would ensure the party's success. They would act as brokers in the localities, mobilising their kinsmen, *murids* and clients to vote for the Unionist Party in return for its promise of access to Government patronage.[139]

The rural constituencies were of the center of this election. For the 138 rural constituencies as many as 364 candidates were contesting which included 90 Unionists, 44 Congress party, 44 Muslim Leagues, 21 Akali Dal and 123 Independents.[140] Out of 175 seats in the Assembly 26 candidates were elected unopposed.[141] And of these, the Unionists had captured 18 seats unopposed as compared to two by the Hindu Electoral Board and one by the Congress and the remaining were captured by the independents.[142]

The polling took place as per schedule. The whole process went on well except for some clashes here and there, like the one between *Ahrars* and *Ittehad-i-Millat* in Lahore at a women polling booth, where police had to be called in, to separate the Burqa-clad female voters.[143] This was, however, a trivial matter. Not a single casualty occurred, nor any seriously violent feud occurred between the contesting parties and candidates, despite the apprehension of the Government that serious event might occurred during the poll.[144]

In total 15,29,890 voters exercised their franchise right out of the total strength of 24,01,637, that is 63.70 per cent polling was held.[145] However, in most urban constituencies the polling was surprisingly low. In some places it has been only fifty per cent of the number of registered voters. It is said that a large number of voters appearing on the register were bogus and agents feared to produce persons answering to the bogus names.[146]

Results were declared in February 1937. Unionist Party emerged the largest one by capturing 95 seats. Congress, Khalsa National Party, Hindu Electoral Board and Akali Dal captured 18, 14, 11 and 10 seats respectively.[147] The details of the results are shown in Table 2.5.[148]

Some of the prominent winners were, Sir Shahab-ud-Din (Unionist Party), Raja Narendra Nath (Hindu Electoral Board), Sir Sikander Hayat Khan (Unionist Party), Sir Manohar Lal (non-party), Sir Sunder Singh Majithia (Khalsa National Party), Sir Gokul Chand Narang (Hindu Electoral Board), Chaudhary Chhotu Ram (Unionist Party), Dr. Muhammad Alam (Ittihad-i-Millat), Malik Barkat Ali (Muslim League), Dr. Saifudin Kitchlew (Independent), Diwan Chaman Lal (Labour), Baba Arur Singh (Congress), Khan Bahadur Nawab Muzzafar Khan

Table 2.5
Results of the Elections, 1937

Parties	*Muslims*			*General*			*Sikhs*			*Others*	*Total*
	U	*R*	*O*	*U*	*R*	*O*	*U*	*R*	*O*		
1. Unionist Party	2	71	1	-	13	-	-	-	-	8	5
2. Indian National Congress	-	2	-	7	3	1	-	4	1	-	18
3. Khalsa National Party	-	-	-	-	-	-	2	11	1	-	14
4. Hindu Electoral Board	-	-	-	1	8	1	-	-	-	1	11
5. Shiromani Akali Dal	-	-	-	-	-	-	-	10	-	-	10
6. Majlis-i-Ahrar	2	-	-	-	-	-	-	-	-	-	2
7. Ittihad-i-Millat	2	-	-	-	-	-	-	-	-	-	2
8. Muslim League	1	-	-	-	-	-	-	-	-	-	1
9. Congress National Party	-	-	-	-	1	-	-	-	-	-	1
10. Socialist Party	-	-	-	-	-	-	-	1	-	-	1
11. Labour Party	-	-	-	-	-	-	-	-	-	1	1
12. Independents	2	2	3	-	9	-	-	3	-	-	19
Total	9	75	4	8	34	2	2	29	2	10	175

Symbols: Same as in Table 2.4.

(Unionist Party), Begam Shah Nawaz (Unionist Party), Nawab of Mamdot (Unionist Party), Malik Khizer Hayat Khan Tiwana (Unionist Party), Jathedar Udham Singh Nagoke (Shiromani Akali Dal) and K.L. Gauba (Ahrars).[149]

The elections of 1937, on the one hand were resounding victory of the Unionist Party, on the other hand, it was a crushing defeat of the Muslim League. Only two candidates were elected on the tickets of Muslim League i.e. Malik Barkat Ali and Raja Ghazanfar Ali Khan.[150] Thus, Muslim League had very poor representation in the Punjab Assembly. There were certain pertinent reasons which led to the victory of the Unionists and the defeat of the Muslim League.

The distribution of the constituencies, according to the Act of 1935, was heavily weighed in favour of the rural areas and the franchise dominated by the land-owning castes.[151] Out of the 157 territorial seats in the Punjab Legislative Assembly, 138 were rural and only 14 urban, that is 80per cent legislative representation were given to the rural land owing classes.[152] With a pro-rural agriculturalist ideological background, the Unionist Party immensely benefited because of this new franchise system. The Unionists had already brought together the landed interests which were still unfettered by the Communalist and Nationalist notions.

Out of these 138 rural constituencies, Muhammandans, general and Sikhs were given 75, 34 and 29 constituencies respectively.[153]The Unionists contested 75 Muhammandans rural and 15 general rural seats[154] and bagged very easily 71 Muhammandans and 13 general rural seats.[155] The party secured 70 per cent votes in the Muslim rural constituencies, 34 per cent in the general rural seats whereas it secured only 25 per cent votes Muslim urban constituencies and it did not contested in the general urban constituencies.[156] So deep was the pro-rural agriculturalist ideology of the Unionist Party that even the other landed based party, the Khalsa National Party, not only extended its support to the Unionists[157] but also joined the new Government.[158]

Secondly, these elections were the victory of the landed elite which was the base of the Unionist Party. The Unionists, in fact, adopted the method of vertical political mobilization. Its landed elite of western Punjab as well as of the eastern Punjab mobilized its respective tenants, *biradari*, community and caste to vote for the Unionist Party. So, did its ally, the Khalsa National Party, under the leadership of Sunder Singh Majithia and Sardar Jogender Singh, in the central Punjab. That was the reason that the Unionist Party did not take keen interest in the process of electioneering as it was the case with the other political parties.[159]

Only a split in the ranks of the rural elite could have saved the Muslim League from humiliating defeat. Jinnah knew this very well, thus, he made his utmost efforts to win over the support of the Muslim landed elite.[160] Frustrated in his futile efforts, Jinnah left Punjab swearing, "I shall never come to Punjab again, it is such a hopeless place."[161] After that the Punjab Muslim League virtually remained a body of the urbanites. Among the fifteen members of the election propaganda committee of the Muslim League, there was only one landlord.[162] The refusal of the landed elite to support to Muslim League had such an adverse consequences that even one of its victorious candidate defected to the Unionist Party.[163] Thus, the Muslim League was represented by only one candidate in the Punjab Assembly.

Thirdly, the elections of 1937 were fought on the old lines with personal, tribal and factional rivalries, not party creeds, dominating the choice of the voters.[164] The Muslim candidates who won these factional struggles in their constituencies agreed to come under the umbrella of the Unionists. The Unionists, therefore, never published a list of the official candidates before polling began and in some constituencies even the victorious candidate was co-opted as the Unionists one. In Ludhiana constituency, for example, immediately after the polling, the victorious independent candidate, Mohammed Hassan, was claimed as a Unionists candidate.[165] Muslim League failed to adopt this strategy nor the victorious factional leaders were willing to join, an already defeated body.

Moreover, the Unionist Party, with its pro-rural agriculturist ideology, was essentially a party of the collaborators. All the collaborating forces and the various classes loyal to the British Raj were willing to vote and support to the Unionists in the hope of getting access to the Government patronage. For example, the new electoral system provided franchise right to the military personel/ex-military personel and also to the war widows.[166] A large number of people of South-East Punjab, which had been a major recruitment ground for the imperial forces,[167] were enfranchised because of this new electoral system. They formed 43 per cent of the total rural voters.[168] This class was immensely benefited because of the concessions and privileges bestowed by the British Raj and was loyal to the Raj. Thus,they have no choice but to vote the Unionists, a party which was pro-Government . The fact, that the Unionists captured all but one of the rural Hindu seats of this region.[169] Another notable example is the support extended to the Unionists by the National Progressive Party, a party of rich Urban Hindu loyalist, immediately after the election.[170] On the other hand, the Muslim League, essentially an anti-Government party could not hope to get the vote and support of these classes.

The assistance and support rendered by the leading *Pirs* and *Sajjada-Nashins* of Punjab also resulted in the success of the Unionists Party. As many as eight *Pirs* and *Sajjada-Nashins* rendered their help to the Unionists. They were—Pir Taunsa of Dera Ghazi Khan district, Pir Golra of Rawalpindi district, Pir Makhad of Attock district, Pir Gilani of Multan district, Pir Qureshi of Multan district, Diwan Pakpattam of Montgomery district, Pir Jamat Ali Shah Alipur of Sialkot district and Mahar Sharif Shaine of Bahawalpur state.[171] The Unionists also approached the two leading Christi shrives, of Ajmer and Delhi. These *Pirs* and *Sajjada-Nashins* were the natural leaders of rural Punjab, as well as they were also large landowners. They mobilized their respective *Murids* to vote for the Unionist Party. In fact these *Pirs* and *Sajjada-Nashins* were enjoying the status of local political leaders and state patronage since the times of Mughal Empire.[172] Their political and landed interests, thus, coincided with the interests of the Unionist Party which compelled them to assist the Unionist. The Muslim League, far away from the political power, simply failed to obtain the valuable support of these *Pirs* not withstanding the exception of Pir Fazal Shal Jalalpur of Jhelum district.[173]

And, lastly the constructive works of the Unionist Government during 1923-36, provided them an edge over the other political parties.[174] Sound economic background of the leaders and candidates of the Unionist Party also became a cause of their success. All above reasons led to the resounding victory of the Unionists and defeat of League and other political parties.

It is obvious from the foregone discussions that the elections of 1937 established the hegemony of the Unionist Party in the politics of Punjab. The Muslim League was not only defeated in the elections but also its existence was threatened. The elections had conveyed a message to the League that it will have to adopt new techniques, strategies and programmes to win over the support of the Muslims of Punjab and will have to wage a relentless struggle against the Unionists.

Foot Notes

1. Dalip Singh (1838-1893), son of Maharaja Ranjit Singh and the Council of Regency signed the treaty and gave up its authority over Punjab. M.A. Rahim, *Lord Dalhousie's Administration of Conquered and Annexed States*, New Delhi; 1963, pp. 40-43, H.R. Gupta, *History of the Punjab 1469-1857*, New Delhi, 1973, pp. 370-72.
2. See, J.G.A. Baird, *Private Letters of Lord Dalhousie*, London, 1868, p. 61.
3. H.R. Gupta, *op.cit.*, p. 376.
4. J.G.A. Baird, *op.cit.*, pp. 61-65.
5. H.R. Gupta, *op.cit.*, p. 378.
6. T.R. Metcalf, *The Aftermath of Revolt 1857-1870*, Princeton, 1965, p. 163 and Lepel Griffen, *Chiefs and Families of Note in the Punjab*, Vol. I, Lahore, 1940, pp. 102-05.
7. Lepel Griffen, *op.cit.*, pp 171-73 and Ian Talbot, *op.cit.*, p. 49.
8. Tan Talbot, *op.cit.*, p. 51.
9. Iftikhar H. Malik, 'Identity Formation and Muslim Party Politics in the Punjab 1897-1936', *Modern Asian Studies*, 29, 2, 1995, pp. 301-02.
10. Ian Talbot, 'Deserted Collaborators: The Political Background of the Rise and Fall of the Punjab Unionist Party', *The Journal of Imperial and Commonwealth History II*, October, 1982, pp. 74-80.
11. For details see G.L. Chopra, *Chiefs and Families of Note in the Punjab*, Vol. 2, Lahore, 1940, pp. 221-31.
12. Ian Talbot, "Deserted Collaborators: The Political Background of the Rise and Fall of the Punjab Unionist Party 1923-1947", *The Journal of Imperial and Common Wealth History*, II, October, 1982, pp. 75-76.
13. Lepel Griffin, *op.cit.*, pp. 229-33.
14. Iftikhar H. Malik, *op.cit.*, pp. 302-03.
15. David Gilmartin, *Empire and Islam—Punjab and the Making of Pakistan*, California, 1988, p. 74.
16. *Ibid.*, p. 75.
17. Amar Nath, *The Development of Local Self-Government in the Punjab*, 1849-1900, Lahore, 1929, pp. 6-24.
18. For details see, Fauja Singh, *A Brief Account of the Freedom Movement in Punjab*, Delhi, 1972, S.C. Mittal, *Freedom Movement in Punjab*, 1905-1929, Delhi, 1977, V.N. Datta, *Ideology of the*

Political Elite in Punjab, 1910-1920, Patiala, 1978, David Gilmartin, *op.cit.*, Nina Puri, *Political Elite and Society in the Punjab*, Delhi, 1987.

19. For details see, Nina Puri, *op.cit.*, pp. 150-52.
20. *Ibid.*, pp. 172-73.
21. K.C. Yadav, *Elections in Punjab*, 1920-1947, Tokyo, 1981, p. 132.
22. For details see Nina Puri, *op.cit.*, pp. 90-100.
23. Azim Husain, *Fazl-i-Husain—A Political Biography*, Bombay, 1946, p. 77.
24. Duni Chand, *The Ulster of India*, Lahore, 1936, p. 51.
25. See Azim Husain, *op.cit.*, p. 96 and S.S. Pirzada (ed.), *Foundation of Pakistan, All India Muslim League Documents*, Vol. I, p. XLIII.
26. *Paisa Akhbar*, Lahore, 3 December 1907 (Citations of the *Paisa Akhbar* are from Ikram Ali Malik, *The History of the Punjab* 1799-1947, Delhi, Reprint 1993).
27. For biographical details of Mian Mohammad Shafi, See Ikram Ali Malik, *op.cit.*, pp. 547-49.
28. *Paisa Akhbar*, 3 December, 1907 in Ikram Ali Malik, *op.cit.*, p. 272.
29. *Ibid.*, p. 281.
30. *Ibid.*, p. 315.
31. *Ibid.*, p. 296.
32. Umar Hayat Khan Tiwana, resigned from the Vice-Presidentship of the Muslim League with the reasons that there were general complaints against the League. *Paisa Akhbar*, Lahore, 11 May, 1916 in Ikram Ali Malik, *op.cit.*, p. 304.
33. *Paise Akhbar*, Lahore, 16 August, 1917, in Ikram Ali Malik, *op.cit.*, p. 315.
34. Ikram Ali Malik, *op.cit.*, p. 426.
35. Iftikhar H. Malik, *op.cit.*, p. 309.
36. A.C. Banerjee, *The Constitutional History of India*, Vol. III, Meerut, 1978, p. 13.
37. Craig Baxter, 'The People's Party vs. the Punjab Feudalist,' *Journal of Asian and African Studies*, Vol. VIII, 1990, p. 167.
38. *Home Public*, No. 145, 10th June 1920.
39. Craig Baxter, *op.cit.*, p. 168.
40. Tan Talbot, 'Deserted Collaborators: The Political Background of the Rise and Fall of the Punjab Unionist Party 1923-1947', *The Journal of Imperial and Commonwealth History II*, October, 1982, pp. 77-78.
41. Craig Baxter, *op.cit.*, p. 168.
42. For biographical details see, Azim Hussain, *Sir Fazl-in-Hussain—A Biography*, Bombay, 1946, Syed Hur Ahmad, *Mian Sir Fazl-i-Hussain*, Lahore, 1936, Waheed Ahmad (ed.), *Letters of Mian Fazl-*

i-Hussain, Lahore, 1977, S.M. Ikram, *Modern Muslim India and the Birth of Pakistan*, Lahore, 1969.

43. *The Punjab Administrative Report*, 1922, p. 17.
44. Syed Nur Ahmad, *op.cit.*, pp. 52-54.
45. Craig Baxter, *op.cit.*, p. 170.
46. Iftikhar H. Malik, *op.cit.*, p. 313.
47. For details about the Party see R. Tanwar, The Unionist Party in Punjab 1923-1947, unpublished Ph.D. Thesis, Kurukshetra University, 1989, pp. 110-43.
48. Ian Talbot, *Punjab and The Raj*, p. 89.
49. David Gilmartin, *op.cit.*, p. 107.
50. S.S. Pirzada (ed.) *op.cit.*, Vol. I, p. 576.
51. Ikram Ali Malik, *op.cit.*, p. 446.
52. David Gilmartin, *op.cit.*, p. 111.
53. David Page, *Prelude to Partition: The Indian Muslims and the Imperial System of Control 1920-1932*, Delhi, 1982, pp. 195-258.
54. Ian Talbot, *Punjab And The Raj*, p. 90.
55. For the biographical details of Sir Muhammad Iqbal, See Ikram Ali Malik, *op.cit.*, pp. 545-46.
56. Presidential Address of Sir Muhammad Iqbal to the All India Muslim League, 21st session, Allahabad, 29-30 December, 1930, See. S.S. Pirzada (ed.) *op.cit.*, Vol. II, pp. 153-71.
57. David Gilmartin, *op.cit.*, p. 107.
58. *Ibid.*, p. 112.
59. Ikram Ali Malik, *op.cit.*, pp. 455-56.
60. For details see Ganda Singh, *History of the Gurdwara Shahidganj*, Lahore, 1935, pp. 64-72 also, Report on the Shahidganj affair by Mian abdul Aziz, *Home Political*, File 5/14/35.
61. David Gilmartin, *op.cit.*, p. 82.
62. A.C. Banerjee, *The Constitutional History of India*, Vol. 111, Delhi, 1978, pp. 137-51.
63. *Government of India Act, 1935*, New Delhi, 1936, p. 41.
64. *Indian Franchise Committee Report, 1932*, Vol. I, Calcutta, 1932, p. 33.
65. *Ibid.*
66. *Home Public*, File No. 305/1937, pp. 58-59.
67. *Home Political*, File No. F. 111/1937, pp. 47-48.
68. These Constituencies were South-East Gurgaon, Karnal-North, Ambala-Simla, Hoshiarpur West, Ludhiana-Firozpur, Jullundur, Amritsar-Sialkot and Lyallpur-Jhang. Source, *Home Public*, File No. 305/1937, p. 63.
69. K.C. Yadav, *Elections in Punjab 1920-1947*, p. 19.
70. *Ibid.*
71. Jawaharlal Nehru, *An Autobiography*, Delhi, 1962, p. 386.

72. *Indian Annual Register, 1936*, Vol. I, p. 294.
73. For details see Tarachand, *History of Freedom Movement in India*, Vo. IV, New Delhi, 1972, pp. 215-17, Anita Inder Singh, *The Origins of the Partition of India 1936-1947*, Delhi, 1987, pp. 2-3 and Ayesha Jalal, *The Sole Spokesman: Jinnah, The Muslim League and the Demand for Pakistan*, Cambridge, 1985, pp. 17-19.
74. Anita Singh, 'Nehru and the Communal Problem 1936-1939,' unpublished M.Phil. Thesis, submitted to Jawaharlal Nehru University, 1976, p. 103.
75. *Indian Annual Register, 1935*, Vol. II, pp. 311-12.
76. See Tara Chand, *op.cit.*, pp. 215-16 and K.L. Tuteja, *op.cit.*, p. 175.
77. Ian Talbot, *Punjab and the Raj 1849-1947*, p. 95.
78. Syed Nur Ahmad, *op.cit.*, p. 127.
79. Iftikhar H. Malik, *op.cit.*, p. 317.
80. Craig Baxter, *op.cit.*, p. 177.
81. Syed Nur Ahmad, *op.cit.*, p. 127.
82. This speculation received strength with criticism levelled against Sir Fazli Husain by some Hindu politician like Gulshan Rai, who wrote to Fazl-i-Husain, "The impression I have gathered during the last few months is that the Europeans want Sir Sikander, and not you to form the first Ministry of the Autonomous Punjab." See Azim Husain, *op.cit.*, pp. 336-37.
83. Sir Sultan Muhammad Shah Agha Khan, had written some letters to Fazl-i-Husain. He offered to give among several other things, Rs. 20,000 for meeting the financial stringency of the party, should Fazli come out to lead it.
    Chaudhary Shahbuddin, a prominent Muslim leader said, "Without You (Fazl-i-Husain) the Muslims will be no where—you must live and lead the Muslims as long as you can." See Azim Husain, *op.cit.*, pp. 300-02.
84. Iftikhar H. Malik, *op.cit.*, p. 318.
85. For example the *Paisa Akhbar*, Lahore, 14.4.1935 (citation of *Paisa Akhbar* is taken from Ikram Ali Malik, *op.cit.*).
86. In a meeting of the Executive Board of the All India Muslim Conference in Delhi in Feb. 1935, Fazli formally announced his intention to reorganize the Unionist Party. He issued a pamphlet entitled, *Punjab Politics*, for this purpose. See Azim Husain, *op.cit.*, p. 304 and Syed Nur Ahmad, *op.cit.*, p. 136.
87. See *The Unionist Party Manifesto* (Urdu), Lahore, 1936, pp. 3-4.
88. *Ibid.*, pp. 5-6.
89. Waheed Ahmad (ed.) *Diary and Notes of Mian Fazl-i-Husain*, p. 346.

90. Speech of Fazl-i-Husain at the inauguration of the Unionist Headquarters on April 12, 1936 wide *Punjab Government Gazette Extraordinary*, 13.11.1936 (Para No. 1331).
91. It was *Two Paise* per rupee for those paying Rs. 10 or more as land-revenue, *one anna* per rupee for those paying income or Hasiat tax. The committees could exonerate poor members from paying these fees. See *The Unionist Party Manifesto* (Urdu), Lahore, 1936, pp. 4-5.
92. Azim Husain, *op.cit.*, p. 337.
93. *Ibid.*, p. 339.
94. After the death of Fazli, this arrangement did not work. Azim Husain, *op.cit.*, p. 341.
95. This money was contributed by the Nawab of Kalabay, Syed Maatab Ali, Sardar Muhammad Nawaz Khan Rs. 5,000 each, Fazl-i-Husain, Zafarulla Khan, Nawab Allaha Bakhsh, Nawab of Mamdot, Sir Chhotu Ram, Malik Umar Hyat Khan Tiwana, Ahmad Yar Khan Daultana and Chaudhary Shahbuddin Rs. 3,000 each. Sir Agha Khan Contributed Rs. 10,000. See Azim Husain, *op.cit.*, p. 340.
96. Waheed Ahmad (ed)., *Letters of Mian Fazl-i-Husain*, p. 592.
97. The poor health and election burden resulted in the death of Sir Husain, thus the Unionist would go to the election without their founder. See Craig Baxter, *op.cit.*, p. 177.
98. See C. Khaliquzzman, *Pathway to Pakistan*, Lahore, 1961, pp. 137-38, Z.H. Zaidi (ed.), *M.A. Jinnah-Ispahani Correspondence 1936-1948*, Karachi, 1976, pp. 10-14, Ian Talbot, *Punjab and The Raj 1849-1947*, pp. 89-90 and Ikram Ali Malik, *op.cit.*, pp. 465-68.
99. Stanley Wolpert, *Jinnah of Pakistan*, Delhi, 1985, p. 140.
100. M. Rafique Afzal, *Malik Barkat Ali: His Life and Writings*, Lahore, 1969, p. 30.
101. Stanley Wolpert, *op.cit.*, pp. 138-42.
102. M.A.H. Ispahani, *Qaid-e-Azam Jinnah As I Knew Him*, Karachi, 1966, p. 20.
103. Jinnah wrote to Fazli on 5 January 1936. See Waheed Ahmad (ed.), *Letters of Mian Fazl-i-Husain*, Lahore, 1976, p. 495, also, Imran Ali, *Punjab Politics in the Decade Before Partition*, Lahore, 1974, p. 75.
104. Azim Husain, *op.cit*, pp. 306-07.
105. *Ibid.*, p. 310.
106. Imran Ali, *op.cit.*, p. 79.
107. Sikander Hyat Khan to Fazl-i-Husain, 1 May 1936. See Waheed Ahmad (ed.), *Letters of Mian Fazl-i-Husain*, p. 423 and Z.H. Zaidi (ed.), *op.cit.*, pp. 13-14.
108. Azim Husain, *op.cit.*, p. 336.

109. Punjab Fortnightly Report for the Second half of April 1936, *Home Political*, File No. 18/4/1936.
110. Z.H. Zaidi, 'Aspects of the Development of Muslim League Policy' in C.H. Philips and M.D. Wainwright (ed.) *The Partition of India: Policies and Perspectives*, London, 1970, pp. 246-47.
111. See C. Khaliquzzman, *op.cit.*, p. 416.
112. Latif Ahmad Sherwani (ed.), *Pakistan in the Making: Documents and Readings*, Karachi, 1987, p. 535 and S.S. Pirzada (ed.), *op.cit.*, Vol. II, pp. 246-58.
113. Punjab Fortnightly Report for the Second half of June 1936, *Home Political*, File No. 18/6/1936.
114. Punjab Fortnightly Report for the Second half of August 1936, *Home Political*, File No. 18/8/1936.
115. For details see, David Gilmartin, 'Religious Leadership and the Pakistan Movement in the Punjab', Mushirul Hasan (ed.), *India's Partition: Process, Strategy and Mobilization*, Delhi; 1997, pp. 210-19.
116. Punjab Fortnightly Report for the Second half of December 1936, *Home Political*, File No. 18/12/1936.
117. See B.N. Pandey, *op.cit.*, pp. 412-13.
118. See Satya M. Rai, *op.cit.*, p. 218.
119. B.N. Pandey, *op.cit.*, p. 413.
120. Satya M. Rai, *op.cit.*, p. 221.
121. Punjab Fortnightly Report for the Second Half of December 1936, *Home Political*, File No. 18/12/1936.
122. Nehru drafted the Congress Election Manifesto, 22 August, 1936. See S. Gopal (ed.) *Selected Works of Jawaharlal Nehru*, Vol. III, New Delhi, 1976, pp. 459-64.
123. See K.L. Tuteja, *op.cit.*, pp. 175-79
124. Sunder Singh Majithia (1872-1941) became M.L.C., then member of Imperial Legislative Council 1915-21, member Executive Council 1921-26, M.L.A. 1937-41. Minister in the Unionist Government 1937-41, Sec. V.N. Datta, *Ideology of the Political Elite in Punjab*, Patiala, 1978, pp. 14-15.
125. Punjab Fortnightly Report For the Second half of May 1936, *Home Political*, File No. 18/5/1936.
126. Stephen Oreh, 'The Sikhs, Congress and the Unionist in British Punjab, 1937-1945', *Modern Asian Studies*, 8, 3, 1974, pp. 399-401.
127. *The Tribune*, November 18, 1936.
128. The Akali Dal Manifesto in *The Tribune*, June 20, 1936. Manifesto of the Khalsa National Party in *Sunder Singh Majithia Papers*.
129. Stephen Oren, *op.cit.*, p. 398.
130. Francis Robinson, "The All India Hindu Mahasabha", in B.N. Pandey (ed.), *Leadership in South Asia*, New Delhi, 1977, p. 411.

131. *Ibid.*, p. 412.
132. Stephen Oren, *op.cit.*, p. 398.
133. Punjab Fortnightly Report for the first half of November, 1936. *Home Political*, File No. 18/11/1936.
134. *Home Public*, File No. 305/1937, p. 59.
135. K.C. Yadav, *Elections in Punjab 1920-1947*, pp. 84-97.
136. Punjab Fortnightly Report for the Second half of December 1936, *Home Political*, File No. 18/12/1936.
137. Punjab Fortnightly Report for the First half of November 1936, *Home Political*, File No. 18/11/1936.
138. Punjab Fortnightly Report for the Second half of November 1936, *Home Political*, File No. 18/11/1936.
139. Ian Talbot, *Punjab and the Raj 1849-1947*, p. 106.
140. K.C. Yadav, *Elections in Punjab 1920-1947*, p. 97.
141. *Home Public*, File No. 305/1937; pp. 59-61.
142. *The Tribune*, 4 December 1936 and 5 to 15 February 1937. Some of the unopposed members were: Sikander Hayat Khan, Raja Narendera Nath, Sir Manohar Lal, Sir Shahab-ud-din.
143. Punjab Fortnightly Report for the Second half of January 1937, *Home Political*, File No. 18/1/1937.
144. Two serious incidents occurred before the polling. A helper of Sir Sunder Singh Majithia was murdered in Gurdaspur district by the supporters of the other side. And, in Amritsar a Hindu Nationalist died after receiving injuries in a scuffle with some Congress supporters. That is why the Government feared violence. *Home Political*, File No. 18/1/1937, Punjab Fortnightly Report of the first half of January 1937.
145. *Home Public*, File No. 305/1937, pp. 59-61.
146. Punjab Fortnightly Report for the Second half of January 1937, *Home Political*, File No. 18/1/1937.
147. *Home Political*, File No. F/111/1937, pp. 47-48.
148. Stephen Oren, *op.cit.*, p. 398, Based on, United Kingdom: House of Commons, *Parliamentary Papers 1937-38, XXI*, 'Returns Showing the Results of Elections in India 1937,' pp. 80-93.
149. *Home Political*, File No. F/111/1937.
150. Ghazanbar Ali Khan was elected from the Pind Datan Constituency with the help of Pir Fazal Shah. See M. Rafique Afzal, *op.cit.*, pp. 36-37.
151. Stephen Oren, *op.cit.*, p. 399.
152. *Home Public*, File No. 305/1937, pp. 58-59.
153. *Home Political*, File No. 305/1937, pp. 58-59.
154. K.C. Yadav, *Elections in Punjab 1920-1947*, pp. 86-87.
155. Stephen Oren, *op.cit.*, p. 399.
156. *Reform Office*, Franchise File No. 20/111/F. 36.

157. Emerson to Linlithgow, December 19, 1937, *Linlithgow Papers.*
158. *The Tribune,* March 3, 1937.
159. The Congress, Muslim League, Majlis-i-Ahrar, Millat and other parties took keen interest in electioneering. See *Home Political,* File No. 18/11/1936.
    Home Political, File No. 18/12/1936.
    Home Political, File No. 18/1/1937.
160. A. Husain, *op.cit.,* pp. 306-07, M. Rafiq Afzal, *op.cit.,* p. 35 and K.B. Sayeed, "The Personality of Jinnah and his Political Strategy," in C.H. Phillips and M.D. Wainwright (ed), *op.cit.,* p. 284.
161. Azim Husain, *op.cit.,* p. 311.
162. These members were: Sheikh Akbal Ali, Mian Abdul Aziz, Professor Inayat Ullah, Abdul Mannan, Sheikh Mohammad Jah, Pir Taj-ud-Din, Mohammad Jabfri, Malik Nur Elahi, Mohammad Azim Khan, Ghulam Rasul, Abdul Malik, Nawabzada Muzaffar Ali Khan, Syed Tassaduq Hussain, Mohammad Shafi and Malik Zeman Mendi Khan (The only landlord). See *Civil and Military Gazette,* Lahore, October 17, 1936.
163. Raja Ghazanfar Ali Khan defected to the Unionist Party and obtained a Parliamentary Secretaryship.
164. Emerson to Linlithgow, October 19, 1936, *Linlithgow Papers.*
165. *Civil and Military Gazette,* February 3, 1937.
166. *Punjab Government Gazette Extraordinary,* 13.11.1936
167. Prem Chaudhary, *Punjab Politics: The Role of Sir Chhotu Ram,* New Delhi, 1984, pp. 297-98 and S.C. Mittal, *op.cit.,* p. 106.
168. Prem Chaudhary, *op.cit.,* p. 302.
169. *The Tribune,* 3-4 February, 1937.
170. *The Tribune,* 5 February, 1937. The elected members of the Hindu Electoral Board formed the National Progressive Party, immediately after the election, under the leadership of Raja Narendra Nath. They extended support to the Unionist Party only with an urge to share power.
171. David Gilmartin, 'Religious Leadership and the Pakistan Movement in the Punjab,' *Modern Asian Studies,* 13,3, 1979, pp. 492-502.
172. *Ibid.,* pp. 489-90.
173. *Ibid.,* p. 497. Pir Fazal Shah Jalalpur of Jhelum district mobilized his *murids* to ensure his uncle's election (Raja Ghazanfar Ali Khan) for the Muslim League.
174. Y.P. Bajaj, 'Unionist Politics and the General Election of 1936-37: An Analysis,' *Punjab History Conference Proceedings,* 20th Session Patiala, 1986, p. 344.

3

Struggle for Survival 1937-1942

The politics of the post-elections period i.e. the period from the year 1937 to 1942, was the ascendancy of the politics of the Unionist Party and the struggle of the Muslim League for its survival. The results of the 1937 elections proved a major setback in the career of the Punjab Muslim League. Faced with the threat of being snuffed out politically, the League urgently needed a new strategy for survival.

The victory of the Unionist Party, on the other hand, was also warmly welcomed by the British officials, since the Unionists were the proven friends of the Raj. On April 2,1937, the new ministry in Punjab[1], under the Act of 1935, took over under the premiership of Sir Sikander Hayat Khan.[2] The other ministers were Sir Chhotu Ram, Mian Abdul Haye, Sir Khizr Hayat Khan Tiwana (all from Unionist Party), Sir Manohar Lal (non-party), and Sir Sunder Singh Majithia (Khalsa Nationalist Party).[3] Thus, a ministry drawn from all the communities was formed, since Sir Sikander wanted to entrench himself firmly in the saddle of power on the basis of the intercommunal structure of the government.

In addition to these ministers Sir Sikander appointed Mian Ahmad Yar Khan Daultana, Mir Maqbool Ahmad, Sardar Ujjal Singh, Begam Jahanawa, Nawab Shah Nawaz, Raja Ghazanfar Ali Khan, Choudhary Tika Ram, Thakur Ripudaman Singh and Sheikh Faiz Muhammad as parliamentary secretaries. Sir Shahabuddin was elected as the speaker of the Assembly and Sardar Dasundha Singh was his deputy.[4]

On the one side, the Unionists were firmly in the saddle and on the other side, the Muslim League was in very poor position. The League lost not only in Punjab but also its performance in other provinces was far from satisfactory. In Bengal, the League had to accept a collision led by Fazlul Huq who did not acknowledge their writ, in Sind they faced an independent ministry and in the N.W.F.P., where almost the entire population was Muslim, a Congress ministry was formed, the worst humiliation of all. Its position in Muslim minority provinces was equally bad as is shown in Table 3.1.

Table 3.1

Results of General Elections, 1937[5]

Provinces	*Total No. of Seats*	*Total No. of Seats Won by Congress*	*Total No. of Muslim Seats*	*No. of Seats Won by Muslim League*	*No. of Seats Won by Muslim Group*
Madras	215	159	28	11	17
Bombay	175	86	29	20	09
Bengal	250	54	117	40	77
U.P.	228	134	64	27	37
Punjab	175	18	84	01	83
Bihar	152	98	39	—	39
C.P.	112	70	14	—	14
N.W.F.P.	50	19	36	—	36
Assam	108	33	34	09	25
Orissa	60	36	04	—	04
Sind	60	07	36	—	36
Total	1,585	714	485	108	377

Before the 1937 elections, Jinnah's plan had been to claim for the League the undisputed spokesmanship of Muslims at the all India level. This plan required the Muslim-majority provinces to come under the banner of League and Muslims in provinces where they were in a minority to vote solidly for the League. However,the election results shattered the plan of Jinnah. The Punjab Muslim League, under the Presidentship of

Sir Muhammad Iqbal, immediately after the elections began the task of reorganizing itself and determined to build a mass base of support in the countryside.[6] The League launched a vigorous rural propaganda campaign.[7] and workers were sent into the villages to form primary branches of the League.[8] The membership fee of the League was reduced from one rupee to only four annas to encourage as many villagers to join as possible.[9] The Punjab League hoped to enroll at this time as many as 20,000 new primary members in the Lahore district alone.[10]

The prominent leaders of the Punjab Muslim League like Sir Muhammad Iqbal, Malik Zeman Mehdi Khan, Ghulam Rasul and Malik Barkat Ali toured rural Punjab to strengthen the task of membership drive.[11] Primary branches were established in the rural areas of Gujranwala, Rawalpindi and Jhelum districts.[12] The League achieved substantial success in enrolling new members from the rural Punjab during the year 1937.[13] However, this new drive of the Muslim League came to an halt in October 1937, with the signing of the Jinnah-Sikander pact at the Lucknow session of the All India Muslim League.[14] Since October 1937 till the death of Sir Sikander i.e. December 1942, the Punjab Muslim League was almost under the control of the Unionists and its activities completely ceased.

The twenty-fifth session of the All India Muslim League, which was attended by Sir Sikander Hayat Khan, the Premier of Punjab and Fazlul-Huq, the Premier of Bengal, was held at Lucknow in October 1937. It was at this session that Sir Sikander along with his Muslim Unionist followers joined hands with Jinnah, this agreement is commonly known as Jinnah-Sikander Pact. The important clauses of this pact were as following-I.

1. That on his return to Punjab, Sir Sikander Hayat Khan will convene a special meeting of his party and advise all Muslim members to sign the creed and join it. As such they will be subject to rules and regulations of the Central Parliamentary Board of the All India Muslim League. This will not affect the continuance of the present coalition of the Unionist Party.
2. That in future elections and by-elections for the

legislature after the adoption of this arrangement, the group constituting the present Unionist Party will jointly support candidates put up by their respective groups.

3. That the Muslim members of the Legislature who are elected on or accept the League ticket will constitute the Muslim Party within the legislature. It shall be open to the Muslim League Party so formed to maintain or enter into a coalition or alliance with any other party consistent with the fundamental principles of the policy and programme of the League. Such alliances may be evolved before or after the elections. The existing combination shall maintain its present name, the Unionist Party.
4. That, in view of the agreement, the Muslim League Provincial Parliamentary Board would be reconstituted.[15]

Why Sikander Hayat Khan joined up with Jinnah at the Lucknow session of the League is a debateable issue. Just one year before, the Unionist Party considered the Muslim League as a biggest enemy and time and again turned down its requests for an alliance. And, now what persuaded Sikander to accept Jinnah as a spokesman of the Muslims at the all India level, on the platform of the All India Muslim League, a party which hitherto be considered a party of the sworn enemy.

It has commonly been asserted that the fervour of the Lucknow session was mainly stimulated by the Muslim reaction to the Congress politics. The Congress has formed ministries in seven provinces out of the eleven provinces of the British India,[16] it has started the Muslim mass contact programme[17] and also refused to have a League Coalition ministry in the United provinces.[18] It is said that Sikander faced a threat from the mass contact programme of the Congress. M.A.H.Ispahani, a close associate of Jinnah, also asserted:

> *Sikander Hayat Khan with his Unionist followers, joined the Muslim League not out of deep conviction but merely as a matter of necessity—as an astute politician, Sikander realized the potential danger to his Ministry. He knew that the Unionist*

> *Ministry by itself could not withstand the tide of Congress totalitarianism unless he secured the support of a Muslim organization functioning on an all-India plane.*[19]

However, it is doubtful that fear of Congress power motivated Sikander to seek political links with the All India Muslim League. The organizational and financial resources of the Congress could be a threat to the inter-communal Unionist coalition. But there was no real prospect of the loss of minority support for the Ministry in the Assembly.[20] Instead, by joining the Muslim League the Unionists ran a greater and more immediate risk of alienating a large block of Hindu supporters. Although, Sikander in 1937 was publicly critical of Congress, especially of its policy towards the minorities.[21] However, the real reason for this criticism was not concern for Muslims, but an effort to support the British position against Congress on the office acceptance issue.[22] Thus, on the basis of the data available, it is difficult to endorse Ispahani's thesis.

Sikander, in keeping with the Unionists tradition, was a non-communal politician, and in associating with Muslim League he risked the weakening of his coalition with non-Muslims and his campaign against communalism. In attending the All India Muslim League session it seems, rather than providing leadership to the Muslim League and Muslim communal consciousness, Sikander wished to immobilize it at its origin. He rightly perceived the League as potentially the most virulent exploiter of the communal issue, and the Punjab Muslim League from its urban base was already thus oriented.[23] Like Fazl-i-Husain, he feared of the League as a Muslim Party which might erode Unionist ranks or attract a rival faction.[24] In his dispatch to Linlithgow, Emerson, the Governor of Punjab, also explains this situation:

> The discontent among Muslims is steadily growing and is finding expression in the Muslim press and in meetings. Feeling is growing that protection of minority may be sound principle, it has so far operated to the detriment of the major community, which has come out worse in most of the communal fights. The Muslim attitude is becoming a cause of anxiety to the Premier.[25]

Sir Sikander, being afraid of losing a grip over the Muslim Unionists, cleverly maintained the status quo by cooperating with the League himself, holding that there were no differences of policy with it on all-India issues, providing Jinnah respected the non-communal composition of the Unionist Party,[26] and would not interfere in the internal affairs of Punjab politics and government.[27] Sir Sikander, therefore, signed a pact with Jinnah to try and reduce the strength of Muslim League in Punjab and as such his intentions were hostile to the role of the League in Punjab.

This further becomes clear from statements by Unionist leaders on their return from Lucknow. The Punjab was astir with rumours that Sikander had made a complete obeisance to Jinnah and would allow the Unionists to be absorbed by the League.[28] Especially critical were the Congress and the Akali Sikhs who wished to discredit the Unionist Party's non-communal stance. Sir Sikander, however, emphatically stated that the pact would have no effect on the existing composition of parties in the Assembly, though Muslim Unionists would be advised to obtain League membership. But in future elections League candidates would have to join the Unionists in the Assembly.[29] This could be regarded as contrary to the wording and spirit of the Sikander-Jinnah pact as it did not encompass the establishment of a League Party in the Assembly.[30] Thus, the Unionists were using the pact for strengthening their position.

That the Sikander-Jinnah pact was a victory for the Unionists is proved by the reaction of Sir Muhammad Iqbal, President of the Punjab Muslim League and the League's urban supporters in Punjab. Muhammad Iqbal wrote to Jinnah that, "I am now definitely of the opinion that Sir Sikander wants nothing less than the complete control of the League and the Provincial Parliamentary Board. In your pact with him it is mentioned that the Parliamentary Board will be re-constituted and the Unionists will have majority in the Board—I personally see no harm in giving him the majority that he wants but he goes beyond that pact when he wants a complete change in the office-holders of the League, especially the Secretary who has done so much for the League. He also wishes that the finances of the League should be controlled by his men. All this to my mind amounts to capturing of the League and then killing it."[31] Malik Barkat Ali and Ghulam Rasool, another prominent Leaguers, also criticised Sikander and warned Jinnah that Sikander wished to minimize the League's influence in Punjab.[32]

It is obvious from the above discussions that Sikander-Jinnah pact further weakened the position of the Punjab Muslim League. Then, why did Jinnah signed this agreement. He, it seems, at that political juncture, was badly in need of the support of the Unionists in all India politics. In order to gain this, he was prepared, for the moment, to see the Punjab League come under Unionist control. The immediate effect of the pact was to strengthen the position of the Muslim League in All-India politics. Choudhary Khaliquzzaman has asserted.

> No one can deny that without this action on the part of Sikander the Muslim League would have been confined to the minority provinces alone and sooner or later they would have gone under—Sikander saved the Muslim India by coming to the League session in Lucknow and by infusing life into the organization. His association with the Muslim League at this crucial hour in the fate of Muslim India is an event in history and must live forever to remind us of his greatness.[33]

Jinnah used this opportunity to strengthen the position of the Muslim League *vis-a-vis* Congress in the All-India politics. He organised his party, provided it a new constitution and passed a resolution, with the following clauses, in order to expand the social base of his party:

1. To fix working hours for factory workers and other labourers.
2. To improve the housing and hygienic condition of the labourers and make provision for slum clearance.
3. To fix minimum wages.
4. To reduce rural and urban debts and abolish usury.
5. To grant a moratorium with regard to all debts, decreed or otherwise, till proper legislation has been enacted.
6. To secure legislation for exemption of house from

attachment or role in, execution of decrees.

7. To obtain security of tenure and fixation of fair rents and revenue.
8. To abolish forced labour.
9. To undertake rural uplift work.
10. To encourage cottage industries and small indigenous industries, both in rural and urban areas.
11. To encourage the use of Swadeshi articles, specially hand-woven cloth.
12. To establish an industrial board for the development of industries and the prevention of exploitation by middlemen.
13. To devise means for the relief of employment.
14. To advance compulsory primary education.
15. To recognise secondary and University education, specially scientific and technical.[34]

Jinnah, thus, knowingly behaved indifferently with Sir Muhammad Iqbal and other leaders of the Punjab Muslim League, who actually acknowledge his authority and whose help he had solicited for the 1937 elections.[35] Jinnah's attitude demonstrated that the price of obtaining Unionist cooperation at the All-India level was to concede to them all rights in Punjab politics. He, it seems, was convinced that this halt to the League's growth would not damage its eventual chances of coming to power in Punjab province.

The arrangements at Lucknow were, in fact in the nature of compromise, and involved advantages as well as disadvantages to both parties. It was not a one sided affair, Jinnah utilized the pact to enhance the prestige of his party in the All-India politics whereas Sir Sikander used this opportunity to assume complete control of the Punjab Muslim League. However, the far reaching consequences of the pact proved beneficial for the Muslim League. Through this pact Jinnah gained ascendency in the national politics and then began to interfere into the internal politics of the Punjab province which led to the growth of the League.

Under the Sikander-Jinnah pact, Muslim Unionists were to join the League, but it was not until April 1938 that Muslim Unionists actually signed the membership forms of the League.[36]

It, nevertheless, indicated the real motives of the Unionists. Sir Sikander wished first to gain control of the Punjab Muslim League, thus he began efforts to remove its office-bearers. He complained to Iqbal that he found it difficult to work with the Punjab Muslim League Secretary, Ghulam Rasul, and suggested his replacement by his own nominee,[37] Nawabzada Khurshid Ali Khan, but Iqbal refused. Ahmad Yar Khan Daultana, one of the close associate of Sir Sikander, had already written to Jinnah about it, as early as in November, 1937:

> Everyone assured Sir Sikander that they would obey his orders and join the League when so desired. But they all expressed their alarm and anxiety over the present state of affairs in the Provincial League. I assured them that you had promised about the reconstruction of the Provincial League. They were not prepared to trust their funds in the hands of Mr. Ghulam Rasul or to acknowledge the present office-bearers of the Provincial League with the possible exception of Dr. Sir Mohammad Iqbal as their leader or representatives—I request you in the interests of Muslims of Punjab to be very careful of what the old Leaguers of Punjab write to you, it is impossible for us to carry on with the people like Mr. Ghulam Rasul and others of the same type.[38]

Sir Sikander, however, continued his efforts to gain control of the Provincial League and in March 1938 he achieved a big success. Mohammad Iqbal, who was fatally ill, was himself replaced as President of Punjab Muslim League by Nawab Shahnawaz Khan of Mamdot, a pillar of the Unionist Party and the largest landowner in Punjab.[39] The Provincial Muslim League was by this time in a state of financial collapse through lack of patronage, and Mamdot succeeded in convincing some of its leaders that his appointment would assure financial viability.[40] Thus, Sir Mohammad Iqbal, the man who had actually reorganized the party in 1935, was ignored and betrayed by the new Leaguers.

With a Unionist as the President of Punjab Muslim League, Sir Sikander acquired a vital source of manipulation. He hoped, now, to check the whatever remaining activities of League in Punjab. His first major move was to obtain the disaffiliation of the Punjab League from its parent body.[41] By March 1938, Provincial Leagues had to submit a full account of their branches and office-bearers for affiliation to the All India Muslim League. At this time also, they had to submit names of members to the All India Muslim Council, for which the Punjab Muslim League sent a list of 90 names. No Unionists were included as none had accepted League membership.[42] Thus, Sir Sikander was suddenly threatened with a complete loss of representation in the legal right to refuse election of these 90 nominees. The only way out was to reject the application for affiliation by Punjab Muslim League.[43]

In March 1938, the All India Muslim League Council, because of the pressure of Sir Sikander, appointed a committee under Nawab Ismail Khan's Presidency to decide on the applications for reaffiliation of its provincial organisations. This committee, in its meeting of April 1938, refused to reaffiliate the Punjab Muslim League on the grounds of fundamental differences between the Punjab Muslim League and All India Muslim League constitutions.[44] It was alleged that Liaquat Ali Khan, the general-secretary of the All India Muslim League, was throughout sympathetic to Sir Sikander, and was instrumental in obtaining disaffiliation.[45] Liaquat Ali Khan perhaps could not afford to antagonize the Sikander Ministry, as he held much land in eastern Punjab and his brother was a Unionist MLA.[46]

The second major achievement of Sir Sikander was to obtain the cancellation of Lahore as the Venue for the 1938 All India Muslim League's session. Mohammad Iqbal had been very eager for this as a means of spreading League popularity, and Jinnah had been sympathetic to it.[47] However, Nawab of Mamdot, President of the Provincial League, under the pressure of Sir Sikander, strongly protested that it would increase communal friction, and Jinnah had no choice but to shift the Venue to Calcutta.[48] Jinnah did it, since there appears to have been an understanding between Jinnah and Sikander that while Jinnah would speak for Muslims at the All India level but he (Jinnah) would not interfere in the provincial matters.[49]

In 1938 Sir Sikander had also begun to influence the decisions of the All India Muslim League. The issue of Shahidganj Mosque was the first example of Sikander's influence on the All India Muslim League. At Lucknow, in October 1937, the All India Muslim League had strongly condemned the Punjab Government's policy on Shahidganj, indicating a readinesss to use the issue for an incursion into communal politics in Punjab.[50] The resolution reads as under:

> The All India Muslim League condemns the wanton demolition of the Shahidganj Mosque at Lahore, as a most intolerable intereference with the law of Islam, and in view of the fact this demolition was carried out in broad daylight, under the protection of British troops and British guns, calls upon the British Government to restore the Mosque to its original conditions, and thus avoid an inevitable conflict between the Muslims of India and the British Government, whose representative in the province failed to perform his elementary duty of protecting an admittedly Muslim Mosque.[51]

Sikander Hayat Khan, on the other hand, did not support the Muslim League on the issue of Shahidganj Mosque. On the contrary, when Malik Barkat Ali, a Muslim League member of Punjab, introduced a bill by which the Muslims could have claimed the Shahidganj Mosque with retrospective effect, Sir Sikander Hayat Khan strongly opposed it and advised the Governor to withhold his consent to it.[52] However, he was always in favour of an honourable agreement between the two communities over the question of Shahidganj. He said:

I would earnestly appeal to all my co-religionists to carefully consider the far-reaching implications of Malik Barkat Ali's move and not to despair difficulties not withstanding of an alternative solution, honourable to all concerned, of this vexed problem.[53]

At the special session of the All-India Muslim League held at Calcutta in April 1938, Sir Sikander's opinion became the voice of the League. The League expressed confidence in the policy of Sir Sikander, decided against a non-cooperation movement and passed the following resolution:

> The All India Muslim League, in view of the fact that the Punjab Government had given an assurance to the effect that they were adopting every means for arriving at an

honourable settlement of the Shahidganj problem, assures them of its co-operation and assistance in bringing about the settlement, and appeals to the Musalmans to create and maintain a peaceful atmosphere in order to facilitate that settlement.[54]

In the Calcutta session of April 1938, Sikander Hayat Khan also persuaded Jinnah to appoint a new organizing committee under the Chairmanship of Sir Sikander with the task of creating a new Muslim League organization in Punjab.[55] The 35 members' committee consisted of only 10 old Leaguers and 25 supporters of Sir Sikander.[56] It was a remarkable success on the part of Sir Sikander. In June 1938, the Punjab Muslim League which consisted of papers of twenty—seven districts and 100 primary Leagues was officially dissolved.[57]

Sir Sikander had now gained full control over the Punjab Muslim League and was, thus, in a position to delay the formation of the League as long as he wanted. The old Muslim Leaguers, however, became increasingly restless as the months passed and still no steps had been taken to create a new Muslim League. At the Patna working committee meeting of the All India Muslim League, held in December 1938, Malik Barkat Ali voiced their frustration by attempting to move a resolution to effect that:

The organising committee appointed at Calcutta to set up and establish the Punjab Provincial Muslim League and its branches under the new League constitution be dissolved and a new organising committee be set up for the same purpose.[58]

Jinnah, who did not want to antagonize Sir Sikander, however, forced Malik Barkat Ali to withdraw his resolution. Jinnah had no alternative but to sacrifice what little organization the League possessed in Punjab in exchange for the limited right to speak for it at the centre. He told his Punjabi supporters that any Muslim ready to accept the League's creed, policy and programme, whatever his political persuasion, is no longer any thing else but a Leaguer and those who had been already in the League are no better than the new Leaguers.[59] Jinnah had already suggested to Malik Barkat Ali that there is no such thing as this group or that group, or that party or this party, because then it really means various cliques.[60] However, the honest and genuine Punjab Leaguers were not contended with this policy of Jinnah and one of them had predicted that the Punjab League, now simply an Unionist creature, a bogus organization, existing only on paper, would soon be absolutely dead.[61]

Sir Sikander took the opportunity and branded the old Punjab Muslim Leaguers as traitors and made it clear that he would not tolerate constant interference in Punjab affairs.[62] He asserted that there were certain traitors in the Muslim League camp who had been intriguing with his opponents with a view to creating dissension in Muslim ranks. It was easier to deal with open enemies, it takes time to expose and deal with secret serpent in the sleeve. The time, however, had arrived to deal with them properly, which would be done by the Provincial organisations.[63]

The old Punjab Leaguers, nevertheless, determined to give a tough resistance to Sir Sikander. At a meeting held at Lahore at the end of February 1939, Mohammad Azam, Secretary of the Sialkot District Muslim League and Mir Ahmad Shah, President of the Campbellpore District League, attempted to pass a resolution demanding action from the organising committee.[64] Sikander's immediate response was to remove Ghulam Rasul, one of the leading spokesmen of the old Leaguers, from the post of the organising committee and replace him with a loyal Unionist, Mian Ramzan Ali.[65] Efforts by the old Punjab Leaguers to discuss in the Council of All India Muslim League the violated state of the League in the Punjab made little headway because Sir Sikander was using such bodies to suppress the activities of the old Leaguers.[66]

The Sholapur session of All-India Muslim League, held in May 1939, was presided over by Sir Sikander.[67] It was a clear demonstration of the dominance of Unionist Party in the All-India politics of the Muslim League and also the influence of Sir Sikander in the Muslim League.[68] This move, however, was not welcomed by the old Punjab Leaguers, who did not consider Sikander as their leader.[69] Thus, the sharp differences between the two, once again, cropped-up in August 1939, over the question of by-elections of Amritsar and Multan Division towns.

According to the Jinnah-Sikander Pact of 1937, the Muslim League's candidates were to be nominated for this by-election and were to be jointly supported.[70] Sir Sikander, without consulting the old Leaguers, nominated Sheikh Sadiq Hasan and Sheikh Mohammad Amin for the Amritsar and Multan seats, respectively. The old Leaguers, however, objected to it and nominated Malik Zeman Mehni Khan as their candidate for Multan.[71] Sir Sikander, in the meantime, used his influence and obtained approval for the candidature of Sheikh Mohammad Amin from Jinnah.[72] Thus, once more, the genuine Leaguers were defeated by the Unionists.

In September 1939, at the meeting of the Muslim League Executive Council, held at Delhi, the old Leaguers once again endeavoured to obtain the dissolution of the organising committee.[73] But, the intervention of Jinnah and Liaqat Ali Khan prevented an open conflict between the two parties and arranged a compromise by saying that a new Punjab Muslim League will be set up by November 15, 1939. The Unionist members of the organising committee unwillingly accepted this compromise.[74] It was also added that the organisation committee will be dissolved after November 15, 1939 irrespective of the fact whether or not its task was completed. Just a week before this deadline, the organisation committee finally announced the formulation of new Punjab Muslim League.[75]

In February 1940, the inaugural meeting of new Punjab League was held in Lahore under the chairmanship of Sikander Hayat Khan. At this meeting, Nawab Shah Nawaz of Mamdot was elected as President, Mian Ramzan Ali, Mian Amir-ud-din and Syed Mohammad Ali Jaafari were elected as Secretary, Financial Secretary and Organizing Secretary, respectively.[76] All of them were staunch Unionists. The honest and genuine Muslim Leaguers were disgusted with this move and violently protested against it. Some district officials of the Muslim League resigned and others requested Jinnah not to affiliate the newly-created Punjab Muslim League.[77] Mian Nurullah, the Arain member for Lyallpur, vehemently protested against this move and appealed to Jinnah to take action against this fictitious Muslim League.

> The Unionist Party has become the complete master of the Punjab Muslim League—I would appeal to Mr. Jinnah in the interests of the League to see that a living Muslim

> League organization is established in the Punjab. The Muslim League under the leadership of the Premier is merely a creature of the Unionist Party packed by honorary Magistrates and Sub-Registrars. Their allegiance is first and last to the Unionist Party in power and they can any day flout Mr. Jinnah on the central body.[78]

The widespread protests finally forced the All-India Muslim League to send a Committee of Enquiry at the end of February, 1940. Nawab Mohammad Ismail Khan, the Raja of Mahmudabad and Choudhary Khaliquzzaman were the members of this committee, who had to decide whether the newly-constituted Punjab Muslim League should be granted affiliation. After a short stay in the province, this Enquiry Committee recommended that the Punjab Muslim League's affiliation should be accepted.[79] This decision was a major victory for Sikander, since, now he had gained control of the Punjab Muslim League with the approval of Jinnah himself.

Thus, the fierce opposition of the old Leaguers nearly came to an end.[80] Now, their efforts, even, to open new League branches proved unsuccessful, for Sikander would not countenance their recognition by the All-India Muslim League and had them rejected.[81] Meanwhile, the new President of the Punjab Muslim League, Nawab of Mamdot, continued to impress upon Jinnah their solidarity with Sir Sikander.[82] Leader like Malik Barkat Ali, disgusted with the actions of Jinnah and Sikander, devoted himself with the organisation and activities of the Punjab Muslim Students' Federation.[83] This dominance of the Unionists, more or less, continued till the death of Sikander in late 1942.

Although, on the one hand, the struggle between the Unionists and Muslim League temporarily came to a halt but, on the other hand, an important international event i.e. beginning of the Second World War, profoundly affected the politics of India as well as the politics of Punjab. The desire of the British to obtain support and co-operation of different political parties in favour of the war efforts,[84] resulted in the growth of the Muslim League. Linlithgow, the Viceroy of India, invited Gandhi and Jinnah on equal footing to seek their co-operation for the war effort[85] which elevated the position of the Muslim League equal to that of the Indian National

Congress in the All-India politics. These developments transformed the relationship which existed between the Muslim League and the Unionist Party.[86] And, more so, the differences between Jinnah and Sikander regarding their approach towards the war effort further brought a change in the relationship of the Unionists Party *vis-i-vis* the Muslim League.[87]

Sir Sikander, essentially a collaborator and loyal to the Raj, was bound to support the war effort.[88] As early as in September 1938, in a speech at Shimla, Sikander pledged Punjab to the unconditional support of Britain in the event of war. "When we offered our hand in the last war (1914-1918), he said,' we were still in our political apprenticeship, it is offered again by a Punjab' which has now attained its political maturity".[89] When in December 1938, Z.H. Lari brought a resolution before the meeting of the Executive Council of the Muslim League, held at Delhi, to criticise Jinnah, the latter made a fierce speech. He warned against the danger of Britain relying on the Congress governments for aid in the war effort and urged that it was in Muslims' interests to maintain the present position. Even, Jinnah supported Sikander, praised his services in the glowing terms[90] and asked Lari to withdraw his resolution.[91]

On August 25, 1939 Sir Sikander repeated his assurance of the previous year. He said, 'the manpower and the resources of the Punjab will be unresistingly and ungrudgingly placed at the disposal of Great Britain and her allies, in the service of our Motherland, and for the sacred cause of justice, rightousness and freedom.'[92] After the beginning of the war, in November 1939, he submitted a resolution to the Assembly declaring its determination to resist aggression, protect the security and honour of Punjab and India. And asked for an assurance that the constitutional position should be reconsidered after the war with a view to India's immediate attainment of Dominion Status with effective protection of minorities and in agreement with all parties concerned.[93] The resolution was carried by 104 votes to 39.

Jinnah did not like this approach of Sikander for rendering unconditional support to the British for war efforts. Jinnah hoped to extract from the Viceroy a promise that the British would jettison the idea of federation and the Congress ministries should be turned out at once in return for his support of the war effort.[94] Linlithgow, however, saw no reason to give up the idea of federation and majority rule altogether.[95]

The Muslim League, then, offered its support for the war effort if the Viceroy would take its leaders into confidence and accept the League as the only organisation that can speak on behalf of the Muslim India.[96] In contrast to Congress, the League was not interested in an independent, united and democratic India.[97] The Viceroy, however, accepted this conditional support of Muslim League.[98] But, the British wanted an agreement between the Congress and the League before reaching a final settlement, however, it was not materialized.[99] Hence, the political impasse continued. However, the new alliance between the Muslim League and the British Raj raised the status of Jinnah and his Muslim League in the All-India politics.

Sir Sikander, on the other hand, continued his unconditional support for the war effort and even instructed his cabinet colleagues to do the needful.[100] Jinnah, however, at this political juncture, and encouraged with the support of the British decided to define the final goals of the Muslim League at Lahore in March 1940. It was expected, because of the political statement, that a demand for the separate Muslim Nation will be raised at this session.

Sir Sikander, expecting such development, had already prepared a scheme of Indian Federation. According to his scheme, the country was to be divided into seven zones.[101] Each zone, according to Sikander, would have a regional Legislature dealing with a group of specified subjects. The Federal Legislature would legislate normally on defence, foreign affairs, customs, currency and communications. The principle of Dyarchy was recognized in respect of the composition of Federal Executive, the Governor-General might nominate the ministers of Defence and Foreign Affairs on his own responsibility and not necessarily from among the members of the Federal Legislature. Each zone should have at least one representative in the Federal cabinet, and at least one-third of its members should be Muslims, Adequate and effective machinery should be set up at the centre and in the units to look after and protect the interests of the minorities. The political goal of India was to be Dominion Status which was to be reached with minimum delay.[102]

In addition to this scheme of Sir Sikander Hayat Khan, some others had also prepared similar schemes before the Lahore Session of March 1940. Abdul Latif of Hyderabad had outlined a plan for a minimal federation of homogenous cultural zones.[103] Choudhary Khaliquzzaman had discussed the possibility of partition with Zetland.[104] Sir Abdula Haroon prepared a scheme of a separate federation of Muslim provinces and States.[105] Syed Zafarul Hasan and M.A.H. Qadri schemed that three sovereign states of British India would be North-West India or Pakistan, Bengal and Hindustan.[106] However, for Muslim League it was not the time to discuss such schemes but to pass the historic 'Pakistan' resolution at Lahore on 23 March 1940, it declared:

> This session of the All-India Muslim League emphatically reiterates that the scheme of federation embodied in the Government of India Act, 1935, is totally unsuited to and unworkable in the peculiar conditions of this country and is altogether unacceptable to Muslim India.
> Resolved that it is the considered view of this session of the All-India Muslim League that no constitutional plan would be workable in this country or acceptable to the Muslims unless it is designed on the following basic principles, viz, that geographically contiguous units are demarcated into regions which should be constituted, with such territorial readjustments as may be necessary, that the areas in which the Muslims are numerically in a majority, as in the North-Western and Eastern zones of India, should be grouped to constitute Independent States in which the constituent units shall be autonomous and sovereign.[107]

Pakistan was not explicitly mentioned, nor was it clear from the language of the resolution whether a single Muslim State of both 'Zones' had been envisioned or two separate 'autonomous' independent states, one in the North-West and other in the Eastern Zone. However, it became clear from the assertion of Jinnah that Muslim League envisaged a single sovereign Pakistan state.[108] The Pakistan resolution exposed the Congress pretensions to represent the whole of India.[109]

The Pakistan resolution stirred the politics of Punjab partly because it gave Jinnah a foothold in the province and partly because of the uncertain future it hold out for the Sikhs and Hindus.[110] Sir Sikander, despite the fact that he did not like this resolution was not in a position to oppose it, because of his political debt to Jinnah. On 28 February, 1940, his Unionist ministry had banned the carrying of arms under the Defence of India Act and the police had fired on the *Khaksars*, a semi-military organization of Muslims, who had defied the ban, which resulted in the death of a scores of *Khaksars* including their lion hearted *salar* (Commander), Agha Zaigham.[111]

On the eve of Muslim League session at Lahore, Sikander's Muslim opponents in the Unionist Party demanded an enquiry into the police firing and urged removal of ban on the *Khaksars*. Banners proclaiming '*Sikander murdabad*'(death to Sikander) were hoisted at the venue of the session. Sikander was indebted to Jinnah for shelving discussion of the issue at the open session of the League. Jinnah, thus, avoided a clash between a government headed by a Muslim and a Muslim organization, safeguarding the position of the Punjab Ministry. By this way, Jinnah also increased his influence over Leaguers in Punjab.[112]

Once the Pakistan resolution was passed, the Punjab Muslim League desired to break the hold of the Unionist Party over its Provincial Organization. Jinnah, on the other hand, did not want to move too quickly against the Unionists because at first he wanted to weaken the influence of the Unionists in all-India Muslim politics, only then, he visualized that the Provincial League will be able to struggle against the Unionists. Moreover, his previous experience of intervention in the politics of Punjab in 1936-37, advised him not to move too quickly against the Unionists.[113]

The Punjab League's local workers, however, did not appreciate this patient approach of Jinnah. Syed Ashraf Ali Tirmize of the Ropar (Ambala) Muslim League had said, 'Ever since the annual meeting of Muslim League in Lahore it is supposed to have had much greater aims and objects, but its workers are not at all active—passing resolution after resolution does not serve any purpose. It is action that is needed—for the last three years those people responsible for running the

Punjab League have proved by their actions that they donot want to achieve its aim—Today those outside the League are overjoyed to see the lack of discipline we have within it.'[114]

The impatient activists of the Provincial League wanted to propagate the goals and aims of the League in the countryside, a task which was, then, carried out by the Punjab Muslim Students Federation. The Punjab Muslim Student Federation was organized in September 1937 under the presidentship of Mirza Abdul Hameed Nizami.[115] The Federation extended support to Pakistan resolution of Muslim League.[116] In 1940, the Federation was reorganized, Abdul Sattar Khan Niazi was elected as its president and Chaudhary Narrulah Khan and Chaudhary Mohammad Sadiq became the other office-bearers.[117] Since 1941 the Federation did remarkable propaganda work to popularise the ultimate goals and aims of the Muslim League.

The Punjab Muslim Students Federation launched its programme in such a way that it extended its activities to some of the district branches rather than limiting itself to the headquarters alone. In February 1941, an educational conference was held at Lyallpur which was presided over by Sir Abdullah Haroon. Regarding the propaganda campaign to be initiated in the villages, Sir Abdullah Haroon advised the Muslim Students saying that, 'during vacations you should enter villages on foot and carry to your people there the message of hope and courage.'[118]

In March 1941, the Federation hold a special Pakistan conference at Lahore in support of the Pakistan resolution of the League. The conference was presided over by Jinnah himself. It was attended by a number of prominent Muslim leaders including Sir Sardullah Khan, Nawazada Liaquat Ali Khan, Choudhary Khaliquazzaman, Sir Abdul Qadir, Nawab of Mamdot, Malik Barkat Ali and Mian Bashir Ahmad.[119]

During the special Pakistan conference, a rural sub-committee was set up to work for the propagation of the Pakistan scheme in the rural areas of the province the rural sub-committee took up this collosal task under the Presidentship of Malik Zafrullah Khan, with Abdul Sattar Khan Niazi as its Secretary.[120] The committee commenced its programme during the summer vacations in May 1941. The committee started intensive and extensive propaganda—intensive, inside to reform the existing Leaguers and extensive, with a view to establishing new Leaguers where there were no Leaguers.[121]

It undertook an extensive tour of carrying the league's message to the Muslim masses in rural areas. It made intensive tour of western Punjab, particularly in those areas where the League's branches had yet not been established, such as the district of Sheikhupura, Sialkot, Rawalpindi, Gujranwala, Lyallpur and Jullundur. In this process they visited at least sixty places and established model Leagues in these districts.[122]

During the propaganda work, the rural committee, at times, was threatened by the Unionists not to propagate the League's creed and its idea of Pakistan. Abdus Sattar Khan Niazi, made reference to this while writing to Jinnah. He wrote, 'we have been under the full blitz of those elements who see their death knel in the organization of a League which should be responsible to you and not a tool in their hands. They coaxed us, they threatened us, they tried every temptation and every terror that they could command and now that they have failed, they are blackmailing us'.[123] Despite such hindrances the Punjab Muslim Students Federation carried on its propaganda programme.

The Punjab Muslim Students Federation organised a Pakistan conference in July 1941 at Lyallpur and then intensified its propaganda programme. The rural committee spent twenty days covering about 500 miles, out of which it travelled 50 miles on foot. The students visited fifty villages, delivered 113 speeches, addressed nearly 22,000 villages and opened 51 Muslim League primary branches.[124] During August 1941, the rural committee propagated the League cause in the Eastern part of Punjab. The committee visited the districts of Ludhiana, Jullundhur, Ambala, Hoshiarpur and Rohtak and covered an area of 1,400 miles.[125] During this whole process of rural propaganda programme, the Muslim students, by and large, were successful in giving a setback to the Unionists cause in the province and thus assisted the Muslim League to challenge the dominance of the Unionists.

Sikander Hayat Khan, who had been, undoubtedly, one of the most powerful leader of the Muslim India during the period 1937-40 and who was controlling the Punjab Provincial

League, did not appreciate the Pakistan resolution of March 1940 nor did he appreciate the decision of Jinnah that Muslim Leaguers should not join the war committees and war boards.[126] Therefore, the issues of Pakistan resolution and joining the war committees created differences between Jinnah and Sikander. In July 1940, in defiance to the decision of Jinnah, as many as thirty-seven members of the Unionists party joined the Provincial War Committee.[127] Nawab of Mamdot, the President of the Punjab Muslim League, was the only Unionists member who resigned from the Provincial War Committee.[128]

In March 1942, because of his antipathy to Pakistan and the need to reassure his Hindu and Sikh colleagues, Sir Sikander openly spoke against the Pakistan resolution. Unity alone could bring freedom, declared Sikander. He said:

> If that is what Pakistan means, I will have nothing to do with it. Let us join hands in order to preserve and maintain peace and harmony within the province, and unite with the rest of India to face with courage and confidence, the danger from without. And let us above all show to the rest of India, that we in Punjab stand unified and will not brook any interference from whatever quarter it may be attempted. Then, and only then, will we be able to tell meddling busy bodies from outside, 'Hands of the Punjab.'[129]

Sir Sikander and other Muslim Unionists stayed away from Jinnah's meetings in Lahore on 1 and 2 March,[130] and he also did not attend the Muslim League conference in Madras in April 1941.[131] To protest against the policies of Jinnah, Sikander proposed to resign from the Muslim League working committee (MLWC), but the idea did not suit Linlithgow. He instructed, Henary Craik, the Governor of Punjab, to persuade Sikander not to resign from the Working Committee.[132] Linlithgow feared that Sikander's resignation from the Working Committee might overthrow his Unionist ministry on the issue of Pakistan which will be harmful for the British since Sikander was successfully organizing the provincial war effort.[133] Secondly, Linlithgow did not want a break between Jinnah and Sikander, because he needed Jinnah at the all-India politics and Sikander at the Provincial politics, thus he preserved the unity between the two.[134]

However, it became obvious from these developments that Sikander's influence in the All-India Muslim politics was weakening. The differences between Jinnah and Sikander once again cropped up in June 1941 when Sikander went to serve on the National Defence Council.[135] Jinnah drew the attention of Sikander to his circular of June 1940, which barrred Muslim Leagues, from joining war committees. Because of the protest of Jinnah, Sikander had to resign from the National Defence Council on August 25, 1941.[136] Sikander's resignation from the National Defence Council cannot be regarded as a concession to Jinnah, but rather as a defensive measure calculated to preserve the situation and avoid an open break. However, this action of Sikander damaged the prestige of Unionist Party in the eyes of the rural elite and also boosted the strength of Provincial Muslim League.[137]

In October 1941, the All-India Muslim League sent an investigation committee in Punjab to know the strength of its Provincial organization. The committee found that no Muslim League organization existed at all in the following ten districts of Punjab: Ambala, Hoshiarpur, Shahpur, Jhelum, Mianwali, Jhang, Kangra, Dera Ghazi Khan, Rohtak and Gujranwala. The total primary League membership of the seven cities and six district branches, which were able to return reasonably accurate figures, was only 14,823. Ferozpur had the largest number of primary members 3,500, Montagomery was the second with 3,200 next came Lahore with 2000. Attock had the lowest numbers with only 491 primary members.[133] Even more worrying for the League that the smallness of its primary membership was the fact that over a third of it came from the towns which were politically unimportant. The League mass membership in the city consisted mainly of members of the Muslim trading community.[139] More or less, the position of the League in the province was still far from satisfactory. The rural elite, still, was not supporting the cause of the League.

In November 1941, Jinnah visited Punjab and presided over the Muslim League Lyallpur conference. This conference was also attended by Sir Sikander and he accepted Jinnah as the greatest Muslim leader of India. He was also forced to reluctantly explain that he fully subscribed to the Lahore resolution of the League which provided for territorial readjustment.[140] This attitude of Sir Sikander indicated that his influence was not only weakening in the All-India Muslim politics but also he was losing his control over the Provincial Muslim League.

Meantime, the Punjab Muslim Students Federation held the second session of the special Pakistan conference at Rawalpindi in March, 1942, under the presidentship of Choudhary Khaliquzzaman. It was in this session that the office of the presidentship of the Punjab Muslim Students Federation passed on to Hameed Nizami.[141] After the session the Federation, once again took up the task of propaganda campaign in rural Punjab. The propaganda committee visited the districts of Patiala, Amritsar, Jullundur and other districts of importance. Such activities continued until November, 1942 and endeavoured to strengthen the cause of the Muslim League.[142]

At the All-India politics, the war-time scenario and the British need for lying back during the war and for creating counterweight to the non-cooperating Congress, led to the prestige of Muslim League and Jinnah. The Cripps Mission, which arrived in India in March, 1942, to negotiate with the Indian political parties for further constitutional reforms, was also favourable towards the Muslim League. It conceded in theory the partition of India but the actual operation of its theory was remote possibility.[143] The Cripps Mission ended in failure, but the Muslim League gained considerably from it as the British had gone a long way towards accepting its demand for Pakistan.[144]

During the 1940-42 period, the prestige and status of the All-India Muslim League was considerably increased in the All-India politics. Jinnah became the undisputed spokesman of the Muslim India which was also acknowledged by the Raj. After consolidating his position in the All-India politics and in the organizational structure of the All-India Muslim League, Jinnah expelled Sir Sikander from the League Council and Muslim League Working Committee in July, 1942.[145] It was said that Sir Sikander was not propagating the ideal of the League and the demand of Pakistan, thus, he was expelled from the League Council. The dismissal of Sir Sikander brought an end to his influence in the All-India Muslim politics.

In November 1942, Jinnah visited Punjab and launched his attack against the Unionist ministry. He asserted, in his meetings, that the League had made enormous strides in recent years towards attaining the goal of Pakistan, the British should acknowledge the right of Muslims to self-determination and promise to give effect to the verdict of a Muslim plebiscite. He publically criticised the Federation scheme of Sikander Hayat Khan.[146] In order to avoid any open rupture with Jinnah, which might risk his position among Muslim Unionists, Sikander proclaimed that he saw eye to eye with the champion of Pakistan. However, this attitude of Sikander further weakened his position in the Provincial Muslim League.[147]

The meetings of Jinnah had attracted large audiences of between ten to thirty thousand parsons and had given the Pakistan movement a fillip. However, it was doubted that the visit and speeches of Jinnah have the lasting influence over Punjab because the Provincial League was, despite the efforts of the Students Federation, primarily confined to the urban classes. Few of the provincial leaders commanded any widespread support.[148] The rural elite of the province was still, not supporting the cause of Muslim League.[149]

The Unionist Party, although it had lost its control over the Provincial Muslim League, was still dominating the politics of the province. Sir Sikander Hayat Khan had maintained political stability in the province and he was highly appreciated by the British Raj. However, the sudden death of Sikander Hayat Khan on the night of December 26, 1942[150] was a great blow to the Unionist Party as well as to the British.[151] The death of Sikander Hayat Khan was the beginning of a new chapter in the politics of the province.

While the Provincial Muslim League, during 1937-1942, was struggling hard for its survival, the Sikh politics and Congress were also endeavouring their best to make their presence felt in the politics of the province. The Sikh politics during this period was divided into two factions. The moderates were working under the banner of Khalsa Nationalist Party while the political body of the radicals one was the Akali Dal. Leadership to these groups were provided by Sunder Singh Majithia and Master Tara Singh, respectively.

The Khalsa Nationalist Party under the leadership of Sunder Singh Majithia, joined hands with the ruling Unionist Party and also secured a seat in the Ministry.[152] On the other hand, the Akali Dal joined hands with the Congress, sitting in the opposition.[153] The Akalis vehemently attacked the Khalsa Nationalist Party because of its alliance with a party of the collaborators[154] and described them traitors and enemies of the *Panth*.[155] Master Tara Singh even attempted to get the theoretically non-political SGPC to condemn Sunder Singh Majithia's action.[156] The Khalsa Nationalist Party, in retaliation also criticised the Akali Dal. Sunder Singh Majithia stated that the destructive policy carried on by other groups during the past 10 to 12 years has yielded nothing but disruption and chaos in the community and their high sounding declaration had ended in nothing but smoke.[157]

The conflict between the Khalsa Nationalist Party and the Akali Dal continued far long since one was aligned with the Unionist and the other was aligned with the Congress. There existed, in fact, no relationship between the Muslim League and any group of the Sikh polity. However, the beginning of the Second World War led to the beginning of a new phase in the Sikh polity. The Khalsa Nationalist Party, in coalition with the Unionists, supported the war effort of the British.[158] The Akali Dal also, contrary to the decision of the Congress not to support the war effort, decided to support the war effort.[159] The Akalis decided to support the recruitment of the Sikhs in the army as Master Tara Singh believed that the future political influence of their community largely depended on their strength in the army.[160]

Penderal Moon, a British Official, believed that the Khalsa Nationalist Party was merely a weak faction of Anglophile Sikhs[161], thus Sir Sikander made efforts to detach the Akalis from the Congress and bring them into a coalition with the Unionists.[162] However, these efforts did not bring any result as Sir Sikander and Master Tara Singh had been feuding ever since the Shahidganj Affair.[163] The Akalis also considered that the period of Unionist rule had been one of the constant persecution of the Sikhs.[164] On the other hand, the relations between the Akali Dal and the Congress constantly deteriorated which resulted in the resignation of Master Tara Singh from the All-India Congress Committee as well as from the Provincial-Congress Committee.[165]

The Pakistan resolution, of March 1940, of the Muslim League led to the emergence of tension between the Muslim League and the Sikhs of Punjab. As the Raja of Mahudabad had suggested at Lahore that Pakistan was to be a Islamic State, based on *Shriat*, the Sikhs had the reasons to be alarmed.[166] Master Tara Singh argued that if Muslims could not trust the Hindu majority in India they should also persume that the Sikhs could not trust the Muslim majority in Punjab.[167]

The Khalsa Nationalist Party asserted that if the Unionists did not denounce Pakistan, the Party would have to leave the Government. It added as the Punjab had belonged to the Sikhs before the British came, it should be returned to the Sikhs if the British left.[168] Master Tara Singh emphasized that Pakistan could only come in a sea of blood and called for the creation of an Akali militia.[169] Baba Kharak Singh said that the Sikhs would not allow the vivisection of India into such an absurd division.[170]

The Pakistan resolution had far reaching impacts on the Sikh politics. The Khalsa Nationalist Party and Akali Dal came closer because of it and in early 1941, these two groups joined hands and stated that a coalition between the all Sikh parties and the Unionists was possible if the Unionists would denounce Pakistan and promise not to introduce legislation of a controversial nature affecting one community far its own political interests.[171] Sir Sikander, too, concentrated on wooing the Sikhs. Meantime, Sunder Singh Majithia died in April 1941 and he was succeeded by Dasundha Singh in the Cabinet.[172]

The Cripps Mission of March 1942 further deteriorated the relations between Muslim League and Sikh politics. The Cripps formula, in fact, made provision for partition before the transfer of power took place, on the basis of the League's demand for Pakistan.[173] This angered the Sikhs as they have demanded an United India.[174] Although the Cripps Mission ended in failure but it increased the internal unrest as Muslims and Sikhs became increasingly suspicious of one another.[175] The prospect of a disruption of Punjab, made natural the coming together of Unionists and Akalis.

In June 1942, Sikander Hayat Khan and Baldev Singh, an

Akali leader, had come to an agreement which is known as Sikander-Baldev Pact. According to the pact, Baldev Singh became a cabinet minister in the Unionist Government.[176] In return, the Unionist agreed to give recognition to *Gurumukhi* script, to give Sikhs 20 per cent representation in the provincial services, to make the change in the Gurdwaras Act without Sikh consent and to give *jhatka* meat the same status as *halal* meat. Sikhs claim for representation in the Executive Council would be supported by the Unionists.[177] The seal of British approval was set on this Union of Unionists and Akalis when a Sikh, Jogender Singh, was appointed to the Viceroy's Executive Council shortly after the pact was concluded.[178] The pact, however, did not serve the purpose quite effectively because the Pakistan loomed threateningly on the political horizons of the Sikhs.

The Congress during this period, was also quite active in the provincial politics. The elections of 1937 made it obvious that Congress is a weak party in Punjab, and in the post election period it had to confront a powerful ruling party i.e. the Unionists. However, to begin with some of the leaders of the Congress like Gopi Chand Bhargwa, Krishan Gopal Dutt, Sohan Singh Josh and Mian Iftikhar-ud-Din gave a very tough time to the ruling party.[179] They availed themselves of all parliamentary modes, like adjournment, cut-motions to attack and expose the government for its anti-people policies.[180]

One of the important issues taken up by the Congress members was the Punjab Minister's Salaries Bill. Dr. Mohammad Alam proposed a postponement of the Bill's consideration till the presentation of budget, and suggested that it should first be circulated for eliciting public opinion. Dr. Gopi Chand Bhargava supporting him said if not in all matters at least in this matter, we should consult our constituencies and the people at large. The motion, however, was lost.[181] The bill was again taken up on April 8, 1937. The Congress members vigorously opposed the high salaries proposed for the ministers.[182] The Congress members criticised the government for neglecting the nation-building departments and spending excessively on unproductive spheres like the police and salaries of high officials. But on account of their small number, they once again suffered a defeat.[183]

During the discussion on budget for 1938-39, the Congress members attacked the economic and political policies of the Unionist Government.[184] Dr. Gopi Chand Bhargava said, "The budget is, to say the least, disappointing. We have been told that the government proposes to create a special development fund with an initial capital of Rs. 55 lakhs. But I fear that it will be used for the development of the Unionist Party and not for the benefit of the poor peasant. There is nothing which will help the welfare of the people."[185] The Congress, thus, continued its task of exposing the government.

However, the attitude of the Congress on the Agrarian Bills, weakend its position in the Assembly as well it weakend the base of the Congress among the Hindu and Muslim peasantry.[186] Even one of the Muslims leaders of the Congress, Mohammad Alam resigned from the Congress, in protest of its opposition to the Agrarian Bills.[187] Meantime, reports of the oppression of Muslims in the Congress governed provinces began to reach Punjab which further weaken the relationship which existed between the Muslims of Punjab and the Congress. The Pirpur committee report into Muslim grievances in the Congress provinces was published in December 1938, which further deteriorated the relations between the two.[188] In May 1939, a deputation of prominent All-India Muslim League leaders toured Punjab to describe the sufferings of the Muslims in the Congress-governed provinces. The visit of this committee destroyed much of the remaining influence which the Congress possessed amongst the Muslims of the province.[189]

The national politics and the relationship which existed between the Raj, Congress and the League also affected the politics of Punjab during this period. The Second World War broke out in the beginning of September 1939. On September 3, 1939, Linlithgow, the Viceroy announced India's entry into the war without consulting political parties, Legislatures and Provincial ministries. The Congress resented the way India was dragged into the war. In the meeting of Congress Working Committee, held on September 14, 1939 Gandhi was alone in suggesting unconditional support for the British on a non-violent basis.[190] The Committee, however, resolved that the issue of war and peace must be decided by the Indian people, and no outside authority can impose this decision upon them, nor can the Indian people permit their resources to be exploited for imperialist ends.[191] The British government was invited to declare in unequivocal terms what their war aims are in regard to democracy and imperialism and the new world order that is envisaged, in particular how these aims are going to apply to India—be given effect to in the present.[192]

In response to the Congress demand for a declaration of British war aims, Linlithgow in his statement of October 18, 1939 only assured that at the end of the war, Government would be prepared to regard the scheme of Federation enshrined in the Act of 1935 as subject to modification in the light of Indian views.[193] Regarding this attitude of Linlithgow, Gandhi remarked, that, 'the Congress asked for bread and it has got a stone'. It will have to go into wilderness again before it becomes strong and pure enough to reach its objective.[194]

The Congress Working Committee finding the Viceroy's statement wholly unsatisfactory, advised the Congress ministries in the province to resign and exhorted the Provincial Congress committees to be ready for any eventuality. The resignation of the Congress ministries provided an opportunity to Jinnah and his Muslim League to consolidate its new found alliance with the British Raj and also to consolidate its position in the All India politics *vis-a-vis* the Indian National Congress. Jinnah, a shrewd politician, took advantage of this political juncture and seize this opportunity with both hands. The Provincial Congress on the other hand, started making preparations to meet any situation following their clash with the government. Political conferences were organised by the Provincial Congress leadership in several district to mobilise public opinion.[195] Local war committees were formed in a number of districts. Meetings were also held to give general publicity to the Congress decision on war issue.[196] Anti-war speeches were delivered in a number of Congress meetings in opposition to the government policy of recruitment.[197]

By September 1940, Gandhi had clearly visualised that a struggle with the British was inevitable. On October 17, 1940, he started the individual Civil-Disobedience movement. Gandhi instructed that one individual should go out at a time in the street showing anti-war slogans or delivering an anti-war speech and should get himself or herself arrested. This was done in order to avoid mass excitement. Only those having faith in non violence and constructive programme were eligible for offering *Satyagraha*.[198] In Punjab, the individual Civil-Disobedience began on November 29, 1940.[199] Mian Iftikhar-ud-Din, Dr. Gopi Chand Bhargava, Sardar Sampuran Singh, Pt. Neki Ram Sharma, Sardar Mangal Singh, Bhim Sen Sachar, Krishan Gopal Dutt and other prominent leaders took active part in this movement,[200] but its overall performance in Punjab was far from satisfactory.[201] The movement, in fact, was not serving its purpose at the All-India level, hence Gandhi withdrew it in December 1941.

The Pakistan resolution of March 1940 and Cripps Mission of March 1942, as discussed earlier, strengthened the cause of the Muslim League, thus, it weakened the influence of the Congress on the Muslims of the province. In August 1942, the Congress launched the Quit-India Movement. Jinnah, however, described the movement as a most dangerous mass-movement intended to force Congress demands at the point of bayonet, which, if conceded, would mean the sacrifice of all other interests, particularly those of Muslims in India. He appealed to Muslims to keep completely aloof from the movement, and to the Hindu public to stop this internecine war before it is too late.[202] The Punjab Provincial Leaguers followed Jinnah's lead.[203] The Provincial Leaguers concentrated on using their influence to keep Muslims away from the Quit India Movement.[204]

In Punjab, the Quit India Movement had began on August 10, 1942 and continued till the Indian National Congress officially withdrew this resolution in March, 1945. There were spontaneous *hartals* and demonstrations in several cities of the province as a mark of protest against the arrest of the AICC leaders.[205] Meetings were also held all over Punjab in which repressive policies of the Government were condemned and the Quit India Movement was popularised among the people. All classes of the people, other than the Muslims, took part in the movement. They flung themselves into the last battle of freedom struggle. Their chief targets of attack were means of communication, post and telegraph offices, telegraph wires and railway and government offices.[206]

The students of different colleges of Lahore remained on strike for a number of days as a protest against the repressive policy of the government. Similarly in Amritsar, Hoshiarpur, Lyallpur, Sialkot, Ferozpur and Gujranwala, students' unrest was reported. Processions organized by students were *lathi-charged.*[207] Prominent Provincial leaders like Gopi Chand Bhargava, Mian Iftikhar-ud-Din, Bhim Sen Sachar, Choudhary Krishan Gopal Dutt, Giani Gurmukh Singh Musafir, Ishwar Singh Majhail and many others were arrested under the Defence of India Rules.[208] Some violent incidents were also reported from Punjab.[209] However, the factionalism within the Provincial Congress[210] and the oppressive policies of the British weakened the movement in Punjab.[211] Above all, the opposition of the Muslim League provided a setback to this movement and established the fact that the Muslim League and the Congress were sworn enemies.

It has become obvious from the foregone discussions that the Punjab Muslim League, during 1937-1942, kept on struggling against all odds. Although, primarily it was struggling against the dominance of the Unionist Party but at the same time it had to take tough stand against the Congress and Akali Dal because of its communal attitude. The issues like Sikander-Jinnah pact, supporting the British for war effort, the Pakistan resolution, the Cripps Mission, Sikander-Baldev Pact and Quit-India Movement profoundly affected the position and politics of the Provincial Muslim League and *vis-a-vis* its relationship with the Unionist Party, Akali Dal, the Congress and the British Raj.

The position and strength of Punjab Muslim League, in fact, depended on the strength of its parent body i.e. All-India Muslim League. And, Jinnah, during this period, became successful to a great extent, to establish the notion that only the All-India Muslim League represented the Muslims of India. This fact was also accepted by the British Raj, who began to treat Jinnah on equal footing with Gandhi at the All-India politics. This position of the All-India Muslim League boosted the strength of the Provincial Muslim League and also encouraged it to challenge the dominance of the Unionist Party, whose support was solicited by Jinnah in order to strengthen the position of the Muslim League in the All-India politics.

No doubt that the Punjab Muslim League till the end of 1942 did not really break the dominance of the Unionist Party in the Provincial politics nor did it really become a mass based party. However, the Provincial League had passed through a period of such intense struggle which would have ruined its very bases in the province as was attempted by the Unionist Party. Once, threat to its very existence was over, the Provincial League began to chalkout strategies to win over the Muslims of Punjab for the cause of the League and Pakistan.

Foot Notes

1. *Civil and Military Gazette,* Lahore, April 3, 1937.
2. *Sir Sikander Hayat Khan (1892-1942).* He belonged to a landed aristocratic family of Wah in Attock District. He was elected to the Provincial Legislative Council in 1921, but was soon unseated in an election petition. In 1923 he was returned again from the Attock seat. In 1928 he headed the Punjab Reforms Committee. In 1929 he became the Revenue member of the government of Punjab and acted as Governor of Punjab in 1932. In 1935 he became the Deputy Governor of the Reserve Bank of India. Remained Premier of Punjab from 1937 to 1942. See Ikram Ali Malik, *op.cit.,* pp. 483-84.
3. *Sir Chhotu Ram (1881-1945),* the Development Minister in the new government, was one of the founders of the Unionist Party. He was elected to the Provincial Legislative Council in 1921. In 1932, he became the Agriculture Minister in the Council. Elected to the Assembly 1937 and worked as a minister under Sir Sikander and Sir Khizr Hayat Khan Tiwana.

   Mian Abdul Haye (1889-1946), Minister of Education, belonged to an aristocratic family of Ludhiana. He was elected to the Legislative Council in 1923 and 1926 and became a member of the Legislative Assembly in 1937 and served as a Minister till 1946.

   Sir Khizar Hayar Khan Tiwana (1900-1975), Minister of Public Works, was son of Umar Hayat Khan, a landed aristocrat of Western Punjab. Remained Minister from 1937-1942 and Premier of Punjab 1943-1947.

   Sir Manohar Lal (1879-1949), Finance Minister, was a close associate of Raja Narender Nath, the President of the National Progressive Party of Punjab. Remained Minister from 1926-1930 in the Legislative Council. Again, served as Minister under Sir

Sikander and Sir Khizr Hayat Khan and was defeated in 1946 by Gopi Chand Bhargava.

Sir Sunder Singh Majithia (1872-1941), Revenue Minister, belonged to a landlord aristocratic family. Remained member of Imperial Legislative Council 1915-21, member Executive Council from 1921-26, and Minister from 1937-1941.

Based on R. Tanwar, 'The Unionist Party in Punjab 1923-1947', unpublished Thesis, Kurukshetra University, 1989, pp. 123-35, Lajpat Rai Nair, *Sir Sikander Hayat Khan: Soldier-Statesman of Punjab*, Lahore, (n.d), pp. 130-32; C. Khaliquzzaman, *op.cit.*, pp. 378-79; K.L. Tuteja, *op.cit.*, p. 202, and V.N. Datta, *Ideology of the Political Elite in Punjab*, pp. 14-15.

4. *Indian Annual Register,* Vol. I, 1938, p. 234.
5. *All India Congress Committee Papers,* File. No. 7/1937.
6. Ashiq Hussain Batalvi, *Iqbal Ke Akhri Do Sal (urdu),* Karachi, 1961, pp. 433-34.
7. *Ibid.,* pp. 434-38.
8. *Civil and Military Gazette,* Lahore, May 4, 1937.
9. Ashiq Hussain Batalvi, *op.cit.,* p. 434
10. *Civil and Military Gazette,* Lahore, July 15, 1937.
11. Ashiq Hussain Batalvi, *op.cit.,* pp. 440-51.
12. *The Tribune,* September 11, 12, 1937.
13. Ashiq Hussain Batalvi, *op.cit.,* pp. 459-60.
14. Ian Talbot, *Punjab and The Raj,* p. 124.
15. For details see Khizr Hayat Khan Tiwana, 'The 1937 Elections and Sikander—Jinnah Pact', *Punjab Past and Present,* Vol. X, Part II, October 1976, pp. 356-85, C. Khaliquzzaman, *op.cit.,* p. 171, M.A.H. Ispani, *op.cit.,* pp. 50-51, and Imran Ali, *Punjab Politics in the decade Before Partition,* Lahore, 1975, pp. 22-23
16. On July 7, 1937, the Congress took charge of government in seven provinces, in the remaining four—Punjab, Bengal, Assam and Sind, the non-Congress governments were already functioning since April 1937. In Sept. 1938, a Congress led combination took office in Assam. See Tara Chand, *op.cit.,* Vol. IV, p. 243.
17. Under the Mass-contact programme the Congress calculated to divide, weaken and break the Muslims See, S.S. Pirzada (ed.), *op.cit.,* Vol. II, p. 270.
18. A.K. Azad, *India Wins Freedom,* Delhi, reprint, 1967, pp. 144-45.
19. M.A.H. Ispani, *Qaid-e-Azam Jinnah as I knew Him,* Karachi, 1966, p. 54.
20. *Indian Annual Register, 1938,* Vol. II, Calcutta, p. 224.
21. *Punjab Legislative Assembly Debates,* Vol. I, 8.6.1937, pp. 405-06.
22. *Punjab Legislative Assembly Debates,* Vol. I, 20.6.1937, pp. 450-51.

23. Ashiq Hussain Batalvi, *op.cit.*, pp. 478-79.
24. Penderef Moon, *Divide and Quit*, London, 1961, pp. 17, 39.
25. Emerson to Linlithgow, Sept. 14, 1937, *Linlithgow Papers.*
26. Ashiq Hussain Batalvi, *op.cit.*, pp. 476-77.
27. Henry Craik to Linlithgow, May 17, 1939, *Linlithgow Papers.*
28. M. Rafique Afzal, *op.cit.* p. 43.
29. Ashiq Hussain Batalvi, *op.cit.*, p. 492.
30. M. Rafique Afzal, *op.cit.*, p. 47.
31. Iqbal to Jinnah, 10 November 1937, See G. Allana (ed.), *Pakistan Movement: Historic Documents*, Lahore, 1968, pp. 148-49.
32. *The Tribune*, November 14, 1937.
33. Choudhary Khaliquzzaman, *op.cit.*, p. 290.
34. S.S. Pirzada (ed.), *op.cit.*, Vol. II, p. 280.
35. JInnah to Barkat Ali, Nov. 20, 1937, in G. Allana (ed.), *op.cit.*, pp. 167-68 and S.Q. Husain Jafri (ed.), *Quaid-i-Azam's Correspondence with Punjab Muslim Leaders*, Lahore, 1977, p. 48.
36. Emerson to Linlithgow, April 12, 1938, *Linlithgow Papers.*
37. Ashiq Husain Batalvi, *op.cit.*, pp. 523-24.
38. Ahmad Yar Khan Daultana to Jinnah November 15, 1937. See S.Q. Hussain Jafri (ed.), *op.cit.*, p. 23 and A.H. Batalvi, *op.cit.*, pp. 502-03
39. Mamdot's estate extended to over 300 villages and the ownership of six inundation canals in Ferozpur District, and Canal Colony land purchased at auctions in Lyallpur and Montgomery Districts. See Lepel Griffin, *Chiefs and the Families of Note in the Punjab*, Vol. I, Lahore, 1940, pp. 229-33.
40. A.H. Batalvi, *op.cit.*, pp. 604-05.
41. A.H. Batalvi, *op.cit.*, pp. 606-07.
42. Emerson to Linlithgow, April 12, 1938, *Linlithgow Papers.*
43. A.H. Batalvi, *op.cit.*, p. 618.
44. *Ibid.*, pp. 623-29.
45. Letter of Malik Barkat Ali to Jinnah, quoted in *Ibid.*, p. 634.
46. M. Rafique Afzal, *op.cit.*, p. 49.
47. Letters of Iqbal to Jinnah, quoted in, A.H. Batalvi, *op.cit.*, pp. 593-94.
48. A.H. Batalvi, *op.cit.*, pp. 613-17.
49. Emerson to Linlithgow, October 21, 1937, *Linlithgow Papers.*
50. The All India Muslim League's resolution on Shahidganj was passed after Sikander had left Lucknow. See S.S. Pirzada (ed.), *op.cit.*, Vol. II, p. 273.
51. Resolution No. Ill, Clause V of the 25th Session of the All-India Muslim League held at Lucknow in October, 1937. S.S. Pirzada (ed.), *op.cit.*, Vol. II, p. 278.
52. Emerson to Linlithgow, March 17, 1938, *Linlithgow Papers.*

53. Statement of Sikander Hayat Khan, *Punjab Legislative Assembly Debates*, Vol V, 1938, p. 806.
54. Resolution No. II of the special session of the All-India Muslim League held at Calcutta in April 1938. See S.S. Pirzada (ed.) *op.cit.*, Vol. II, p. 296.
55. S.S. Pirzada (ed.), *op.cit.*, Vol. II, p. 290 and *Indian Annual Register, 1938*, Vol. I, pp. 386-87.
56. For details see, *Indian Annual Register, 1938*, Vol. I, p. 387.
57. *The Tribune*, Lahore, June 7, 1938.
58. G. Allama (ed.), *op.cit.*, p. 230, M. Rafique Afzal, *op.cit.*, p. 61 and *Indian Annual Register*, 1938, Vol. II, p. 340.
59. Ayesha Jalal, *op.cit.*, p. 39.
60. Jinnah to Barkat Ali, November 20, 1937, in G. Allama (ed.), *op.cit.*, pp. 167-68 and also in S. Qaim Hussain Jafri(ed.), *op.cit.*, p. 48.
61. Sheikh Zafar Ali to Jinnah, December 21, 1938, in G. Allama (ed.), *op.cit.*, p. 232.
62. *Indian Annual Register, 1938*, Vol. II, pp. 346-47.
63. Sir Sikander's speech at the Twenty-sixth session of the All-India Muslim League (AIML), held at Patna in December 1938, see S.S. Pirzada (ed.), *op.cit.*, Vol. II, p. 313.
64. Ian Talbot, *Punjab and the Raj 1849-1947*, p. 127.
65. *Ibid.*
66. *Indian Annual Register, 1939*, Vol. I, pp. 374-75.
67. Henry Craik to Linlithgow, May 2, 1939, *Linlithgow Papers*.
68. *Indian Annual Register, 1939*, Vol. II, p. 348.
69. Henry Craik to Linlithgow, March 12, 1939, *Linlithgow Papers*.
70. Khizer Hayat Khan Tiwana, 'The 1937 Elections and Sikander Jinnah Pact', *Punjab Past and Present*, Vol. X, Part II, October, 1976, pp. 356-85.
71. Punjab Fortnightly report for the second half of August 1939, *Home Political*, File No. 18/8/1939.
72. *Ibid.*
73. Henry Craik to Linlithgow, October 17, 1939, based on the report of central intelligence officer, Lahore, *Linlithgow Papers*.
74. Ian Talbot, *Punjab and the Raj 1849-1947*, p. 128.
75. Ian Talbot, 'Deserted Collaborators : The Political Background to the Rise and fall of the Punjab Unionist Party 1923-1947', *The Journal of Imperial and Commonwealth History*, Vol. No. 1, October, 1982, p. 81.
76. *Civil and Military Gazette*, Lahore, February 10, 1940.
77. *The Tribune*, Lahore, February, 12, 1940.
78. *Ibid.*, February 14, 1940.
79. Ian Talbot, 'Deserted Collaborators', *op.cit.*, pp. 81-82.

80. *The Tribune*, Lahore, February 24, 1940.
81. Choudhary Khaliquzzaman, *op.cit.*, pp. 228-29, 235.
82. *Indian Annual Register, 1940*, Vol. II, pp. 12-13.
83. *Ibid.*, pp. 112-35.
84. Linlithgow to Zetland, August 31, 1939, *Linlithgow Papers.*
85. Linlithgow to Zetland, September 5, 1939, *Linlithgow Papers.*
86. Anita Inder Singh, *op.cit.*, pp. 46-60.
87. Ashiq Hussain Batalvi, *op.cit.*, p. 621.
88. Henry Craik to Linlithgow, July 29, 1938, *Linlithgow Papers.*
89. See *The Tribune*, September 28, 1938.
90. Ashiq Hussain Batalvi, *op.cit.*, p. 623.
91. Craik to Linlithgow, December 8, 1938, *Linlithgow Papers.*
92. See *The Tribune*, August 28, 1939.
93. *Punjab Legislative Assembly Debates*, 1939, Vol. X, p. 543 also, Craik to Linlithgow, November 16, 1939, *Linlithgow Papers.*
94. Linlithgow to Zetland, September 5, 1939, *Linlithgow Papers.*
95. *Ibid.*
96. Linlithgow to Zetland, September 24, 1939, *Linlithgow Papers.*
97. *Ibid.*
98. Linlithgow to Zetland, October 24, 1939, *Linlithgow Papers.*
99. Linlithgow to Zetland, January 16, 1940, *Linlithgow Papers.*
100. Henary Craik to Linlithgow, November 16, 1939 and February 15, 1940, *Linlithgow Papers.*
101. The Seven Zones were as under:
    1. Assam, Bengal and Sikkim.
    2. Bihar and Orissa.
    3. United Provinces and the Princely States in the Province.
    4. Madras, Travencore and Coorg.
    5. Bombay, Hyderabad, Mysore, Western Indian States and Central Provinces States.
    6. Central Provinces, Rajputana States (except Bikaner and Jaisalmer), Gwalior and the States of Central India, Bihar and Orissa.
    7. Punjab, Sind, North-West Frontier Province, Baluchistan, Kashmir, Punjab States, Bikaner and Jaislmer.

    Sikander Hyat Khan, *Outlines of a Scheme of Indian Federation*, Lahore, 30 July, 1939.
102. See V.P. Menon, *The Transfer of Power in India*, Delhi, 1957, pp. 451-67.
103. R.J. Moore, 'Jinnah and the Pakistan Demand', in Mushirul Hasan (ed.), *India's Partition*, p. 174.
104. Choudhary Khaliquazzaman, *op.cit.*, pp. 205-08.
105. See Mushirul Hasan, *op.cit.*, p. 170.
106. *Ibid.*, p. 173.

107. This resolution was purposed by Sir Fazlul Haq, the Premier of Bengal, and was seconded by Choudhary Khaliquazzaman and was supported by Maulana Zafar Ali Khan, Sardar Aurangzeb Khan and Sir Abdullah Harbon.
See S.S. Pirzada (ed.), *op.cit.*, Vol. II, pp. 340-44.
108. *Ibid.*, Vol. II, p. 337.
109. Henary Craik to Linlithgow, April 30, 1940, *Linlithgow Papers.*
110. Anita Inder Singh, *op.cit.*, p. 59.
111. Stanley Wolpert, *op.cit.*, p. 179.
112. Henary Craik to Linlithgow, March 31, 1940 and April 8, 1940, *Linlithgow Papers.*
113. Ian Talbot, *Punjab and the Raj 1849-1947*, p. 155.
114. *Ibid.*
115. Sarfaraz Hussain Mirza, *The Punjab Muslim Students Federation : An Annotated Documents (1937-47)*, Lahore, 1978, pp. 22-24.
116. *Ibid.*, pp. 102-03.
117. *Ibid.*, pp. 127-28.
118. *Ibid.*, pp. 131-32.
119. *Ibid.*, p. 138.
120. *Ibid.*, p. 153.
121. Abdus Sattar Niazi to Jinnah, June 6, 1941, in S.Q. Husain Jafri (ed.), *op.cit.*, pp. 282-83.
122. Sarfaraz Husain Mirza, *op.cit.*, p. 154.
123. Abdus Sattar Niazi to Jinnah, May 16, 1941, in S.Q. Husain Jafari (ed.), *op.cit.*, pp. 274-75.
124. Sarfaraz Husain Mirza, *op.cit.*, p. 167.
125. *Ibid.*, p. 169.
126. Linlithgow to Amery, June 10, 1940, *Linlithgow Papers.*
127. Henary Craik to Linlithgow, September 24, 1940, *Linlithgow Papers.*
128. This action of Mamdot was no more than a token gesture as he had earlier personally written to Jinnah asking him to change his mind over this issue and had led the deputation which had gone to Bombay in order to argue the case for exemption from the ban. Henary Craik to Linlithgow, July 16, 1940, *Linlithgow Papers.*
129. Craig Baxter, 'Some Aspects of Politics in the Punjab 1936-45', in *Pakistan : The Long View*, New York, 1977, pp. 52-53.
130. Craik to Linlithgow, March 4, 1941, *Linlithgow Papers.*
131. Punjab Fortnightly Report for the Second Half of April 1941, *Home Political*, File No. 18/4/41.
132. Craik to Linlithgow, March 1, 1941, *Linlithgow Papers.*
133. Anita Inder Singh, *op.cit.*, p. 66.
134. Linlithgow to Amery, May 15, 1941, *Linlithgow Papers.*

135. Linlithgow to Amery, June 19, 1941, *Linlithgow Papers.*
136. Linlithgow to Amery, August 30, 1941, *Linlithgow Papers.*
137. Punjab Fortnightly Report for the First half of October 1941, *Home Political,* File No. 18/10/1941.
138. Ian Talbot, *Punjab and the Raj 1849-1947,* p. 155.
139. *Ibid.,* pp. 155-56.
140. *Civil and Military Gazette,* Lahore, 19 November, 1941.
141. Sarfaraz Husain Mirza, *op.cit.,* p. 177.
142. *Ibid.,* pp. 178-82.
143. G. Rizvi, *Linlithgow and India : A Study of British Policy and the Political Impasse in India, 1936-43,* London, 1978, p. 183.
144. *Ibid.,* p. 186.
145. A.H. Ispahani, *op.cit.,* p. 58.
146. Punjab Fortnightly Report for the Second Half of November 1942, *Home Political,* File No. 18/11/1942.
147. B.J. Glancy to Linlithgow, November 28, 1942, *Linlithgow Papers.*
148. Fortnightly Report of the Punjab for the Second half of November 1942, *Home Political,* File No. 18/11/1942.
149. *Eastern Times,* Lahore, 29 November, 1942.
150. Gilancy to Linlithgow, December 27, 1942, *Linlithgow Papers.*
151. Linlithgow to Amery, December 28, 1942, *Linlithgow Papers.*
152. *The Tribune,* March 11, 1937.
153. Stephen Oren, 'The Sikhs, Congress and the Unicnists in British Punjab 1937-1945', *Modern Asian Studies,* 8, 3, 1974, p. 399.
154. *The Tribune,* March 7, 1937.
155. Lajpat Rai Nayyar, *op.cit.,* p. 132.
156. *The Tribune,* March 25, 1937.
157. *The Tribune,* March 11, 1937.
158. *Punjab Legislative Assembly Debates,* Vol. X, November 3, 1939, p. 471.
159. *Ibid.,* p. 501.
160. *The Tribune,* October 19, 1939.
161. Penderal Moon, *op.cit.,* p. 32.
162. Penderal Moon, *op.cit.,* p. 33.
163. Durlab Singh, *The Valiant Fighter: A Biographical Sketch of Master Tara Singh,* Lahore, 1942, p. 130.
164. *The Tribune,* November 19, 1939.
165. Fortnightly Report of Punjab for the Second half of September 1940, *Home Political,* File No. 18/9/1940.
166. S.S. Pirzada (ed.), *op.cit.,* Vol. II, p. 342.
167. *The Tribune,* March 25, 1940.
168. *The Indian Annual Register, 1940,* Vol. I, p. 257.
169. *The Tribune,* April 18, 1940.
170. *Ibid.,* April 11, 1940.

171. Stephen Oren, *op.cit.*, p. 409.
172. *Ibid.*
173. Cripps Interview with Jinnah on 25 March 1942, See Nicholos Mansergh and Penderal Moon (ed.), Constitutional Relations Between Britain and India, The Transfer of Power 1942-47, London, 1970, Vol. I, pp. 480-81.
174. Cripps interview with Sikh Leaders on March 27, 1942, See *Ibid.*, pp. 496-97.
175. B.J. Glancy to Linlithgow, May 1, 1942, *Linlithgow Papers.*
176. *The Tribune*, June 25, 1942.
177. Fortnightly Report for Punjab for the First half of June 1942, *Home Political*, File No. 18/6/1942.
    Jhatka Meat and *Halal Meat*, means meat killed according to Sikh and Muslim law, respectively.
178. *The Tribune*, July 9, 1942.
179. Gopi Chand Bhargava, *Punjab Legislative Assembly Debates*, Vol. V, 6 July, 1938, p. 721.
    Sohan Singh Josh, *Ibid.*, July 18, 1938, p. 1385.
180. Satya M. Rai, *op.cit.*, p. 247.
181. *The Punjab Legislative Assembly Debates*, 1937, Vol. I, pp. 35-47.
182. *Ibid.*, p. 58.
183. *The Tribune*, May 30, 1937.
184. *The Punjab Legislative Assembly Debates*, 1938, Vol. III, pp. 339-40.
185. *Ibid.*, p. 480.
186. Stephen Oren, *op.cit.*, pp. 401-03.
187. G.A. Meegar, 'The Growth of the Congress Movement in the Punjab 1920-1940', *Journal of Asian Studies*, 32, I, 1972, p. 50.
188. *Pirpur Report: The hardship, ill treatment and injustice that meted out to the Muslims in Congress Governed Provinces*, Lucknow, 1938, pp. 156-60.
189. *The Tribune*, May 12, 1939.
190. *Harijan*, September 23, 1939.
191. P. Sitaramayya, *History of the Indian National Congress*, Vol. II, pp. 130-35
192. *Harijan*, September 25, 1939.
193. Linlithgow to Zetland, September 21, 1939, *Linlithgow Papers.*
194. *Harijan*, October 21, 1939.
195. Punjab Fortnightly Report for the Second half of September, 1939, *Home Political*, File No. 18/9/39.
196. Punjab Fortnightly Report for the Second half of October, 1939, *Home Political*, File No. 18/10/39.
197. Bhagwan Josh, *op.cit.*, p. 153.
198. R.C. Majumdar, *History of Freedom Movement*, Vol. III, p. 607.
199. Punjab Fortnightly Report for the First half of December, 1940, *Home Political*, File No. 18/12/40.

200. S.L. Malhotra, *op.cit.*, pp. 117-23.
201. *Ibid.*, p. 132.
202. *The Statesman*, Bombay, August 10, 1942.
203. *The Eastern Times*, Lahore, August 17, 1942.
204. *Ibid.*, September 8, 1942.
205. Fortnightly Report for Punjab for the First half of August, 1942, *Home Political*, File No. 18/8/42.
206. *Ibid.*
207. *The Tribune*, August 17, 1942.
208. Fortnightly Report for Punjab for the Second half of August, 1942, *Home Political*, File No. 18/8/42.
209. *The Tribune*, August 21, 1942.
210. S.L. Malhotra, *op.cit.*, pp. 152-53.
211. Fortnightly Report for Punjab for the Second half of September, 1942, *Home Political*, File No. 18/9/1942.

4

Rapid Growth of the Muslim League 1943-1945

The Punjab Muslim League during the years 1943-1945 made a rapid progress. The Provincial League during this period not only successfully challenged the dominance of the Unionist Party in the provincial politics but also made roads into the country-side of Punjab. The new life breathed into the League by the Pakistan demand which contributed to a fundamental change in the balance of Punjab politics. The right of self-determination for the Muslim nation was directed particularly at the Muslim-majority provinces and Punjab was an important Muslim majority province. The League's demand armed it with a positive doctrine that was effectively to regenerate and exploit the religious fervour of Punjabi Muslims. This implied that provincial politics were to be radically affected by the Pakistan movement and this could not fail to alter the pattern of relations between the League and Unionists, and tip the balance in favour of the former.

After Sikander's death the growing strength of this resurgent Muslim consciousness brought the League into a conflict with the Unionist Ministry. But this clash was to be only outwardly one of ideologies. That the League was composed of the most reactionary element was clear in the Punjab, for Jinnah had preferred linkages with the landed gentry to links with the rural and urban masses or even the urban bourgeoisie. By manipulating national and communal symbols, this landed elite began to legitimize its control over the Pakistan movement. With the growth of the Muslim League's influence in Punjab during these years, the class basis of its leadership did not change. In fact, during these years the Unionist Party ceased, and the League began to be the caucus of the Muslim elite, for a large section broke its Unionist links and assumed leadership of the Punjab Muslim League. The details of this rapid growth of the Punjab Provincial Muslim League will be discussed in this chapter. The factional rivalry among the Unionists, the tussle between the League and the Unionists, the propaganda made by the Punjab Muslim Students Federation, effects of the war time policies of the Unionist Government and the national level politics of the Indian National Congress and the All India Muslim League further strengthened the cause of the Provincial Muslim League.

The sudden death of Sikander Hyat Khan was a serious blow to the Unionist Party and to the British, who acknowledged that they owed the success of the war effort in Punjab to him.[1] No plans had been drawn up for choosing his successor and it was doubtful if anyone else could held together the rural Assembly members as well as he had done. Sir Chhotu Ram was now the senior most member of the Unionist Party but he knew that it would be impossible for a Hindu to become Premier.[2] The Premier had to be a Muslim, this was proposed by Chhotu Ram himself.[3]

There were two main opposing factions to contest the Premiership. The Noon-Tiwanas and Hayats-Daultanas, both staked their claims.[4] A lot of tussle and lobbying followed and eventually Sir Khizar Hayat Khan Tiwana succeeded.[5] A motion of confidence, moved by Chhotu Ram, the Revenue Minister, at the meeting of the Unionist Party, was seconded by Mamdot, President of the Punjab Muslim League, and Khizar Hayat was chosen as the new leader of the Unionists. Earlier, Muslim Unionists had unanimously passed a vote of confidence in Khizar.[6] B.J. Glancy, the Governor of Punjab, also wrote to the Viceroy that:

> After a period of wise-pulling only four serious candidates for vacancy of Premiership have emerged. These are, Khizar Hayat Khan Tiwana now Minister of Public Works,

> Liaqat Hayat Khan, Nawab Muzaffar Khan and Firoz Khan Noon. Of these the last two have stated that they do not wish to be considered and No. 2, who is not a M.L.A. and commands a very small following, seems unsuitable. All existing Ministers and a strong body of supporters are in favour of Khizar and as an early decision to stop intrigues is essential, I am inviting him to form a ministry. He proposes to keep on all existing Ministers who will resign and be reappointed. Solution is very satisfactory in my opinion.[7]

Khizar Hayat Khan Tiwana belonged to an aristocratic landed family of West Punjab. The Tiwanas had strong martial traditions, having furnished successive Punjab Governments with military recruits. During the Ranjit Singh period, the Tiwana cavalry troop had formed an important part of the army. The Tiwanas transferred their allegiance to the British during the Anglo-Sikh wars and thereafter remained their most loyal supporters, even during the troubled times of 1857. The Tiwanas were highly respected by the other landlords of the West Punjab and were the leading tribe in the Shahpur district. The *Kalra* estate of the Tiwanas was acknowledged as one of the finest properties in the Rawalpindi Division.[8]

Despite all these social advantages Khizar Hayat Khan was a weak premier in comparison to Sikander Hayat Khan. Factional rivalry among the Unionists and the growing pressure of the Provincial Muslim League further weakend the position of the new premier. Linlithgow, the Viceroy of India, also doubted Khizar's ability to stand up to Jinnah, but he thought that Glancy, who had become Governor of Punjab in 1942, was now well in the saddle and in a position to give him a great deal of assistance.[9] The Viceroy also wrote to the Governor of Punjab that, "Khizar is not of the caliber of Sikander, but I have no doubt that under your expert guidance he will do well. I do hope that Khizar will be able to keep things together and to maintain the communal balance with the same care and skill that Sikander showed. He may count himself fortunate in having you to guide and help him."[10]

Linlithgow, in fact, was not trusting Jinnah and he thought that Jinnah might hamper the war effort in Punjab if he managed to tighten his hold over the Unionist ministry, or actually establish a Muslim League Ministry in the Province. Linlithgow feared that the break up of the tenuous alliance between the Muslim and non-Muslim ministers would led to purely communal politics in Punjab, which in turn would create instability in the province. Therefore Glancy must make it clear that he would use his special powers to prevent the fall of the Unionist Minister.[11]

The Premier, in order to weaken the factional rivalry with in the Unionist Party and to check the growing pressure of the Muslim League, appointed Sardar Shaukat Hayat Khan, the eldest son of Sikander Hayat Khan, as a cabinet minister. However, to begin with, the Premier did not face any challenge from the League. Jinnah, the pragmatist one, was more concern about his strategy at the centre. He, therefore, adopted a policy of watching the situation and see how things develop. Jinnah even discouraged Malik Barkat Ali to organise a separate League party in the Punjab Assembly.[12]

In January 1943, a Muslim League Workers' Conference was held in Lahore with Nawabzada Rashid Ali Khan, the Lahore city League's President, in the chair. The Conference elected seven permanent members on the Workers' Board with Maulana Zafar Ali Khan as President, Malik Barkat Ali as senior Vice-President, Nawabzada Rashid Ali Khan as General-Secretary and Khan Rab Nawaz Khan as propaganda Secretary. The Board wanted all Muslim members of the Assembly to resign from the Unionist Party and join the League Assembly party. However, Jinnah, who was following a policy of watch and wait, denounced this Board and cautioned these Leaguers to behave.[13]

At a meeting of the All-India Muslim League Council in Delhi in March 1943, Jinnah's strategy brought some fruits. In this meeting, Khizar Hayat, appeared with the policies of Jinnah, who was discouraging the provincial Leagues against the premier, acknowledged the general leadership of Jinnah and affirmed his adherence to the Sikander-Jinnah pact. Khizar also agreed to establish a separate Muslim League Assembly Party in accordance with the wishes of Jinnah.[14] Khizar said:

> We in the Punjab felt proud of the great services rendered by the All India Muslim League under the leadership and

> guidance of the Quad-e-Azam to the cause of the Muslims. You will never find me and my Muslim colleagues failing in our loyalty to the cause of the Mussalmans and to their sole representative body—the All India Muslim League.[15]

Khizar Hayat Khan, however, vehemently opposed a resolution advocating more active interference by the League in the affairs of Punjab and the resolution was ultimately withdrawn.[16] Thus, Khizar provided only the lip-service to the Muslim League and by doing so he hoped to continue to keep Punjab out of Jinnah's influence. However, there was always the danger that some Muslim politicians might sell the Unionist fort for their own personal advantage.[17] The growing enthusiasm for Pakistan in Muslim circles was a political resource which was encouraging some ideologues and more numerous opportunities to undermine the Unionist coalition.

The tussle between the Muslim League and Unionist Party continued. Nawab Iftikhar Husain Khan of Mamdot, President of the Punjab Muslim League, and Jinnah told Khizar that the Unionist Ministry, should be redesigned as Muslim League Coalition. Khizar retorted that he intended to abide by the Sikander-Jinnah pact and to maintain the name 'Unionist'. He pointed out that he himself had been elected to the Assembly on the Unionist ticket. Jinnah was annoyed with the attitude of Khizar but he realized that he could not go further as he did not have a majority in the Provincial Assembly. So he instructed Mamdot to come to a satisfactory agreement with Khizar.[18] Moreover, the establishment of a Muslim League Ministry in Punjab was not an ultimate goal of Jinnah but his sights were set on a far higher goal i.e. Pakistan.[19]

At the annual session of the All India Muslim League held at Delhi in April 1943, Jinnah appealed to the Muslim leaders of Punjab to assemble under the flag of the Muslim League and to work for the establishment of the Muslim Nation. He said that:

> I regret to say that the Punjab has not yet played the part that it ought to play and is entitled to play-because, remember, the Punjab is the corner stone of Pakistan. I particularly appeal to the delegates from Punjab—people are alright in the Punjab—when you go back, please—I

> would not say anything more—please substitute the love of Islam and your nation in the place of sectional interests, jealousies, tribal notions and selfishness. For these evils have overpowered you and you are being ground down for the last 200 years. But I see a light—a very bright light. Because, I say, when I went to the Punjab in November last, throughout my tour, it really made me happy to see that the solid body of the people were all right and sound. My appeal is to the leaders—and we have got very able men, very capable men. If they were to make up their minds, I feel confident that within six months the face of the Punjab would be changed.[20]

Jinnah's efforts brought some fruits and by May 1943, Shaukat Hayat Khan, who has been appointed a cabinet minister by the Premier, fell in with him. Shaukat Hayat Khan joined hands with two other prominent and influential League leaders, Nawab of Mamdot and Mumtaz Daultana. The Sikander-Jinnah pact, which gave the Unionists hard local bases in Punjab, was now coming to be questioned by the very politicians in whose provincial interest it had been made. Nawab of Mamdot even claimed that the Sikander-Jinnah Pact had come to an end.[21] He wrote to Jinnah that', we have now reached a stage where nobody has the guts to say anything against the League. I have purposely tried to involve the Muslim Ministers knowing that none of them will have the courage to say "no". "We must assert ourselves because we know that the masses are with us."[22] Jinnah, however, was not in a hurry and he remarked, 'All I can say is patience. The League is bound now to go ahead. I have full confidence that our opponents and enemies will fail.'[23]

The increased activities of the Muslim Leaguers throughout the summer months of 1943 created uneasiness in Ministerial and political circles. Shaukat Hayat Khan's unpardonably indiscreet references to 'Pakistan' in the course, of his tour in August 1943 came near to bringing matters to a head.[24] Now Shaukat Hayat Khan, Nawab of Mamdot, Mumtaz Multans and others were ready to make a bid for power. Their tactic was to challenge Khizar either to reaffirm his allegiance to the League or to declare his independence from it. The survival of

Khizar and his Unionist coalition depended on their taking a stand on Sikander-Jinnah pact.[25]

Although Shaukat Hayat Khan, Nawab of Mamdot, Mumtaz Daultana and others tried to pull members of the Assembly out of the Khizar camp under the convenient pretex of backing "Pakistan", however, Khizar survived. Khizar survived because he was shrewder than Shaukat, Mamdot and Daultana and because he still had the votes of most Muslim politicians in the Assembly, the support of some Hindus and Sikhs. Glancy was also supporting Khizar because he did not want a League ministry since it was bound to aggravate communal tensions and undermine the war efforts.[26] The Viceroy was, even, intended to impose Governor's rule instead of establishing Muslim League ministry in case of the collapse of the Unionist Government.[27]

In September 1943, Khizar had an inconclusive meeting with Jinnah during which the latter claimed that the Unionist Party has ceased to exist as soon as the Jinnah-Sikander Pact has been drawn up. Khizar did not accept it, however, in order to avoid any pressure, he agreed to pay more vocal lip-service to Jinnah. This involved going through the motions of establishing a specifically Muslim League Assembly party which would be subject to League party discipline and organization according to the wishes of Jinnah. Thereafter, Jinnah, also instructed to the anti-Khizar group that Muslims in the Assembly should patch up their differences.[28]

In November 1943, in a meeting of the Muslim Unionists, Khizar established a Muslim League Assembly party. He said that the Muslim League Assembly party shall be subject to the control and discipline of the Central and Provincial Muslim League Parliamentary Boards and in all matters relating to Muslim interests. The members of the party vote in accordance with the decision arrived at in the party meeting.[29] However, these paper arrangements did not alter the fact that the League Assembly party was effectively under Unionist management. The Sikander-Jinnah Pact has been unanimously ratified by the meeting and by a majority vote it was decided to incorporate it into the Assembly party's constitution. The Unionists, in fact, remained independent because of the terms of the pact. Thus, in practice the things remained as they had always been.[30] It was obvious that Jinnah would not be able to content with such a state of affairs for long.

To challenge the Unionist Party and Khizar, Jinnah, began work at all India level. The Working Committee of the All-India Muslim League at its meeting held on November 13, 1943 appointed a three men committee, consisting of Nawab Mohammed Ismail Khan, Choudhary Khaliquzzaman and Khawaja Nazimuddin to examine whether the constitution framed for the Muslim League Assembly Party was in conformity with the fundamental principles, policies and programmes of the All India Muslim League.[31] At the Karachi session of the All India Muslim League held in December 1943, Jinnah appointed a six-member Committee of Action under the chairmanship of Nawab Mohammad Ismail Khan to undertake the work of organising, co-ordinating and unifying the Provincial League and the entire Muslim League organisation in consonance with the Constitution, Rules and Programme of the All-India Muslim League. Its sub committees were entrusted to control, direct and regulate all the activities of the various Provincial Leagues and to take disciplinary action against any member of the League who violates the decisions of the League or to dissolve or disaffiliate any Provincial League who fails in its duties.[32]

In February 1944, Wavell, the new Viceroy, announced that the Cripps Offer was still open to India.[33] Encouraged with this announcement, Jinnah streamlined his efforts to establish a Muslim League Ministry in Punjab. The three newly created committees—the Election Enquiry Committee, the Committee of Action and a committee to examine the Punjab Muslim League's Constitution were sent to Lahore, to see if a ministry more overtly in the League camp could be formed.[34] But the situation remained much the same and these committees failed to elicit Khizar's cooperation and those who wanted to do down Khizar could not claim any wide Muslim support.[35]

The Muslim League now declared an open war against the Unionists. Jinnah, himself, came to Lahore in March 1944 for talks with Khizar and determined to settle the issue once and for all. Mumtaz Daultana, General Secretary of the Punjab Muslim League, outlined an ambitious mass contact programme to mobilize Muslims against the Hindus and the British.[36]

Jinnah while discussing the situation with Provincial Muslim Leaguers emphasized that the Unionist Party should be liquidated.[37] Jinnah also asserted that the policies and programmes of the Unionist Party were mainly in the interest of one class—the *Zamindars*—whereas the Muslim League stood for independent Pakistan—and was a people's party pledged to safeguard the interest of all classes that constituted the Muslim nation. Therefore, the fundamental and basic principles of the Muslim League were quite different from those of the Unionist Party.[38]

Jinnah aimed to repudiate the Jinnah-Sikander Pact and to replace the Unionist Ministry with a Muslim League Government. He told Khizar "You cannot owe allegiance to two political parties. There can be no divided loyalty, so far as the League is concerned. The so-called pact clearly lays down that we may continue the present coalition or enter into any other coalition before or after the elections. The present coalition is merely at will and formed for specific purpose."[39] Jinnah held that the League rather than the Unionist Party formed the coalition Ministry with non-Muslims, and that its name be changed to "Muslim League Coalition Party."[40] Although Khizar did not want open conflict with the Muslim League but he was not intented to meet Jinnah's demand to abolish the pact as it symbolized the guarantees of the Muslim members of the Unionist to their Hindu and Sikh colleagues.[41]

Khizar told Glancy that he had no appetite for politics and wanted to retire as soon as the war was over. But he was anxious not to leave his followers in the lurch or to be relegated to political oblivion since the future belonged to two political parties, Indian National Congress and Muslim League. Admitting that the Unionist Party existed only in name, all the members of the Unionist Party were also members of the Provincial Muslim League and in fact, a majority of them owe allegiance to the Muslim League rather than the Unionist Party, thus Khizar confessed that its disappearance would cause little regret. Of course, Khizar assured the Governor, he did not believe in Pakistan, yet his disheartened politician felt that the Pakistan slogan is bound to gain momentum and and it is likely to become a decisive factor in the next elections. Khizar estimated that the number of his Muslim supporters in the

Assembly who would defect to Jinnah stood at thirty-two, and he told Glancy that even after these defections the Unionist would have a comfortable majority in the House. Khizar, in fact, wanted an order from Glancy that he should stand up to Jinnah in the interests of the war effort and he got these orders from Glancy.[42] Wavell also favoured the encouragement given by Glancy to Khizar to stand up to Jinnah.[43]

In order to help Khizar, Glancy decided to take action against one of his ministers, Sardar Shaukat Hayat Khan, who was openly upholding the cause of Muslim League. At a cabinet meeting, certain charges were made against Shaukat Hayat Khan and Glancy without giving him an opportunity to defend himself, dismissed him on the ground that his colleagues had lost confidence in him. Glancy wrote to Wavell that, 'I do not altogether like this course of action, but larger issues are at stake—the tranquillity of the province and the continuance of the war effort'.[44]

Shaukat Hayat Khan's dismissal from the Unionist ministry added a new dimension to the Unionist—League tussle for Shaukat claimed that he resigned a week before this dismissal on the issue.[45] At the Sialkot session of the Punjab Provincial Muslim League held in May 1944, Jinnah demanded an explanation from Khizar and Glancy, asserting that Shaukat Hayat had been dismissed for his sympathy with the League.[46]

Later, the Council of the All India Muslim League passed a resolution condemning the action of the Governor of Punjab in dismissing Sardar Shaukat Hayat Khan, as apart from the question of his power to dismiss an individual minister by virtue of the power conferred upon him under Section 51 of the Government of India Act, he never furnished the particulars of allegations or charges against Sardar Shaukat Hayat Khan, nor did he allow him any opportunity to give his explanation or defense before dismissal.... The Council called upon the Government of India and the British Government to recall the Governor.[47]

Meanwhile, Jinnah-Khizar negotiations finally broke down on April 27, 1944. Khizar issued a statement explaining that the repudiation of the Jinnah-Sikander Pact would amount to a breach of faith and that he could not accept Jinnah's demand, 'involving interference in provincial affairs and the inner working of the Ministerial Party formed under the Jinnah-Sikander pact as this would be contrary to the accepted democratic principle that the wishes of the electorate and legislature should prevail.[48] Khizar further said that he was prepared to extend his whole-hearted and full support to Jinnah in all questions which related to the Muslim community and also promised to strengthen the Punjab Muslim League, but warned that he will not allow to disturb the communal harmony of the province.[49]

On April 27, 1944, Jinnah wrote a letter to Khizar Hayat Khan and requested him for a written reply so that there should be no room for misunderstanding. In this latter, Jinnah made three proposals, that every member of the Muslim League Party in the Punjab Assembly should declare that he owes allegiance solely to the Muslim League Party in the Assembly and not to the Unionist or any other party, that the present label of the coalition, namely the Unionist Party should be dropped, and that the name of the proposed coalition should be the Muslim League Coalition Party.[50]

On the same day, Jinnah wrote another letter to Khizar which was personally handed over to him by Nawab of Mamdot and Mumtaz Daultana. This second letter was also not replied by Khizar. In this letter Jinnah had requested him to give a written reply immediately failing which the Muslim League Council will have to decide what course of action should be taken against him.[51]

After the collapse of Jinnah-Khizar negotiations, a Conference of Punjab Provincial Muslim League was called at Sialkot under the presidentship of Sardar Abdur Rab Nishtar. Jinnah attended the Conference and took the opportunity to explain the whole position to the Muslims who had assembled from all over the province. Jinnah asserted that Khizar Hayat Khan should have come to this Conference in order to explain his position. He has thus violated the discipline of the party of which he was a member.[52] Jinnah also asserted that an assurance of non-interference in Punjabi politics had never existed in his pact with Sikander and that in accordance with it, it was open to the League Party in the Assembly to terminate any coalition arrangement.[53] Jinnah further said that he wanted to kill the very name Unionist and see its funeral.[54]

The non-muslim Ministers of the Unionist cabinet i.e., Sir Chhotu Ram, Sir Manohar Lal and Sardar Baldev Singh, on May 3, 1944 issued a joint statement on the League-Unionist controversy and suggested that the negotiations could be a part of an All-India settlement. Jinnah stated that an All-India understanding could not be achieved with only three non-Muslim ministers in Punjab. He said, together they did not represent more than 20 members out of the total number of 175 members of the Punjab Assembly. Thus the demand that the Muslim League should come to all-India settlement with them was preposterous.[55]

It was against this background that the whole matter was referred to the Committee of Action and the committee issued a notice to Khizar Hayat Khan to explain his position and also invited him to meet members of the Committee. Khizar Hayat, however, did not respond to the Committee. The Committee, thereupon, resolved to remove him from membership of the Muslim League in view of the breach of the party discipline and contravention of rules, principles and policies of the Muslim League that he had committed.[56] The Council of All-India Muslim League which meet at Lahore on July 30, 1944, also took up the matter and passed the following resolution. 'This Council approves and endorse the action taken by the committee of Action in expelling Malik Khizar Hayat Khan, the Premier of Punjab, from the Muslim League for his utter disregard of the wishes of the Muslims of India in general and the Muslims of Punjab in particular'.[57]

Thus a League-Unionist alliance which had survived for seven years came to an end. This marked the beginning of a new era in the provincial politics. Although the League failed in its efforts to gain control of the Ministry of the province, but it had freed itself from the clutches of the Unionist Party. As many as eighteen members from the Unionist benches defected to the League and an independent Muslim League Party was constituted in the Assembly under the leadership of Sardar Shaukat Hayat Khan.[58] The League, now, more vigorously began to construct a rural base and endeavoured to win over some local notables from the Unionist camp while taking advantage of the factional rivalry among the Unionists.

In fact the sole aim of the Muslim League was not to gain control of the ministerial power in Punjab but to attain Pakistan and for this the determined support from the Muslim MLAs in the Provincial legislature was essential. Since Khizar Hayat Khan, the Premier, refused to allow Muslim MLAs to be controlled by the League Parliamentary Board thus the men like Nawab of Mamdot, Mumtaz Daultana and Shaukat Hayat Khan with the blessing of Jinnah endeavoured to capture the Ministry. Since the aim of the Provincial Muslim League was to attain Pakistan, it was not only trying to consolidate its position in the Provincial Legislative Assembly but it was also making a drive to widen its rural and urban mass base and the League had made a rapid progress in this direction during the years 1943-45.

Meanwhile, the Provincial Muslim League, in January 1943, held meetings at Shahkot, Hoshiarpur, Kasur, Jullundur, Patti and Ludhiana in the Ambala and Jullundur divisions.[59] In February 1943, meetings were held at Gujranwala, Wazirabad, Sialkot, Gujrat and Jhelum.[60] Emphasis was placed on the establishment of new primary Leagues and on holding district conferences which were hoped to galvanise League activities througout their surrounding areas.[61] Some primary Leagues were established in February 1943 and a district conference was held at Fazilka.[62] In March, three more district conferences took place at Karnal, Amritsar and Jhang.[63]

In January 1943, a Muslim League Workers Board was established at Lahore under the presidentship of Maulana Zafar Ali Khan. This Board was aimed to establish new district and primary Leagues and to revitalize those which already existed so that half a million two annas League members could be enrolled within Punjab.[64] This unauthorized action was, however, condemned by other Provincial League's leaders. Thus Jinnah, as had already been mentioned, ordered Nawabzada Rashid Ali Khan to suspend the activities of the Board.[65]

The Provincial Muslim League meantime continued to conduct public meetings, district conferences and to establish primary branches of the League under the leadership of Nawab of Mamdot, Mumtaz Daultana, Malik Barkat Ali, Mian Bashir Ahmed and others. But, Maulana Zafar Ali Khan, Khan Rabb Nawaz Khan and Nawabzada Rashid Ali Khan criticised the functioning of Nawab of Mamdot, - President of the Provincial Muslim League. In March 1943, Nawabzada Rashid Ali Khan wrote to Jinnah that Nawab of Mamdot was an obstacle to the growth of League. He also stated that the Nawab refused to allow primary League branches to be established on his Ferozepur estate.[66]

Glancy, the Governor of Punjab, also had a low opinion about Nawab of Mamdot. He wrote to the Viceroy that, "It is no doubt fortunate for Khizar that Mamdot is a man of very ordinary ability. Indeed I think that one of the features of the Muslim League, at the moment, is the extraordinary lack of the men with ability apart from Jinnah himself. The Provincial Muslim League for all its increase in influence and in spite of its success in starting quite a good daily paper in English, had very great weakness in its lack of leaders."[67] Despite all such shortcomings and complaints, Jinnah did not remove Nawab of Mamdot from the presidentship of the Provincial Muslim League since apart from being the richest and biggest Muslim landowner in East Punjab. Mamdot was influential amongst the Pathan community of the Province[68] and, with the passage of time he acquired political experience and became popular among all the Muslim Leaguers.

The Provincial Muslim League, during its campaign programmes and meetings, adopted religious symbols. The League appealed to the Punjabi Muslims to support the demand of Pakistan in the name of Islam. The religious festivals such as *Id* were used by the League to spread its message and to promote unity and social solidarity amongst the Muslims of Punjab.[69] Mosques, because of their importance as centres of Muslim life, were used to spread League propaganda. League's meetings were regularly held in mosques especially after the Friday prayers.[70] The Quran was also frequently paraded as the League's symbol and pledges to support it being made on it.[71] The Muslim League's workers always delivered emotional speeches, their appeals always commence with a text from the Quran, invoking God's protection and praising his wisdom. Very often, poems from Iqbals's poetry were also declaimed at such meetings.[72]

The new generation of the Provincial Muslim League especially Nawab of Mamdot, Shaukat Hayat Khan, and

Mumtaz Daultana also endeavoured to make a departure from the traditional political system based on landlordism and clan leaders instead they made propaganda by defining the concept of community.[73] In the Press and public meetings, these leaders had defined a Muslim community in Punjab that was, like that of the *Ulema*, politically independent of the colonial administrative structure.[74] These young leaders argued that the power of the Unionist Party was a product of the bureaucratic system developed by the British to maintain their own power. Mumtaz Daultana asserted that the Britishers had imposed a leadership of large owners, and who in their turn, have been completely subjected to the bureaucracy by a subtle distribution of partonage and privilege.[75] To establish their independence of colonial ideology, these leaders of the League wedded themselves with the Islamic concept of community rather than to be encapsulated within the bureaucratic structure.

In the wake of Jinnah's final split with the Unionist in 1944, the young leaders of the Provincial Muslim League especially Nawab of Mamdot, Shaukat Hayat Khan and Mumtaz Daultana assumed the task, as Khizar Hayat Khan remarked ironically, of undoing the work their fathers, the great builders of the Unionist Party had done.[76] They primarily attacked the ideology of mediation on which Unionist power was based. These League's leaders argued that the Unionist Party, as an inheritors of the structure of colonial authority had claimed to protect Punjab's local structure but the communities it claimed to protect was wholly artificial. The colonial state in fact, Leaguers asserted, through the Unionist Party had manipulated local loyalties for its own purposes and it is less concerned with the interests of the communities.[77]

The Provincial Muslim League leaders also attacked the Punjabi tribal associations, such as *Jat Maha Sabha and Rajput Conference*, which were supported by the Unionist Party. It was argued that these tribal associations ignored the differences between Hindus, Muslims and Sikhs. It was said that *Jat Mahasabha* was trying to create Jat consciousness among the Muslim Jats, simply to undermine the Muslim League.[78] It was argued by the Muslim Leaguers that there was nothing common between the Hindu Jats of eastern Punjab and the Muslim Jats of western Punjab, neither they interdine, nor they intermarry nor they participate in the domestic festivals of one another.[79] Similarly, the Muslim Leaguers also attacked Khizar Hayat Khan's efforts to include non-Muslim Rajputs in the Rajput Conference.[80] The Provincial Muslim Leaguers, in fact, stood for and campaign for only one thing i.e. the Muslim Community and Pakistan.

During the summer months of 1944, the Provincial Muslim League made vigorous campaign in rural Punjab, conducted large number of public meetings, established primary branches of the League and also enrolled new members. It was decided that the divisional workers would complete a tour of the province by the end of June. In July they will hold large meetings at *tehsil* headquarters followed by district conferences at short intervals.[81] Accordingly during the months of June and July, Nawab of Mamdot, Shaukat Hayat Khan, Mumtaz Daultana and Raja Ghazanfar Ali Khan along with the workers of the Muslim League toured all the five divisions of the province and addressed Muslim League Conferences at Montgomery, Lyallpur, Sheikhupura, Sargodha, Jhang, Sialkot and Rawalpindi.[82] These meetings attracted large audiences, over 15,000 attended the meeting at Multan and 10,000 at Montgomery.[83] Primary Leage branches were established even in the remote rural areas of Sargodha and Mianwali, and by the end of July nearly 7,000 members were enrolled in these two districts.[84] Five orgainising secretaries were appointed in each of the Five divisions of the Punjab. Besides taking up the task of the propaganda programme these Secretaries also laid the basis of organisation in various districts of the five divisions. Syed Mustafa Shah Gilani, the Organizing Secretary of the Rawalpindi division, may be singled out for his energetic work.[85] Efforts were also made to contact MLAs and to bring them toward the League, particularly in the Multan Division.[86]

A training school was established at Lahore in order to provide intensive agitational training to the workers of the Muslim League.[87] Sardar Shaukat Hayat Khan made an extensive tour of Ambala and Jullundur divisions and held meetings in almost every important centre of these two divisions.[88] Regarding their campaigning programme Nawabzada Rashid Ali Khan also wrote to Jinnah:

> Every Friday at prayer time I go to mosques in the city accompanied by leading workers and explain the policy and programme of the League to the Muslims. Three times a week I lead a deputation to leading wards and mohallas in the city accompanied by leading Muslims of the locality and enroll members of our League in large numbers.[89]

Nawab of Mamdot, president of the Punjab Muslim League, also wrote to Jinnah that, "We are having great success in our public meetings. I attach great importance to the Montgomery meeting because it was exactly ten days after an official meeting which was attended by Khizar Hayat Khan and Sir Chhotu Ram. The attendance in their meeting was 492 while in spite of all official resistance the gathering in our meeting was decidedly more than ten thousands. Not only that, the Montgomery people gave us a purse of Rs. 10,000 for the provincial fund. Even the big *Zamindars* have discarded the bar and have started attending the meetings freely."[90]

Mumtaz Daultana, Secretary Punjab Provincial Muslim League, in his report of the Muslim League submitted in July 1944, had stated,

> "The public response in our meetings had been much more than we could expect. Big demonstrations, huge meetings and boundless enthusiasm had greeted us everywhere. Our weakness have been so far our inability to effectively plan our agitation. It is now becoming clear that in view of the determined Government opposition, our basic strength must come not from the landlords or the Zaildars-Lamberdar class but from the broad masses of the Muslim people."[91]

Nawab of Mamdot and Mumtaz Daultana in order to weakened the opposition of the Government and to weakened the Unionist ideology, decided to sought support of Muslims in the Punjab Communist party. The Communists, in fact, had never claimed much support among the Punjabi Muslims although they had considerable influence among a section of the Sikhs.[92] Nawab of Mamdot and Mumtaz Daultana, however, realised that an alliance with the Communists would help to legitimize their position as rural Muslim leaders, independent of the ideology of the Unionist Party and would also assist them to assert their pressure against the policies of the Unionist Government. On the other side, the Communists were also willing to had an alliance with the Muslim League realizing that the rural League leaders would play a critical role in stimulating popular rural consciousness in Punjab, in spite of their largely landlord backgrounds.[93] The two parties came close to each other when the Communist Party decided to recognize the legitimacy of the Muslim demand for Pakistan as a just, progressive and national demand.[94]

In July 1944, Daniyal Latifi, the Office Secretary of the Provincial Muslim League drafted the manifesto of the Punjab Muslim League.[95] This manifesto was shaped by Communist influence and it was unanimously adopted by the Provincial League working committee in October 1944 and circulated over the signatures of Nawab of Mamdot and Mumtaz Daultana. Though it dealt with a wide range of issues, the Manifesto provided at its heart a comprehensive plan for redefining the structural and cultural relation between the state and society.[96]

The manifesto proposed to transform the economy of the province. A radical national reconstruction was suggested that would transform the contours of the colonial system with a sweeping series of state-sponsored economic and administrative reforms, ranging from the acceleration of rural road construction to the development of a system of state-planned industrialization. Such reforms would also transform the position of Punjab's peasantry. The state would take a direct role in marketing the peasants' produce and it would also guarantee to the peasants a fair return on their labour.[97]

The Muslims must be trained, the manifesto further declared, in the spirit of Islamic brotherhood and in traditions of their religion so as to recreate a moral basis for their conduct. Practical skills were to be joined with the message of Islam. The Quranic religious education would be a compulsory subject for all Muslims in the primary and secondary school standards and a study of Islamic history and culture a compulsory subject for all Muslims in secondary and higher education. To guarantee that such instruction would permeate the lives of all Punjabi Muslims, this religious education was also for women.

The non-Muslim minorities would be allowed to organise education in accordance with their religious and cultural traditions.[98] Educational reform and moral regeneration thus went hand in hand with a structural transformation of Punjab.

The contribution of the manifesto, however, was more theoretical than practical. Although the Communist ideas had proved useful in differentiating the goals of the Muslim Leaguers from those of the Unionists, but few took the manifesto very seriously. In fact, most League leaders showed little interest in making the radical transformation an immediate reality. Moreover, in its call for a radical transformation the manifesto, served, more to highlight than to resolve the immediate political dilemmas of the Muslim League. The influence of the Communist organization was so weak in Western Punjab that its help proved almost immaterial for the Provincial Muslim League. The Provincial Muslim League, thus, continued to hold public meetings, district conferences and League Workers Conference on the bases of Islamic appeals, using religious symbols and thus strengthened the movement for Pakistan.

In December 1944, the Provincial Muslim League started province-wide campaign to enroll new recruits for the Legislative Assembly. The League leaders, Nawab of Mamdot, Mumtaz Daultana, Sardar Shaukat Hayat Khan, Ghazhafar Ali Khan and others, also started extensive tour programme of the province in order to conduct public meetings and worker conferences.[99] Nawab of Mamdot said, "These tours will infused new and progressive life into the League. Our intention is to awaken our workers regarding the benefits of the Islamic State and to tell them more about the aims and ideals of the Muslim League, so that the workers can more vigorously participate in their political struggle."[100]

The Punjab Muslim League in its public meetings was warmly welcomed and responded. Nawabzada Rashid Ali Khan, president of the Lahore city Muslim League, wrote to Jinnah, 'A huge mass meeting was held in Lahore, where attendance was 15,000 which is a record for public meetings in Lahore. The Muslims of Lahore welcomed the stand of the Muslim League party and also pledges their full support to it.[101] Nazir Ahmad Khan, a Muslim League worker of

Montgomery, reported about the tour programme of his district and states that the Muslim League Speaker's party which had spent only four days in that district, attracted the attention of Muslim masses and also aroused enthusiasm among them for the cause of the League.[102]

Nazir Ahmad Khan reported that a huge public meeting was held at Shergarh on December 30, 1944 and had four noticeable features. Firstly, it was a purely *Zamindar* gathering—the landlords and the tillers of the soil all coming from the backward areas but all eager to know. Secondly, the nobles of the area the *Pirs* of Shergarh, Huseingarh, Mustafabad and Dipalpur etc. were present in large numbers several of them being *Zaildars* and *lambardars* the class that is generally under the Unionist thumb. Thirdly, the outstanding work was done by Pir Syed Ishaq Husain and his nephew and the spontaneous present of a purse of Rs. 5,500 by these gentlemen and their kinsmen are landmark in the League movement of the province. Fourthly, the presence of police reporters and officials in uniform at the meeting was perhaps a special gift of the Unionist ministry to the people.[103]

The report further elaborated that the meetings were also held at Okara, Pakpattam, Arifwala, Chichawanti and at Montgomery. Resolutions calling upon Muslim members of the Assembly, from Montgomery district, to join the League were enthusiastically passed at each of the meetings and this is sure to have a good effect provided it is backed up by personal persuation. At Montgomery a contribution of Rs. 10,000 to the Provincial League was announced on behalf of the district. The Muslim League speakers' party travelled in a lorry fitted with loud speakers and decorated with Muslim League flags, mottos and slogans. Every where this lorry evoked considerable interest. The Party's members deserve the thanks of all sane Muslims for the great service they are doing to the League cause by undertaking this long and arduous tour.[104]

The Muslim League speakers' Party made an extensive tour of the Lahore and Multan divisions and held a number of public meetings and Workers Conferences at Lahore, Lyallpur, Jhang, Sheikhupura, Multan, Gujranwala, Sialkot, Muzafargarh, Gurdaspur and Kasur.[105] Rana Nasarullah Khan, Chaudhary Attaullah Jahania and Chaudhary Roshanuddin were also the members of the League Speakers' party.[106] At a public meeting at Gurdaspur, Rana Nasarullah Khan, the Divisional Organizing Secretary of the Jullundur division, retorted that:

> Muslim League is not an organization of Khan Bahadurs and Nawabs but is a party of the masses. Thousands of Khan Bahadurs and Nawabs can be sacrificed on the altar of the Muslim Kaum (community) but the Kaum cannot be sacrificed for the sake of Nawabs and Khan Bahadurs... persons like Nawab of Mamdot, Mumtaz Daultana, Sardar Shaukat Hayat Khan, Raja Ghazhafar Ali Khan, Chaudhary Roshanuddin have sacrificed their titles and offices for the sake of Kaum. It appears that the tide were turning in favour of the League in the rural areas.[107]

The League Speakers' party also toured Jullundur division and held public meetings and workers meetings at Firozpur, Jullundur, Batala, Hoshiarpur and Ludhiana.[108] Rana Nasarullah Khan during these meetings vehemently attacks the British rule and the Unionist Government, highlighted the features of the Islamic State and appealed to the people to support the demand of Pakistan. He asserted that the Muslim League will also take care of the interest of the workers, peasants and the downtroddens.[109] While making an assessment of these tour programmes, Nawab of Mamdot, President of the Provincial Muslim League, asserted that these tours of the Muslim League had infused new life into the League and had arised the workers and the masses for the cause of Pakistan and Islam.[110]

Apart from making this propaganda work and making Islamic appeals in favour of the demand for Pakistan, the League leaders decided to took up some local issues in order to expose the weaknesses and functioning of the Unionist Government. Mumtaz Daultana said, there is no doubt about the deep sympathy of the people for the Muslim League, but to shake off the deep-rooted fear of the bureaucracy, to combat the firm hold of nepotism over Punjabi public life, we need tireless and prolonged agitation. Apart from the appeal of Pakistan, the League must formulate a more concrete and immediate programme which is suited to local needs of the province and is democratic and anti-bureaucratic and which will distinguish the League from Khizar's party of the 'Friends of the Governor' as a People's party'.[111]

The war time grievances of the people of Punjab and the food policy of the Unionist Government during the war time caught the attention of the Provincial Muslim League and the League got an opportunity to expose the weakness and contradiction in the ideology and functioning of the Unionist Government. The Second World War brought considerable hardships to the people of Punjab in the shape of inflation and growing shortage of consumer goods. Inflation, infact, wiped out the profits of the agrarian class which resulted them from the increase in price of such crops as wheat, maize and gram. As the war progressed, the consumer goods such as cloth, iron, cement, sugar and kerosene, all became virtually unobtainable in the villages.[112] Although the shortage of the consumer goods was first felt in the towns, the rural population however, increasingly suffered from its effects. Shortage of foodgrains were reported from thirteen districts and of consumer goods from ten districts.[113] This led to a rapid rise in inflation which caused great distress amongst the poor.[114]

The Unionist Government instead of controlling the rising inflation and removing the shortage of consumer goods and foodgrains, in accordance with the order of the government of India, established a price ceiling for wheat, Punjab's most important surplus foodgrain commodity. This move of the Unionist government caused deep resentment among rural producers and led to their widespread withholding of grain stocks from the market. The Punjab Government even began the export of wheat to Bengal to compile the order of the Government of India and appointed purchasing agents who alone could act as middlemen between Punjab and outside.[115] This policy of the government pushed the Unionist Party into close cooperation with the non agriculturalist Hindu interests who had long dominated the Punjab's grain trade. And it provided an opportunity to the Provincial Muslim League to claim that the Unionist Party was functioning against the interests of the Punjabi Muslim agriculturalists.[116]

The Unionist Government, in September 1943, by obeying the order of the Government of India, introduced the policy of rationing and requisitioning of foodgrains. In accordance with the instructions from the central authorities, the Punjab Government ordered its district officials to induce the release of all surplus stocks of foodgrains lying in the villages or in the markets.[117] The introduction of requisitioning of the foodgrains and rationing of grain annoyed the rural Muslim population. The League leaders attacked this policy as it was benefiting only the non-Muslim from the economic opportunities the war has created.[118]

The Muslim League frequently organised protest meetings against the policy of requisitioning and rationing of the foodgrains and attempted to win the support of Muslim agriculturalists. Raja Ghazanfar Ali Khan argued in the Assembly that the government regulations were benefiting only the Hindu and Sikh grain traders and were excluding rural Muslims from the government's bounty, consigning Muslim agriculturalists to a permanently backward position. Agriculturists are already very backward in trade and commerce and in the presence of these regulations it becomes totally impossible for them to better their lot in these fields.[119] The Provincial Muslim League also resented the increase in governmental interference which accompanied requisitioning, it was said that the houses of the agriculturists were being invaded and their families insulted under the pretext of requisitioning.[120]

As early as in November 1943, the Provincial Muslim League adopted an unofficial resolution to the effect that any attempt to control the price of wheat would result in very keen resentment and discontent among the agricultural classes.[121] However, the Unionist Government did not bothered about it and in October 1944, the government fixed the agricultural prices.[122] The operation of the statutory price ordinance encouraged the growth of large scale smuggling of the foodgrains between Punjab and United Provinces.[123] Many farmers regarded the high black market prices which they obtained for their produce as a legitimate compensation for their other economic difficulties. As a result of this smuggling operations the foodgrains specially the wheat began to disappear from the open market. The Punjab Government, thus, began to use force to requisition grain from the villages. This policy of the Unionist Government was vehemently criticised by the Muslim League.[124]

Rationing policy of the Punjab Government, gradually, acquired a communal colour. The Muslims of Lahore and other towns in which it was first introduced complained that Hindu and Sikh civil supply officers regularly discriminated against them in the distribution of rationed goods.[125] The Muslim League frequently organized protest meetings against the communal favouritism in rationing. The League leaders asserted that the Unionist Government was taking no steps to control inflation and to curb the profit making deeds of the Hindu community.[126]

The Provincial Muslim League attempted to win over the support of the rural Muslim population by helping them in their war time distress. The League workers took medical supplies, which had become increasingly expensive and difficult to obtain during the war, with them on their tour to the countryside.[127] The League also distributed other essential consumer goods, attempted to obtain increased ration allowances for the villages and wherever possible they gained control of the rationing machinery.[128] The Provincial League, thus, attempted to win over the support of the rural Muslims by solving their economic miseries and assisting them in their struggle against the highhandedness of the Unionist Government.

The food policy of the Punjab Government, in fact, exposed the contradictions in the ideology and functioning of the Unionist Party. The Unionists always claimed to act as a custodian of the interests of agriculture class and the same class became the worst sufferer of the food policy of the government. The discriminatory and hated food policy thus eroded the base of the Unionist Party amongst the agriculture class and the rural Muslims. More significantly, the League workers linked the solution of the economic miseries with the demand of the establishment of Pakistan.

The Punjab Muslim Students Federation during the years 1943-45, played an active role in campaigning for Pakistan. Although their immediate practical influence on Punjab politics was limited, however, their strategic role in the evolution of the Pakistan movement proved substantial. Their propaganda of the demand for Pakistan proved very important for Jinnah as it helped him to dramatize the Muslim League's public commitment to a communal ideal. As S.M. Ikram, a historian, has asserted that the value of Students Federation was quite obvious to Jinnah as it was free from the handicaps of the Unionists and more broad based than the small urban and other groups.[129] The Punjab Muslim Students Federation, in fact, played a symbolic role in Punjab, provided a visible form to the demand for Pakistan and aroused personal commitment of the Muslim community in its favour.

In the absence of an effective Provincial League Organisation, the Muslim students devoted themselves to the propagation of the demand for Pakistan. In February 1943, a delegation of the Punjab Muslim Students Federation, comprising Hamid Nizami, President of the Federation, Raja Iftikharullah and Mohammad Ilayas Qureshi toured to Attock, Rawalpindi, Jhelum, Gujrat, Wazirabad, Sialkot and Gujranwala and held meetings in support of the demand for Pakistan. The same delegation also met William Phillips, an emissary of the US President, F.D. Roosevelt, in the Governor House, Lahore and convincingly acquainted him with the Pakistan scheme.[130]

The Muslim Students Federation, as a part of its propaganda campaign, set up Pakistan Study Circles at many places, particularly in the colleges of the province. Reading material and literature on Pakistan was provided by the Home Study Circle and 'Pakistan Library' of the Federation situated at its Provincial office. The Provincial Federation had also issued instructions to its primary branches to establish Pakistan Study circles of their own.[131]

On March 23, 1943, the Punjab Muslim Students Federation celebrated 'Pakistan Day' and held a public meeting at Islamia college, Lahore. Abdul Hameed Nizami in his presidential remarks said:

> Today the 23rd of March is a day of great significance for Muslim India. On this auspicious day, three years ago, was declared at Lahore, for the first time authoritatively from the platform of the All India Muslim League, the final goal of Muslim India, which later on came to be known as the Pakistan Scheme, we have embodied our

> goal in it ... I particularly appeal to our intelligentsia and Muslim students to come forward and rise to the occasion. Train yourselves, equip yourselves for the task that lies before us. The final victory depends upon you and is within our grasp.[132]

To make propaganda on a wider scale, the Punjab Muslim Students Federation resolved to launch a re-organization movement throughout the province. In the months of May-June, the students had sufficient time to devote to the League work. With this in mind, Nizami decided to launch a campaign programme and he wrote to Jinnah, "we have divided the province into four zones and have allotted each zone to a group of three students. An elderly League worker, preferably a local man, will be with them for their help and guidance. The Provincial Muslim League will pay for the railway fare. The students will meet the other expenses from their own pockets. We hope to reach every town in these two months."[133]

The Federation commenced its propaganda programme on May 13, 1943. Its delegates toured Lyallpur, Jhang, Gujranwala, Wazirabad, Gujrat, Sialkot, Muzafargarh, Multan, Montgomery and Ambala.[134] Commenting on his impressions of these tours Nizami wrote to Jinnah that, 'the masses are very sincere. They can be relied upon but they are hopelessly unorganized. Everywhere we hear murmur against the middle leadership. We must create a band of genuine workers to inspire confidence in the masses'.[135] During this propaganda programme, the Punjab Muslim Students Federation organized Jullundur Divisional Conference in Hoshiarpur on May 29-30, 1943. It was the first Conference held in this district in favour of the Muslim League.[136]

By the middle of the year 1943, the Punjab Muslim Students Federation had become a solid body and the Muslim youth had shown their loyalty and selfless devotion to the League. The Federation continued its propaganda work for Pakistan during the months of July-August 1943. In October 1943, Abdul Hamid Nizami, president of the Punjab Muslim Students Federation resigned on health grounds and Zia-ul-Islam was nominated to work as officiating president.[137] Nizami wrote to Jinnah, 'I am not giving up the job because I am dissatisfied with the work of the Federation or I have any differences with my colleagues. I am rather proud of these youngmen. I am proud of their work also ... but I feel that in the present state of my health it would be more honest on my part to vacate for a person who can spare more time.'[138]

The Punjab Muslim Students Federation, through its propaganda work, kept alive a particular conception of community identity that proved essential, in the end, to the triumph of the Pakistan campaign. This conception of community identity owed its origins largely to Iqbal, thus, the leaders of the Punjab Muslim Students Federation looked to Iqbal, sometimes more than to Jinnah, as the special ideological patron of their movement. In his poetry and his philosophical writings, Muhammad Iqbal, stressed the active, individualistic and itensive personal commitment to Islam that defined the Muslim community in India.[139] According to him the most intensive personal commitment to Islam by the individual Muslims was the only legitimate way of the political foundation for the Pakistan movement.[140] The Punjab Muslim Students Federation during their campaign programme attached great importance to Iqbal's view of Pakistan and embodied the essence of this personal commitment.[141]

In March 1944, the Punjab Muslim Students Federation held its annual session at Lahore which was presided over by Jinnah. On his arrival in the *Pandal*, Jinnah was given a rousing reception amidst shouts of *Pakistan Zindabad* and *Quaid-i-Azam Zindabad*. Muslim Students Guards escorted him with naked swords. Ten guns were fired as a mark of respect.[142] After recitations, Mian Mumtaz Daultana, president, reception committee, outlined the importance of the session and said:

> It is the proper function and the proper duty of the Muslim youth of the Punjab to extricate us. Your task is great and a difficult one, but it is a task which has an abiding significance for all Muslims of India. It is time you should girded up your loins and took your position by the barricades ... go to your masses. Explain to them, argue with them convince them of the message of the League. They are, I tell you, ready and willing to accept you ... you

are privileged to be their guides, their preceptors and their shepherds.[143]

Zia-ul-Islam, president of the Punjab Muslim Students Federation, remarked that the session proved a great success and the propaganda work of the Federation was widely appreciated.[144] Soon after this session, the Federation played an important role in neutralizing the *All India Jat Mahasabha* conference, which was organized at Lyallpur in April 1944. The Federation thought it to be damaging for the cause of Pakistan and the unity of the League. The workers of the Federation undertook an extensive tour of almost all the villages of the Lyallpur district[145] and made their best efforts to dissuade the Muslim Jats from attending the said conference. They told the villagers that the Jat Conference was intended to create friction among the Muslim community and thus to weaken the cause of the Muslim League and Pakistan. They appealed to the people to refrain from attending such conferences and as a result of the efforts made by the Federation only a few attended the Conference and even hundreds of them returned from there with shouts of *Muslim League Zindabad and Pakistan Zindabad*.[146] Immediately after the failure of the Jat Mahasabha the Federation successfully conducted a Pakistan Conference at Sialkot on May 1, 1944.[147]

During the summer months of 1944, the Punjab Muslim Students Federation, as usual decided to undertook the propaganda work. It was officially announced by the Secretary of the Federation that two hundred students would participate in the propaganda campaign.[148] The campaign was launched in the first week of June, 1944 and the student delegates toured the districts of Rawalpindi, Multan, Gujrat, Jhelum, Attock, Sheikhupura, Layallpur, Jhang, Montgomery and Muzaffar-garh.[149] During this campaign programme, the students re-organized primary branches of the Federation and the League and impressed upon the local MLAs to support the League and the demand of Pakistan.[150] Making an assessment of this tour programme, Zia-ul-Islam, said that the most remarkable observation of this campaign was how the love of the Islam has penetrated every Muslim including the homes of the MLAs, who today for personal interests are supporting the Government and the Unionist Party. The Government can intimidate and bribe the MLAs but it cannot corrupt the spirit of freedom—loving youth who are rising up in arms against their own fathers.[151]

During the Pakistan propaganda campaign, the Punjab Muslim Students Federation, hold an effective Pakistan Conference at Rawalpindi on June 17, 1944 which was inaugurated by Nawabzada Liaqat Ali Khan and was presided over by Sardar Shaukat Hayat Khan. The conference approves the action of the committee of action of the All India Muslim League in expelling Malik Khizar Hayat Khan Tiwana, the Punjab Premier, from the Muslim League. The Conference also appealed for unity amongst the Muslims of the province. It was appealed to *Ahrars, Ulema, Momins, Rajputs, Jats, Awans* and others to sink their differences in the name of the community and make united efforts for the cause of the Pakistan.[152]

After the successful campaign in the Western Punjab districts, the Federation decided to cover some districts of the Eastern Punjab. In July 1944, a deputation of the Federation toured Ambala division and addressed a few students meetings at Ambala, Karnal and Panipat. The deputation also visited Rohtak and was successful in getting assurance from Ashiq Ali, President of Rohtak Municipal Committee, for establishing a League party in the Municipal Committee.[153]

In addition to the propaganda campaign, the Punjab Muslim Students Federation resolved to organise a Summer School of Politics with a view to give training to the students which could help them in the propagation of the League's demand of Pakistan. The Summer School training camp, was inaugurated on July 23, 1944 by Mian Abdul Bari, President Lyallpur District Muslim League. The daily routine of the trainees during a fortnight training programme included morning prayers, recitation and teaching of the Holy Quran, lecturers on the ideology of the Pakistan, history of the freedom struggle of the Muslims and the methodology regarding further course of action. After the evening prayers, the programme was resumed for physical training and would end with a note on the contemporary politics.[154]

Immediately after the successful completion of training, the students spread out in various deputations to different districts to propagate the creed of the League. The students deputations went round several villages of the districts of Jhang, Multan, Montgomery, Sargodha, Sialkot, Lyallpur, Rawalpindi, Ludhiana and Ambala.[155] These deputations, addressed several meetings and stressed that Pakistan was necessary for leading an Islamic way of life which was essential for establishing *Hukumat-i-Ilahi*.[156] These deputations worked with a missionary spirit and were able to bring a number of rural people to the League.[157] Referring to the tour activities undertaken by the student workers, the daily *Dawn* remarked that:

> On each occasion they toured various districts in the province, established their branches and enthused the office-bearers with true spirit of Islam ... the members of the Punjab Muslim Students Federation have shown by their hard work how theories are translated into practice. They deserve not only moral support from everyone, but more encouragement than has been shown to them so far. The establishment of Summer School of Politics in Lahore is yet another step towards developing their activities.[158]

In order to make the propaganda work more effective, the Punjab Muslim Students Federation, hold divisional conferences in all the five divisions of the province during October, 1944.[159] On November 13, 1944, the Federation called a general meeting of the presidents and general secretaries of all the district branches which was presided over by Zia-Ul-Islam. Reviewing the past achievements of the Federation, the President of the meeting put forth the future course of action that was to be carried out in the following year. The secretaries of all the districts submitted reports of the activities of their respective areas. The propaganda committee prepared the campaign programme and urged upon the representatives of the different districts to speed up the campaign programme.[160]

On March 23, 1945, the students federation celebrated 'Pakistan Day' and a huge public meeting was conducted at Islamia College, Lahore under the presidentship of Nawabzada Rashid Ali Khan. 'Pakistan Day' was celebrated by most of the branches of the Federation throughout the province.[161] After the collapse of the Simla Conference, the Punjab Muslim Students Federation vigorously took up the propaganda work.[162]

After 1944, one of the powerful voices in Punjabi Muslim politics, committed to the propagation work of the Punjab Muslim Students Federation and the demand of Pakistan, was the daily *Nawa-i-Waqt*, a newspaper edited by a former president of the Federation, Abdul Hameed Nizami. Strongly influenced by his background in the students movement, Nizami started the *Nawa-i-Waqt* in 1940 as a fortnightly for the promotion of Urdu and for the popularisation of the message of the League and the demand of Pakistan.[163] To begin with its influence was minimal, however, in July 1944 at Jinnah's urging, the paper was converted to be a daily one to serve as a mouthpiece for the Muslim League in Punjab. Very soon the paper became not only the most popular urdu vehicle for the Provincial Muslim League but also a powerful voice for the Punjab Muslim Students Federation and their propaganda campaign for Pakistan based on the idea of most personal and individualistic commitment to Islam. The paper in fact played an important role in disseminating the ideas of the Federation and its propaganda work for Pakistan.[164]

Thus, the efforts made by the leaders of the Provincial Muslim League and the propaganda work of the Punjab Muslim Students Federation strengthened the cause of the Muslim League and the demand for Pakistan. The Islamic appeals and the concept of community (quam) propagated by the League and Federation brought home the demand of Pakistan to every nook and corner of Western Punjab. There developed an individual commitment to Islam among the Punjabi Muslims which in turn weakened the factional, professional, caste, *biradari* and rural-urban consciousness. The development of the League in the province and the growth of the demand for Pakistan attracted the attention of the rural elite, landlords and rival factions among the Unionists and they began to extend their support to the League and ultimately defected to it.[165]

The support of the rural elite, landlords and rival factions among the Unionists proved substantially important for the cause of the League. For example, in district Shahpur after the expulsion of Khizar Hayat Khan Tiwana, the Premier, from the Muslim League the rival Qureshi group provided the backbone of Muslim League support, in the district. Similarly in district Muzaffargarh, the powerful and influential landlord, Abdul Hamid Khan Dasti along with his followers supported the League and provided strength to it. Lust of power, was the other important reason because of which the rural notables and factional leaders extended support to the Muslim League, since the enthusiasm for Pakistan among the Punjabi Muslims had shifted the balance of politics in favour of the League and it appeared that the League would capture the power in Punjab innear future. Since long, these rural notables had been enjoying the political power and privileges, thus they did not, simply, intend to be out of the political power. There even emerged a trend among, nearly every important landlord family, to extend support to both the political parties, that father and son intentionally to join different parties, in order to gain advantage from the party in power.[166]

In addition to the tussle between the Provincial Muslim League and the Unionist Party, efforts made by the leaders of the Provincial League and the propaganda campaign of the Punjab Muslim Students Federation, the politics at the national level, and the relationship which existed between the Indian Nation Congress and the All India Muslim League also profoundly effected the growth of the Muslim League in Punjab. In April 1944, Rajagopalachari in order to had a final settlement between the Indian National Congress and the All-India Muslim League and to end the political impasse prepared a plan and presented it to Jinnah, this plan is known as Rajagopalachari formula.[167]

The terms of the formula were as follows. The Congress and League should co-operate in a provisional government and when the war ended, a commission would demarcate the contiguous districts in North, West and East India having an absolute majority. In the areas thus demarcated, a plebiscite of the adult population would be taken. If the majority votes for a separate sovereign state, it would be given effect to, but border districts would have the option to join one of the new states. In the event of separation, mutual agreements would be entered into for safeguarding defence, commerce and communications. These terms would be binding when the British transferred full power to India.[168]

The formula clearly conceded the principle of Pakistan and embodied Rajagopalachari's belief that this would satisfy the Muslims and they would, in time, cease to want Pakistan.[169] In May 1944, Gandhi was released from the prison, Rajagopalachari had talks with him and announced that Gandhi was prepared to accept the formula if only Jinnah agreed to it. Punjab Provincial Muslim Leaguers were jubilant that Gandhi had accepted Pakistan in principle.[170] The Sikhs, the Hindu Mahasabha and the Unionists were alarmed that the success of this formula would prejudice their position in Punjab.[171] However, Congressmen were surprised and did not know what to make of Gandhi's attitude.[172]

Gandhi's move was calculated to strengthen the hands of Jinnah and further the cause of the Muslim League at a time when the Unionist Party was refusing to submit to the League.[173] Jinnah, however, replied that he could not accept the formula but he would place it before the Muslim League Working Committee and he also insisted on having the formula directly sent to him by Gandhi. This would have served no purpose, so Rajagopalachari ended the correspondence.[174]

Although Jinnah rejected the Rajagopalachari formula but at the same time he agreed to talk with Gandhi, in order to keep open the doors for the future of the Muslim League. Gandhi-Jinnah talks was held at Jinnah's Malabar Hill house in Bombay from September 9-27, 1944. Once again during these talks, the two nation theory of the League proved to be the main trouble. For Jinnah the only acceptable solution was to accept the two-nation theory and division of India into Pakistan and Hindustan.[175] Gandhi could not accept the two nation theory and said that Muslims could not be a separate nation by reason of acceptance of Islam. Will the two nations become one if the whole of India accepted Islam... The majority of Muslims in India were after all converts to Islam.[176]

Gandhi rejected the two-nation theory and was advocating some form of self determination for Muslims in United India.[177] According to Gandhi the proposals meant a common centre concerned with defence, commerce and communications. This did not command itself to Jinnah who insisting upon Gandhi agreeing to the two-nation theory, partition without plebiscite amongst the whole population and that India be divided before it received independence.[178] Gandhi had hoped in vain that Jinnah might be satisfied with the union of the Muslims areas into larger political units within India.

An annoyed Jinnah wrote to Gandhi on September 25, 1944, 'As a result of our correspondence and discussions, I find that the question of the division of India as Pakistan and Hindustan is only on your lips, and it does not come from your heart, and suddenly at the eleventh hour you put forward a new suggestion saying let it be a partition as between two brothers ... it is difficult to deal with you any further, unless it comes from you in your representative capacity ... why not then accept the fundamentals of the Lahore resolution and proceed to settle details.'[179] Gandhi replied by asking Jinnah, 'to think fifty times before throwing away an offer which has been made entirely in the spirit of service in the cause of the communal harmony.'[180]

Jinnah responded by rejecting all Gandhi's overtures, including his appeals to address the League Council or open session, coldly explaining that only a member or delegate is entitled to participate in the deliberations of the meeting of the Council or in the open session respectively[181] Thus the Gandhi—Jinnah talks finally broke down on september 27, 1944 and Jinnah informed the Press that day, 'I regret to say that I have failed in my task of converting Mr. Gandhi. Nevertheless, we hope that the public will not feel embittered and we must trust that this is not the final end of our effort.'[182] Gandhi also told the press that the breakdown is only so-called. It is an adjournment sine die. Each of us must talk to the public and put our view points before them. The chief thing is for the press and the public to avoid partisanship and bitterness.[183]

The breakdown of these negotiations shows the extent of Jinnah's commitment to Pakistan. His refusal was actuated by the fact that he was unwilling to accept anything less than an autonomous and independent Pakistan and it has increasingly added to the prestige and status of Jinnah and the League. The Unionists, the Sikhs and the Hindu Mahasabha were pleased at the breakdown of the talks but at the same time Punjab Provincial Leaguers were also pleased, because the demand of Pakistan, in principle, was accepted by the Congress,[184] which led to the growth of the League in the province. Wavell also recorded his observations, "The two great mountains have met and not even a ridiculous mouse has emerged. This surely must blast Gandhi's reputation as a leader. Jinnah had an easy task, he merely had to keep on telling Gandhi he was talking nonsense, which was true, and he did so rather rudely, without having to disclose any of the weaknesses of his own position. I suppose it may increase his prestige with his followers."[185]

Wavell, the Viceroy, hoped to pave the way for co-operation between the Congress and the League by bringing them together into an interim government at the centre and which will help him to have a constitutional settlement for the future.[186] Bhaulabhai Desai, leader of the Congress in Central Legislative Assembly, encouraged by his talks with the Viceroy, in January 1945, began negotiations with Liaqat Ali Khan, leader of the Muslim League in Central Legislative Assembly, in order to form an interim government at the Centre. Both of them reached to an agreement which is known as *Desai-Liaqat* Pact. According to this pact Congress and the League would join the interim government at the Centre. Each party would have 40 per cent of the seats and 20 per cent would be reserved for minorities. The government would work under the Act of 1935, though the Viceroy should not use his powers to enforce a measure not passed by the Legislature. If the coalition was formed at the Centre, the next step would be to form coalitions in the provinces.[187]

Bhaulabhai Desai met Gandhi and got his consent for this formula. He also gathered from Liaqat Ali Khan that he had mentioned the matter to Jinnah. Desai, thus, assured Wavell and his Secretary, Sir Evan Jenkins, that both Gandhi and Jinnah had approved the formula.[188] However, Jinnah, surprisingly, reported that he knew nothing of the Desai-Liaqat scheme. Jinnah notified to press that, "There is absolutely no foundation for connecting my name with talks which may have taken place between Nawabzada Liaqat Ali Khan and Mr. Bhaulabhai Desai."[189] Now, Gandhi warned Desai not to go ahead without the approval of the Congress Working Committee.[190] Under such a circumstances, the Desai-Liaqat formula finally did not materialize. However, the Desai-Liaqat dialogue introduced and popularised the idea of parity between

Congress and the Muslim League in a interim government which itself strengthened the League at the national level as well as at the provincial level.

Wavell, during March-April 1945, repeatedly requested the Whitehall to allow him to open negotiations with the Indian leaders, in order to include them in his Executive Council. It was, however, only in May 1945, once the war ended in Europe, that the Whitehall granted permission to Wavell to convene a Conference of Indian leaders to help him form a new executive Council that would represent the main communities and would include equal proportions of caste Hindus and Muslims.[191]

On June 7, 1945, Wavell informed his current Council of the impending changes. And, on June 15, 1945, in a public broadcast Wavell announced that he would invite Indian leaders to discuss the formation of a new Executive Council which would be more representative of organized political opinion. The reconstituted Council would continue the war against Japan; tackle problems of post-war development until a new and permanent constitution could be agreed upon.[192] To create an appropriate atmosphere for negotiations, Wavell released all members of the Congress Working Committee from jail.

Wavell's provision for parity between caste Hindus and Muslims elicited a sharp reaction from Gandhi.[193] Neither Congress nor Gandhi was willing to admit that the Congress represented the caste Hindus alone and Gandhi argued that although Congress had an overwhelming Hindu membership, it always had striven to be purely national. Gandhi regretted in a telegram on June 18, 1945 to the Viceroy that, "You will quite unconsciously but equally surely defeat the purpose of the Conference if parity between caste Hindus and Muslims is unalterable."[194] The Congress also made it clear that it would not accept the right of the Muslim League to nominate all the Muslim members of the new Government.

Khizar Hayat Khan Tiwana, Premier of Punjab, and the Unionists were also asserting that at least one of their member would be represented in the Executive Council among the Muslim members. Glancy, the Governor of Punjab, also supported their move since they had from the very beginning of the war consistently and unconditionally supported the war efforts. The Unionists finally got an assurance from Wavell through Glancy.[195]

Jinnah feared that the Muslims would always be in a minority in the new Council because the other minorities would always vote with the Hindus and that the Viceroy would be reluctant to use his veto. Jinnah, therefore, proposed that a majority of Muslims were opposed to any decision, it should not go by vote and also claimed that the League had the right to nominate all Muslim members to the Council. Wavell would not accept this and further told him that he also had it in mind to nominate a Unionist Muslim. Wavell also said that the Congress could nominate Muslims and schedule castes but the principle of parity must be maintained.[196]

Twenty-two political leaders were invited to took part in the Conference which opened up at Simla on June 25, 1945. Maulana Abul Kalam Azad, President of the Indian National Congress, first spoke for the Congress, stressing its non-communal character. Jinnah spoke next for the League and said that Azad's points were largely irrelevant to the immediate proposals and further said that Congress representated only Hindus, he asserted that League would not agree to any constitution except on the fundamental principle of Pakistan.[197]

The main problem at Simla was, however, the method of selecting new members of the Executive Council.[198] Jinnah adopted a rigid attitude regarding the nomination of the Muslim members only by the Muslim League. The Congress, on the other hand, reiterated that they would not accept the League's demand for the exclusion of Congress Muslims. Khizar Hayat Khan Tiwana, meanwhile, was insisting for the nomination of a Unionist Muslim, independent of the League, since he feared that a Congress-League bargain would be disastrous for his ministry. The main stumbling-block was the attitude of Jinnah, that is, his claim to nominate all Muslim members.[199] On June 29, 1945, the Viceroy asked all party leaders to give him panels of names of candidates for his new Council. Azad readily agreed, but Jinnah refused, arguing that he could not submit any list before consulting his Working Committee. So the Conference adjourned until July 14, 1945.[200]

Jinnah finally refused to submit a list, on the ground that Wavell had not accepted his right to nominate all Muslim members for the Executive Council.[201] Wavell, after then, prepared a provisional list and sent it to Amery, the Secretary of State, for his approval. The British cabinet, however, did not support the course of action suggested by Wavell and raised certain objections.[202] Even then, Wavell continued his efforts and showed his list to Jinnah which included the names of four Muslim Leaguers and a Unionist Muslim, Wavell even, excluded the names of Nationalist Muslims. Jinnah, however, became adamant and demanded the absolute right to select all Muslims and some guarantee that any decision which the Muslims opposed in the Council could only be passed by a two-third majority.[203] Wavell told him these conditions were entirely unacceptable and he decided to close the Conference.[204]

At the last meeting of the Conference on July 14, 1945, Wavell commented, "It shows that he (Jinnah) had never, at any time an intention of accepting the offer and it is difficult to see why he came to Simla at all".[205] Two other prominent Muslim Leaguers, Khaliquzzanan and Nazimuddin also told Francis Mudie, the Home Member, that Jinnah was anxious to get out of the whole thing. Quite apart from his right to nominate, he was afraid that if the League came into a Central Government they might have to take action that would prejudice their Pakistan demand.[206]

The failure of the Simla Conference is significant since it exercised a vital influence on the Pakistan Issue. Though Jinnah was not allowed to nominate all the Muslims, he was convertly allowed to wreck the Conference. The British by bringing the Conference to an end ensured that the Muslim League's position was not jeopardised. Jinnah's view was that if a Punjab Unionist Muslim and two Congress Muslims were allowed on the Council it would have cut at the very root and the very existence of the Muslim League and the object surrender of all what Muslim League stand for, it would have been a death knell to the Muslim League.[207]

The success of the Conference as desired by the Congress and Wavell would have seriously effected his position as the sole spokesman of the Muslims and thereby weaken his authority to establish his claim for a separate homeland. Though the British considered Jinnah's claim to be wrong and unfounded, yet they allowed Jinnah's intransigence to wreck the Conference.[208] Thus, the status of Jinnah was elevated to new heights and Pakistan gathered more adherents. The position of the Unionist Muslims, who had been seriously opposing the Muslim League was effectively impaired and it became clear to them that only Jinnah and Muslim League could deliver the goods. The wavering Unionist Muslims began to gravitate towards the Muslim League and its demand of Pakistan. Therefore, the failure of the Simla Conference strengthened the cause of the Muslim League in Punjab. The wrecking of the Simla Conference brought home the fact that the Punjabi landlords' and rural elites' future access to high office would be cut off if they remained out side the ranks of Muslim League, thus, there followed a large scale exodus from the Unionist Party to the Muslim League, even the Muslim leaders of the Congress also defected.

The growing influence and prestige of the Provincial Muslim League and the increasing popularity of the demand of Pakistan effected the Sikh polity of the province. The Sikh polity during 1943-45, was represented primarily by Sardar Baldev Singh of United Punjab Sikh party, which was involved in the coalition government, Master Tara Singh of Shriomani Akali Dal, Sardar Kharak Singh of Central Akali Dal and Sohan Singh of the Progressive Akali Dal i.e. the Communists. The Sikh polity, consisting of different groups, remained implacably opposed to the scheme of Pakistan of the Muslim League and adopted different measures to register their protest and opposition to the demand of Pakistan.

To avoid being steam-rolled by the Muslims, the Working Committee of the Shiromani Akali Dal, under the leadership of Master Tara Singh, in its meeting held on June 7, 1943 resolved to go for separate homeland for the Sikhs, that is *'Azad Punjab'*.[209] It was said in the resolution that the Sikh Panth notes that at the present moment, on the eve of expected far reaching changes in the Constitution of the country, the desire on the part of the majorities to dominate the minorities is rising with great tempo, as is evident by the slogans of Akhand Hindustan and Pakistan.

It further notes that in a situation so greatly charged with aggressive communalism, the minorities and especially the Sikhs, find themselves placed in a position, in which, they cannot safeguard their national existence against the high handedness of a political organized communal majority, resulting in grave attacks being made on the cultural, civic and political rights of the Sikhs in Punjab.[210]

It was further said that in order to ensure free and unfettered growth of the Sikh Panth, the Panth demands the splitting up of the existing province of Punjab, with its unnatural boundaries, so as to constitute a separate autonomous Sikh state in those areas of the Central, Northern, Eastern and South Eastern Punjab in which the overwhelming part of the Sikh population is concentrated, and which, because of the proprietors in it, being mostly Sikhs, and its general character being distinctly Sikh, is also the de-facto-Sikh homeland—the area, extent, the status and constitutional framework of such a state being left to be settled by negotiation between the accredited representatives of the Sikh Panth and the other interested parties, such as the British Government, the Hindus and the Muslims.[211]

The Sikh community, however, had spilt on the issue of the scheme of Azad Punjab. The leaders of the Central Akali Dal took part in a Punjab-Pan-Hindu Conference organised by the Hindu Sabha leaders, which bitterly attacked the Pakistan idea and any other concept that held India to be something other than a single entity. It also proclaimed the solidarity of the Hindus and the Sikhs.[212] By late 1943, an anti, Azad Punjab Conference was called where the leaders of the Central Akali Dal and of the Progressive Akali Dal denounced the schemes of Azad Punjab and Pakistan and both Jinnah and Master Tara Singh were accused of being British agents who were disrupting Indian unity and, more specially, the unity of Hindus and Sikhs.[213] The Conference also condemned the coalition government and called it a sellout to the British.[214] A further source of opposition to the idea of Azad Punjab came from Rawalpindi Division, whose Sikhs would be left in a strongly Muslim Province if Azad Punjab was formed, the Rawalpindi delegation opposed the scheme and said that it was merely a clever effort of the Unionist to divide Hindus and Sikhs while splitting up the Sikh community.[215]

It appeared, however, that Master Tara Singh himself was not serious about the scheme of the establishment of a separate home-land for the Sikhs. By advocating 'Azad Punjab' demand, Master Tara Singh and other Akali leaders wanted to act as an effective check on the demand for Pakistan. Master Tara Singh asserted that the Sikhs neither wished to be dominated by the Muslims nor to be absorbed by the Hindus.[216] At a later stage, Master Tara Singh also remarked that the Hindus and Muslims could always look upon the provinces, where their co-religionists were in a majority for security and protection of their rights, but the Sikhs did not enjoy similar position for they did not have majority anywhere. Thus he insisted upon this form of protection, Azad Punjab, until a better and more practical form of protection was proposed of their rights.[217]

The Sikh leadership remained adamant in their opposition to the Muslim League. At the final stage of the League-Unionist tussle, during 1944, the Sikhs declared that they would oppose Jinnah because they opposed Pakistan and because Jinnah's victory would mean the end of the Sikander-Baldev Singh Pact which Jinnah did not regard as valid.[218] The Sikh leadership, at this crucial hour, even allowed Khizar to change the communal balance of the cabinet by appointing a fourth Muslim to secure the support of some factional Muslim leaders,[219] and once the panic was over the Sikhs demanded the restoration of the old communal balance.[220]

The Sikh leadership also opposed the Gandhi-Jinnah talks of September 1944, based on the Rajagopalachari formula, which called for the partition of Punjab with its Muslim-majority districts going to Pakistan and its other districts going to Hindustan. An all parties Sikh Conference was held in September 1944, and the conference bitterly attacked Pakistan, Muslim rule, and the division of Punjab along population lines as meaning political suicide for the Sikhs. Giani Sher Singh, an Akali Leader, demanded that if Pakistan was conceded to the Muslims, a Sikhistan including both the Azad Punjab territory and various Sikh-ruled states should be given to the Sikhs.[221]

Jinnah, meanwhile, declared that the Sikhs would be much better off in Pakistan than in Hindustan and he stated that he was waiting for them to present their ideas to him so that he might consider them. Master Tara Singh, however, said that the Sikhs recognized neither Gandhi nor Jinnah as their masters and would not negotiate with either or both of them except on equals.[222] The Sikh leadership were, thus pleased at the break down of Gandhi-Jinnah talks.[223] The adamant attitude of Jinnah at the Simla Conference of June 1945 and subsequently its failure provided an other opportunity to the Sikh leadership to oppose the demand of Pakistan.

The Sikh leadership during 1943-45, for from persisting in their alliance with the Hindu parties, in fact, made a definite effort to establish themselves as an independent party. The Sikh leadership, however realised their need to achieve an understanding with those Punjabi Muslim leaders who, for their part, realized that a united Punjab could not be run by a single community alone. But, the factional divisions amongst the Sikhs did not help this strategy. On the other hand, while the Unionist Muslims were willing to cooperate with the Sikhs, the Muslim Leagues, animated with the idea of Pakistan, were not willing for cooperation. Thus, there was no ground for compromise between the Muslim League and the Sikhs.

It has become obvious from the foregone discussions that the Provincial Muslim League during 1943-45, made a rapid progress in the provincial politics. In early 1944, the League successfully challenged the dominance of the Unionist Party in the provincial politics, freed itself from the clutches of the Unionist Party and for the first time established an independent League Assembly Party in the Provincial Legislative Assembly. Henceforth, the Muslim League Assembly Party under the leadership of Sardar Shaukat Hayat Khan and Nawab Iftikhar Hussain Khan of Mamdot provided a tough time to the ruling benches. With the passage of the time some rival factional leaders of the Unionist Party and other MLAs, especially after the failure of the Simla Conference of June 1945, defected to the Muslim League which further strengthened its cause.

The Provincial League also made-roads into the country areas of Punjab. The efforts made by the Provincial League leaders, the various public meeting, conferences and tours conducted by them in rural as well as in urban areas led to the increasing popularity of the Muslim League and the demand of Pakistan became popular among the Punjabi Muslims. The League took advantage of the war time grievances of the people of Punjab especially of the rural

Muslims and told them that only the Muslim League and the successful establishment of Pakistan will solve their social and economic problems.

The national level politics and the attitude of the British further consolidated the position of the Provincial Muslim League and the demand of Pakistan. Moreover, the propaganda campaign of the Punjab Muslim Students Federation based on Islamic appeals, religious symbols and the concept of Muslim community further stimulated the cause of the Muslim League and the demand of Pakistan echoed from every nook and corner of the Muslim of Punjab.

Foot Notes

1. Linlithgow to Amery, December 28, 1942, *Linlithgow Papers,* and Linlithgow to glancy, December 27, 1942, *Linlithgow Papers.*
2. K.C. Yadav, 'Partition of India: A study of the Muslim Politics in the Punjab,' *The Punjab Past and Present,* Vol. XVIII, April 1983, p. 135.
3. *Ibid.*
4. For details see Craig Baxter, 'The people party vs. the Punjab Feudalists,' *Journal of Asian and African Studies,* Vol. VIII, Oct. 1973, pp. 176-89.
5. Penderel Moon, *op. cit.,* p. 58.
6. *The Tribune,* January 24, 1943.
7. Glancy to Linlithgow, January 3, 1943, *Linlithgow Papers.*
8. Lepel Griffin, *Chiefs and Families of the Note in the Punjab,* Vol. II, Lahore, 1940, pp. 167-68.
9. Linlithgow to Amery, January 11, 1943, *Linlithgow Papers.*
10. Linlithgow to Glancy, January 4, 1943, *Ibid.*
11. Linlithgow to Glancy, February 1, 1943, *Ibid.*
12. Jinnah to Malik Barkat Ali, January 3, 1943 in M. Rafique Afzal (ed.), *op. cit.,* pp. 309-10.
13. Jinnah to Nawabzada Rashid Ali Khan, February 13, 1943, in S.Q. Hussain Jafri (ed.), *op.cit.,* pp. 318-19.
14. *The Tribune,* Lahore, March 8, 1943.
15. *Civil and Military Gazette,* Lahore, March 9, 1943.
16. *Ibid.*
17. Glancy to Linlithgow, April 17, 1943. *Linlithgow Papers,* N. Mansergh and Penderel Moon (ed.), *The Transfer of Power 1942-47,* Vol. III, p. 899.
18. *Civil and Military Gazette,* Lahore, March 30, 1943.

19. Ayesha Jalal, *op.cit.* , pp. 85-86 and Ian Talbot, *Punjab and the Raj 1849-1947*, pp. 170-71.
20. Jinnah's address to the All India Muslim League Session at Delhi, April 24, 1943, in S.S. Pirzada (ed.), *Foundations of Pakistan*, Vol. II, p. 406 and N. Mansergh and Penderel Moon (ed.), *op.cit.*, Vol. II, pp. 919-20.
21. *Eastern Times*, Lahore, May 10, 1943
22. Nawab of Mamdot to Jinnah, May 19, 1943 in S.Q. Husain Jafri (ed.), *op.cit.*, p. 222.
23. Jinnah to Barkat Ali, June 23, 1943 in S.Q. Husain Jafri (ed.), *Ibid.*, p. 72.
24. Glancy to Linlithgow, August 6, 1943, *Linlithgow Papers.*
25. *Ibid.*
26. Glancy to Linlithgow, July 6, 1943, *Linlithgow Papers.*
27. Linlithgow to Glancy, July 16, 1943, *Ibid.*
28. Jinnah to Mamdot, September 11, 1943 in S.Q. Husain Jafri (ed.), *op.cit.*, p. 224.
29. *Eastern Times*, Lahore, November 10, 1943.
30. *Ibid.*, November 11, 1943.
31. Ikram Ali Malik, *op.cit.*, p. 565.
32. S.S. Pirzada (ed.), *Foundations of Pakistan*, Vol. II, pp. 487-88.
33. *Punjab Legislative Assembly Debates*, 1944, Vol. I, pp. 342-43.
34. *Eastern Times*, Lahore, February 21-28, 1944.
35. Imran Ali, *op.cit.*, p. 61 and Ayesha Jalal, *op.cit.*, p. 90.
36. *Eastern Times*, Lahore, March 20, 1944.
37. *Ibid.*, March 23, 1944.
38. *Ibid.*, April 5, 1944.
39. Ikram Ali Malik, *op.cit.*, p. 567.
40. *Indian Annual Report*, 1944, Vol. I, pp. 217-19.
41. *Eastern Times*, Lahore, April 10, 1944.
42. Glancy to Wavell, April 14, 1944, in N. Mansergh and Penderel Moon (ed.), *op.cit.*, Vol. IV, pp. 880-81.
43. Wavell to Glancy, April 15, 1944, *Ibid.*, p. 882.
44. Glancy to Wavell, April 24, 1944, *Ibid.*, pp. 922-25.
45. *Punjab Legislative Assembly Debates*, 1944, Vol. III, pp. 239-40.
46. *Eastern Times*, Lahore, May 2, 1944.
47. S.S. Pirzada (ed.), *Foundations of Pakistan*, Vol. II, p. 497.
48. *Eastern Times*, Lahore, April 28, 1944.
49. Punjab Fortnightly Report for the Second half of April, 1944, *Home Political*, File No. 18/4/1944.
50. Ikram Ali Malik, *op.cit.*, p. 569.
51. *Ibid.*, pp. 569-70.

52. Punjab Fortnightly Report for the Second half of April 1944, *Home Political*, File No. 18/4/1944.
53. *Ibid.*
54. *Eastern Times*, Lahore, May 2, 1944.
55. *Ibid.*, May 3-4, 1944.
56. *Ibid.*, May 6, 1944.
57. S.S. Pirzada (ed.), *Foundations of Pakistan*, Vol. II, p. 498.
58. Wavell to Amery, May 16, 1944 in N. Mansergh and Penderel Moon (ed.), *op.cit.*, Vol. IV, p. 969.
59. S. Q. Husain Jafri (ed.), *op.cit.*, p. 77.
60. *Ibid.*, p. 79.
61. *Ibid.*, p. 77.
62. *Ibid.*, p. 78.
63. *Ibid.*, p. 80.
64. Ian Talbot, *Punjab and the Raj 1849-1947*, p. 159.
65. Jinnah to Nawabzada Rasid Ali Khan, February 13, 1943 in S.Q. Husain Jafari (ed.), *op.cit.*, pp. 318-19.
66. Nawabzada Rashid Ali Khan to Jinnah, March 25, 1943 in S. Q. Husain Jafri (ed.), *op.cit.*, pp. 327-28.
67. Glancy to Linlithgow, July 12, 1943, *Linlithgow Papers.*
68. Lepel Griffin, *op.cit.*, Vol. I, p. 205.
69. S.S. Pirzada (ed.), *Foundations of Pakistan*, Vol II, p. 480
70. *Ibid.*, p. 482.
71. *Shamsul Hasan Collection*, Punjab, Vol. I, General Correspondence, p. 35.
72. *Ibid.*, p. 36.
73. *Eastern Times*, Lahore, July 6, 1943.
74. *Ibid.*, August 10, 1943.
75. *Ibid.*, March 16, 1944.
76. *Ibid.*, July 6, 1944.
77. *Punjab Legislative Assembly Debates*, 1944, Vol. III, p. 415.
78. *Eastern Times*, Lahore, March 31, 1944.
79. *Ibid.*, April 11, 1944.
80. *Ibid.*, April 5, 1944.
81. Mumtaz Daultana to Jinnah, May 31, 1944 in S.Q. Husain Jafri (ed.), *op.cit.*, p. 249.
82. *Shamsul Hasan Collection*, Punjab, Vol. I, General Correspondence, pp. 6-7.
83. *Ibid.*, p. 6.
84. *Ibid.*, pp. 6-7.
85. *Ibid.*, pp. 6-7.
86. *Ibid.*, p. 6.
87. *Ibid.*, p. 8.
88. *Ibid.*, pp. 6-7.

89. Nawabzada Rashid Ali Khan to Jinnah, July 4, 1944 in S.Q. Husain Jafari (ed.), *op.cit.*, p. 336.
90. Nawab of Mamdot to Jinnah, July 11, 1944 in *Shamsul Hasan Collection*, Punjab, Vol. III, pp. 2-3.
91. Punjab Provincial Muslim League's Report for the Month of June-July 1944 in *Shamsul Hasan Collection*, Punjab, Vol. I, p. 7.
92. Bhagwan Josh, *op.cit.*, pp. 121-24.
93. David Gilmartin, *Empire And Islam*, p. 196.
94. Punjab Fortnightly Report for the Second half of May 1944, *Home Political*, File No. 18/5/1944.
95. Punjab Fortnightly Report for the Second half of July 1944, *Home Political*, File No. 18/7/1944.
96. *Civil and Military Gazette*, Lahore, November 8, 1944.
97. *Ibid.*
98. *Ibid.*, November 23, 1944.
99. *Civil and Military Gazette*, December 7, 1944.
100. *Ibid.*, December 8, 1944.
101. Nawabzada Rashid Ali Khan to Jinnah, December 18, 1944 in *Shamsul Hasan Collection*, Punjab, Vol. I, p. 28.
102. Nazir Ahmad Khan, 'Thoughts on the League Speakers' 'Party Tour of Montgomery District', *Shamsul Hasan Collection*, Punjab, Vol. I, p. 30.
103. *Ibid.*
104. *Ibid.*, pp. 30-31.
105. *Eastern Times*, Lahore, May 4-10, 1945.
106. *Ibid.*, May 10, 1945.
107. *Ibid.*, May 23, 1945.
108. *Ibid.*, June 3-10, 1945.
109. *Ibid.*, June 13, 1945.
110. *Ibid.*, June 16, 1945.
111. *Shamsul Hasan Collection*, Punjab, Vol. I, p. 6.
112. Ian Talbot, 'Deserted collaborators : The Political Background to the Rise and Fall of the Punjab Unionist Party', *Journal of Imperial and Commonwealth History*, October, 1982, p. 82.
113. Punjab Fortnightly Report for the Second half of January 1943, *Home Political*, File No. 18/3/1943.
114. Punjab Fortnightly Report for the Second half of March, 1943, Home Political, File No. 18/3/1943.
115. *Punjab Legislative Assembly Debates*, 1943, Vol. XX, pp. 270-71.
116. Ian Talbot, "Deserted Collaborators: The Political Background to the Rise and Fall of the Punjab Unionist Party 1923-47," *Journal of Imperial and Commonwealth History*, October, 1982, pp. 83-85.
117. Linlithgow to Glancy, September 23, 1943, *Linlithgow Papers*.

118. Ian Talbot, The Growth of the Muslim League in the Punjab, 1937-1946", *Journal of Commonwealth and Comparative Politics*, March, 1982, pp. 17-18.
119. *Punjab Legislative Assembly Debates*, 1944, Vol. XXIII, p. 261.
120. *Ibid.*, p. 310
121. *Civil and Military Gazette*, November 6, 1943.
122. Punjab Fortnightly Report for the Second half of October 1944, *Home Political*, File No. 18/10/1944.
123. Punjab Fortnightly Report for the Second half of April 1945, *Home Political*, File No. 18/4/1945.
124. *Eastern Times*, April 23, 1945.
125. *Ibid.*, May 1, 1945.
126. *Ibid.*, May 27, 1945.
127. *Ibid.*, June 23, 1945.
128. *Ibid.*, August 28, 1945.
129. S. M. Ikram, *Modern Muslim India and Birth of Pakistan*, Lahore, 1970, p. 263.
130. Abdul Hameed Nizami to Jinnah, February 16, 1943, in Sarfaraz Hussain Mirza, *The Punjab Muslim Students Federation : An Annotated Documents*, Lahore, 1978, p. 228
131. Sarfaraz Hussain Mirza, *op.cit.*, p. 229.
132. *Eastern Times*, March 24, 1943.
133. Sarfaraz Hussain Mirza, *op.cit.*, p. 233
134. *Eastern Times*, May 28, 1943.
135. Sarfaraz Hussain Mirza, *op.cit.*, p. 236.
136. *Eastern Times*, May 31, 1943.
137. *Ibid.*, October 28, 1943.
138. Nizami to Jinnah, September 28, 1943 in Sarfaraz Hussain Mirza, *op.cit.*, p. 242.
139. Rajmohan Gandhi, *Understanding the Muslim Mind*, Delhi, 1986, pp. 63-65.
140. *Ibid.*, p. 76.
141. *Eastern Times*, June 28, 1943.
142. *Ibid.*, March 20, 1944.
143. *Ibid.*
144. *Ibid.*
145. *Ibid.*, April 12, 1944.
146. *Ibid.*, April 22, 1944.
147. *Ibid.*, May 2, 1944.
148. *The Dawn*, Delhi, June 7, 1944.
149. *Ibid.*, June 20, 1944.
150. *Ibid.*, June 29, 1944.
151. *Eastern Times*, June 30, 144.

152. *The Dawn*, June 19, 1944.
153. *Ibid.*, July 11, 1944.
154. Sarfaraz Hussain Mirza, *op.cit.*, pp. 264-66.
155. *Eastern Times*, August 29, 1944
156. *Ibid.*, August 26, 1944.
157. *Ibid.*, August 28, 1944.
158. *The Dawn*, August 24, 1944.
159. *Ibid.*, October 14-19, 1944.
160. *Eastern Times*, November 16, 1944.
161. *Ibid.*, March 25, 1945.
162. *Ibid.*, July 16, 1945.
163. S.M. Ikram, *op.cit.*, p. 266.
164. *Ibid.*, pp. 267-68.
165. David Gilmartin, *Empire and Islam*, p. 200.
166. *Ibid.*, p. 201.
167. Rajagopalachari to Jinnah, April 8, 1944 in *Indian Annual Register*, 1944, Vol. 2, p. 129.
168. *Ibid.*, pp. 129-30.
169. Wavell to Amery, July 11, 1944, N. Mansergh and Penderal Moon (ed.) *The Transfer of Power 1942-1947*, Vol. III. pp. 1077-79.
170. *Eastern Times*, July 10, 1944.
171. Punjab Fortnightly Report for the Second half of July 1944, *Home Political*, File No. 18/7/1944.
172. *Ibid.*
173. *The Tribune*, July 14, 1944.
174. Jinnah to Rajagopalachari, July 2, 1944 and Rajagopalachari to Jinnah, July 4, 1944, *Indian Annual Register*, 1944, Vol. 2, pp. 129-30.
175. Jinnah to Gandhi, September 10, 1944, *Collected Works of Mahatma Gandhi*, Vol. LXXVIII, pp. 89-90.
176. Gandhi to Jinnah, September 11, 1944, *Ibid.*, p. 98.
177. *Ibid.*
178. Gandhi to Jinnah, September 15, 1944, *Ibid.*, p. 101.
179. Jinnah to Gandhi, September 25, 1944, *Indian Annual Register*, 1944, Vol. 2, p. 157.
180. Gandhi to Jinnah, September 25, 1944, *Collected Works of Gandhi*, Vol. LXXVIII, pp. 130-31.
181. Stanley Woelpert, *op.cit.*, p. 235.
182. *Indian Annual Register*, 1944, Vol. V, p. 262.
183. *Ibid.*
184. Punjab Fortnightly Report for the First half of October 1944, *Home Political*, File No. 18/10/1944.

185. Wavell to Amery, September 29, 1944, N. Mansergh and Penderel Moon (ed.), *op.cit.*, Vol. V, pp. 56-57.
186. Wavell to Amery, October 20, 1944, *Ibid.*, Vol. V, p. 93.
187. Desai-Liaqat Pact, *Bhaulabhai Desai Papers* and Nicholas Mansergh and Penderel Moon (ed.), *op.cit.*, Vol. V, p. 400.
188. Wavell to Amery, January 14, 1945, N. Mansergh and Penderel Moon (ed.), *op.cit.*, pp. 401-02.
189. *Indian Annual Register*, 1945, Vol. I, p. 33.
190. Gandhi to Desai, January 27, 1945, *Bhaulabhai Desai Papers.*
191. N. Mansergh and Penderel Moon (ed.), *op.cit.*, Vol. V, p. 1078.
192. *The Tribune,* June 15, 1945.
193. Press statement by Gandhi, N. Mansergh and Penderel Moon (ed.), *op.cit.*, Vol. V, p. 1125.
194. N. Mansergh and Penderel Moon (ed.), *op.cit.*, Vol. V, p. 1140.
195. *Ibid.*, p. 1104.
196. Wavell to Amery, June 25, 1945, Penderel Moon (ed.), *Wavell: The Viceroy's Journal,* Oxford, 1973, p. 146.
197. N. Mansergh and Penderel Moon (ed.), *op.cit.*, Vol. V, pp. 1155-56.
198. *Ibid.*, p. 1157.
199. Wavell to Amery, June 27, 1945, *Ibid.*, pp. 1165-67.
200. Wavell to Amery, June 29, 1945, *Ibid.*, pp. 1171-73.
201. Wavell to Amery, July 9, 1945, Penderel Moon (ed.), *Wavell : The Viceroy's Journal*, pp. 152-53.
202. *Ibid.*, p. 154.
203. Wavell to Amery, July 11, 1945, *Ibid.*, p. 154.
204. Wavell to Amery, July 12, 1945, *Ibid.*, p. 155.
205. Wavell to Amery, July 14, 1945, *Ibid.*, pp. 155-56.
206. Mudie to Jenkins, July 17, 1945, N. Mansergh and Penderel Moon (ed.), *op.cit.*, Vol. V, p. 1269.
207. Ayesha Jalal, *op.cit.*, p. 132.
208. R.J. Moore, 'Jinnah and the Pakistan Demand', *Modern Asian Studies,* October, 1983, p. 580.
209. Master Tara Singh's Azad Punjab Scheme, *The Tribune*, July 23, 1943.
210. Gurbachan Singh and Lal Singh Giani, *The Idea of the Sikh State,* Lahore, 1946, pp. 1-3.
211. *Ibid.*, pp. 56-57.
212. *Indian Annual Register*, 1943, Vol. I, p. 270.
213. *Ibid.*, pp. 295-98.
214. *Ibid.*, p. 301.
215. Stephen Oren, 'The Sikhs, Congress and the Unionists in British Punjab 1937-45', *Modern Asian Studies,* July 1974, p. 413.

216. *Indian Annual Register*, 1943, Vol. II, p. 269.
217. *The Tribune*, June 25, 1945.
218. *The Tribune*, May 11, 1944.
219. *Ibid.*, May 18, 1944.
220. *Ibid.*, July 6, 1944.
221. Stephen Oren, *op.cit.*, p. 414.
222. *Ibid.*, pp. 414-15.
223. Punjab Fortnightly Report for the Second half of October 1944, *Home Political*, File No. 18/10/1944.

5

Elections of 1946

The period from July 1945 to March 1946, i.e., the period between the collapse of the Simla Conference and the provincial elections of 1946, was an important landmark in the history of Provincial Muslim League, in the history of Punjab, as well as it also affected the courses of national history. During this phase the Provincial Muslim League propagated the ideals of the League and the idea of Pakistan to the every nook and corner of the Muslim of Punjab, achieved grand victory in the elections of 1946 and thus, now, it was very near to its striking goal of Pakistan.

In July 1945, the general elections were held in Britain which brought the Labour Party into power. Attlee became the Prime Minister of Britain and Pethick-Lawrence was appointed Secretary of State for India. The new government was expected to resolve the Indian political problem.[1] Meanwhile, a Governors meeting was held in Delhi on August 1-2, 1945 to decide the next political move and to discuss the issue of holding elections in India. B.J. Glancy, the Governor of Punjab, argued vigorously against any elections till an economic planning meeting could be called to expose the potential pitfalls of Pakistan. He said that unless the Muslim League could be steered away from the crude version of Pakistan, there would be civil war in Punjab and immediate Central and Provincial elections might consolidate the Muslim League position.[2]

The Conference, however, unanimously resolved that an official government could not solve post-war problems, thus, the elections to the provincial and Central legislatures should be held in the coming winter.[3] The government of Attlee accepted the recommendations of the Governors Conference and on August 20, 1945, Wavell was invited home for consultation with the new cabinet and authorised him to announce that elections would be held throughout British India during the next winter. Accordingly, on August 21, 1945, Wavell announced that the elections would take place and also sent his summary analysis of the Pakistan problem to Pethick-Lawrence. He argued that the Punjabis are tougher than the Bengalis, and the Sikhs, who were the rulers in Punjab before it was annexed by the British, would fight rather than see their Holy Land pass under permanent Muslim rule. Wavell further argued that he had always hoped to be able to avoid any full-scale public inquiry into the feasibility and implications of Pakistan, since he anticipated that Jinnah would boycott such a Conference or Commission and it might only stir up communal feeling. He felt, however, that continuing to ignore the possibility of its birth would not make Pakistan fade away.[4]

The Prime Minister, Attlee's announcement in the Parliament that the Cripps proposals, with the right of provinces to opt out of the Indian Union, continued to be the basis of the British policy provided immense significance to the elections.[5] Pethick-Lawrence also wrote to Wavell that the elections would be followed by positive steps to set up a Constituent Assembly which would frame a new constitution.[6] Obviously, the imminence of the British departure was clear to all political parties of India. For the Muslim League, thus, elections provided another front on which to wage the battle for Pakistan. To achieve a sovereign Pakistan, Jinnah shrewdly calculated that the number of seats the League could win on the Central and Provincial Assemblies was more important than its ability to form ministries in the Muslim majority provinces.[7] The Muslim League, all over the country, fought the election campaign, on the sole issue of Pakistan. The main object of the League in these elections was to demonstrate the support which the League has among the Muslims and force the issue of Pakistan.[8]

The provincial elections of 1946 were quite crucial for the Punjab Provincial Muslim League since it had to prove that the demand of Pakistan was popular in this key Muslim area, that is the heartland of future Pakistan. Pakistan and Islam were the main issues for the leaders of the Provincial Muslim League and after the failure of the Simla Conference, these leaders had already launched vigorous attack against the Unionist Party and began to strengthen the cause of the League. The leaders of the Punjab Provincial Muslim League issued a statement against the attitude of Khizar Hayat Khan Tiwana at the Simla Conference and called him a traitor of Islam and which had tremendous effect on the politics of the province.[10] Jinnah also wrote to Mian Mumtaz Daultana, the General-Secretary of the Punjab Muslim League, 'that the Simla results had a marvellous effect on the public opinion and it has done more to rouse the Punjab Muslims than anything that has happened hitherto. It is for you now to take the fullest advantage of this wave of enthusiasm and whole-hearted support in favour of the Muslim League'.[11]

Defections from the Unionists to the Muslim League now became thick and fast. Moreover, the Unionist Party was not an organised party and its cross-communal arrangements depended critically upon local notables whose allegiance was always a matter of calculation not commitment. It has now become obvious that the Muslim League rather than the Unionist will provide the benefit of the office in future, thus the rural notables from all sections began shifting their allegiance. Malik Firoz Khan Noon, a member of the Viceroy's Executive Council and a kinsman of Khizar Hayat Khan Tiwana, was an important defector. Firoz Khan Noon resigned from the Executive Council of the Viceroy, joined the Muslim League and his desire was to help the Muslim League in Punjab with a view to bring all Muslim M.L.As in the Muslim League. He also requested Khizar Hayat Khan to join the League, the only party, he said, under which the Muslims can be united, and asked him not to divide Punjab Muslims—the heart of Muslim India.[12]

The influential *Pirs* of Jalalpur, Jahanian Shah and Shah Jiwana and Gilani Pirs of Multan had also joined the League.[13] All the Muslim M.L.As of the districts of Jhang and

Sheikhupura also defected to the Muslim League.[14] Khizar Hayat Khan was even deserted by his Private Parliamentary Secretary, Syed Amjad Ali and his kinsman, Malik Sardar Khan Noon and Major Mohammad Mumtaz Khan Tiwana.[15] A large number of Congressmen also defected to the League, prominent among them were Mian Iftikhar-ud-Din, President of the Provincial Congress Committee and Malik Lal Khan, a former leader of the Congress Party in the Legislative Assembly.[16] The Provincial Muslim League was gaining strength day after day and it emerged as a powerful force in the elections of 1946. The brunt of Muslim League's attack was directed against the Unionists. Ghulam Bhik Nairang, the organisation Secretary of the Ambala Division, wrote to Jinnah that:

> The coming general elections are fraught with far reaching consequences and so every political party will strain every nerve to obtain results most favourable to itself. For the Muslims, particularly, these elections are a matter of life and death, but nowhere will the contest be keener than in the Punjab. While all political parties are likely to make a common cause against the Muslim League, the most powerful enemy appears to be the Unionist Party.[17]

The Provincial Leaguers observed that the Unionist Party represented the *Jagirdars*, honorary magistrates and government grantees and who in turn had profound influence upon the peasantry and rural population. The Muslim League, thus, could not depend only on the upper strata of the Punjab Muslims and continued its propaganda among the rural class in order to make it a mass movement and in order to check the interference of the government officials in the election work.[18] Vicky Noon, wife of Sir Firoz Khan Noon, also observed that the Muslim League in Punjab has truly become a mass movement but, she said, the official pressure is being used against the Muslim League. She further observed that the administration was at the lowest ebb and requested to Jinnah to impress upon the Governor of Punjab to state publicly that he does not want government servants to use undue influence in the coming elections.[19]

In addition to the official interference and indifferent attitude of the Punjab Government in the election work, it was reported that some of the Punjab Muslim Leaguers, were wasting their time in personal quarrels. Wavell, the Viceroy, observed that the Punjab Muslim League may suffer at the poll because of these personal quarrels.[20] Vicky Noon also observed that there were many uncontrolled elements in the Punjab Muslim League. It is unwise, she said, when the pupils try to excel their master. She requested Jinnah to visit Lahore and to check these uncontrolled elements.[21] Mian Bashir Ahmad, a prominent leader of the Provincial League, also observed that a visit of Jinnah to Lahore at this juncture will prove to be of inestimable value for Punjab.[22]

Despite the undue interference by the officials of the Unionist government and the trivial differences among the Muslim Leaguers, the cry of 'Islam in danger' and the slogan of Pakistan was gaining strength and each and every Muslim was responding to it. A Muslim League Workers Centre was established at Lahore, where a batch of 30 to 50 workers would come and stay and have their training for a week and then would leave for the propaganda campaign.[23] Moreover, the attitude of Jinnah and his vigorous campaign in favour of Pakistan at the All-India level was also rousing the Muslims of Punjab. In the last week of October 1945, at a public meeting at Ahmedabad, Jinnah uttered, 'Pakistan is the question of life and death for us. All Muslims believed in one God and were one nation. They wanted Pakistan and would attain it.'[24]

This enthusiasm for the Pakistan and the Islamic appeals echoed from every nook and corner of the Muslim Punjab. In November 1945, Mian Bashir Ahmad wrote to Jinnah, that, 'the general situation in the Punjab has undergone a tremendous change. The League movement is spreading even to the rural areas with unexpected rapidity. Our workers have not yet reached the villages in adequate numbers and yet one hears sensational stories of conversion to the League. Some say the League will capture sixty seats out of the eighty nine, others put it even higher than seventy.'[25]

The League workers and propagandists, during their election campaign also tried to exploit the wartime grievances of the soldiers, who have began to return to the province once the war was over. The League, in fact, in order to win the election in the name of Pakistan and Islam, was trying to placate every conceivable interest group within the province.[26] As many as 8,00,000 men, 27 per cent of the total number of Indian Army recruits during the war, from Punjab fought for the *Raj in* the war.[27] Once, these soldiers returned to the province they assumed significant political importance and this was increased by their constituting a large proportion of the electorate in a number of key constituencies such as those of Rawalpindi, Jhelum and Mianwali.[28] The Unionist Party had endeavoured to maintain the traditional loyalty of the recruiting areas by a series of measures designed to aid the servicemen's dependents whilst they were abroad and after the war the Unionists began promises and prepared plans for providing employment and land grants to the demobilized soldiers of the recruiting areas.[29]

However, despite the efforts of the Unionist Party many grievances existed amongst the Punjabi Servicemen on the eve of elections. The slump which had hit the Punjab's trade and industry as a result of the fall in the high war time level of demand meant that many servicemen returned home to face the same high levels of unemployment which had originally prompted their enlistment. Even by the end of 1945, less than 20 per cent of the demobilized soldiers registered with employment exchanges had found work.[30] Ayesha Jalal, a historian, argued that there was no rewards for the demobilized soldiers despite all the promises and plans of the Unionist Party and she has suggested that if before the elections these soldiers had been given land in canal colonies, this may just have tipped the balance in the Unionist favour in some districts.[31]

The Provincial Muslim League took advantage of this situation and made much of the discontent among demobilized Muslim soldiers through its propaganda campaign. Shaukat Hayat Khan, who had been serving in the army before his return to Punjab, was the chief spokesman of the League on this matter. He delivered a series of hard-hitting speeches against the Unionist Party in the main recruiting areas in September-October 1945.[32] The Muslim League gained great popularity in the major recruiting areas of Rawalpindi, Jhelum and Mianwali by providing work to the demobilized soldiers in its organization as well as by setting up committees to look into their problems.[33] The Muslim League also addressed itself to the soldiers' wider area of concern which included such issues as the fate of the Punjabi members of the Indian National Army. The League's decision to follow the Congress lead and establish a Defence Committee for the Indian National Army members who were on trial was well received in the main recruiting districts.[34] The Muslim League, thus, by exploiting the war time grievances of the demobilized soldiers simply eroded the base of the Unionists in the main recruiting districts. Similarly, the Congress also exploited the war time grievances of the soldiers of the South-East Punjab and secured victory in this area in the elections of 1946.[35]

Meantime, the official interference in favour of the Unionist continued. Mohammad Zafarullah, President of the Simla District Muslim League, wrote to Jinnah that the active persuasion of permanent Government officials to coerce the illiterate masses into voting against the Muslim League has been going, of late, at a brisk pace. Influential public servants are being summoned and plainly told to enlist support for the Unionist cause in their circles of influence and necessary transfers to suit this purpose are being made in scores.[36] The Provincial Muslim League passed a resolution demanding the dismissal of the ministry and the liquidation of the bureaucratic machinery, because of this undue official interference.[37] Glancy, the Governor of Punjab, however, rejected this demand and even declined a demand by the Provincial League to issue a communique assuring voters that the provincial elections would be entirely free from official interference.[38]

M.A. Jinnah, visited Punjab in the last week of January 1946, in order to survey the election campaign and to give practical and concrete help to the Provincial Muslim League. Jinnah was also informed about the undue official interference in favour of the Unionists. Jinnah said, 'The methods and the manoeuvres, that the Unionists are resorting to, are both disgraceful and unlawful. There is the grossest and undue interference by the officials in these elections. The prospective voters and the workers of the Muslim League are being coerced, threatened, intimidated and persecuted. The attention of the Viceroy and the Governor has been repeatedly drawn to all these manoeuvres of the Unionists, but these representations have met with a deaf ear and nothing has been done to prevent these shameful and criminal tactics on the part of the ministry which is headed by Malik Khizar Hayat Khan. But, in spite of all this, I was very glad to see with my oven eyes that there is a tremendous upsurge and compelte solidarity amongst the Muslims of Punjab. They are now determined to resist, lawfully and by all legitimate methods, all the obstacles and difficulties that are put in their way.'[39]

In addition to this official interference, the sound economic condition of the Unionist Party, sometime, also created tension among the leaders of the Provincial League. Ghulam Bhik Nairang, Organising Secretary of the Ambala Division, wrote to Jinnah that, 'The Unionist Party has got big funds and will bear the financial burden of the election and where necessary it will pay good prices to the voters for their votes. It is said that the Unionist Party will give every Unionist candidate Rs. 12,000 for fighting his election ... Will the Muslim League be in a position to render financial help to individual candidates, and in case such help be possible, I would ask you to allot Rs. 30,000 to each candidate'.[40] Similarly, as late as in January 1946, the District Muslim League of Amritsar,[41] Mian Mumtaz Daultana, General Secretary of the Provincial Muslim League[42] and Mian Amiruddin,[43] one of the leabers of the Provincial League, also demanded financial help from Jinnah.

Appreciating that the Provincial League was fighting the hardest battle against the most treacherous foes in Punjab, Jinnah agreed to give some money from the Central fund.[44] However, Jinnah cautioned the Leaguers to meet their financial demands only from the Provincial funds[45] and also warned them not to spend the money lavishly, he said, 'I say to our workers and voters, who want to support the League candidates that if you cannot get conveyance, if you cannot get petrol, trudge to the polling stations to vote, go to the polling booths walking, may be you have to walk five miles or ten miles, after all it is not such a great sacrifice.'[46] Jinnah and the Muslim League endeavoured to meet the financial difficulties and the financial pressure of the Unionists with the fervor of Pakistan.

There was a profusion of religious symbolism in the Muslim League's election campaign. According to the Provincial League, it held forty to fifty meetings a day all over the province. Almost a statement a day was issued from the League office in Lahore, Ghazanfar Ali Khan used to preside over a daily round table Conference with a number of journalists working for the League.[47] The leaders and workers of the Muslim League attempted to convince Muslims of the benefit of Pakistan and they identified Pakistan with Islam. The Leaguers would often preach in the mosques and would exploit the religious sentiments of the Muslims.[48] Firoz Khan Noon, for example, openly preached that a vote caste for the League was in favour of the prophet.[49] A poster issued in Urdu over the signature of Raja Khair Mehdi Khan, the League candidate in Jhelum district, asked Muslims to choose between 'Din' and 'Dunya'; in the battle of righteousness and falsehood. Analysing it, he explains the difference between the two as follows:

	DIN	*DUNYA*
1.	On one side is your belief in the Alimighty and your conscience	On the other side you are offered squares and *Jagirs*
2.	Righteousness and faithfulness are on one side	The other side has to offer *Lambardaris*, and *Zaildaris*
3.	One side is the rightful Cause	On the other is *Sufedposhi*
4.	One side has Pakistan for you	The other has *Kufristan* (region of infidels)
5.	On the one side is the problem of saving Muslims from slavery of Hindus	As opposed to this there is only the consideration of personal prestige of one man
6.	On one side you have to bring together all those who recite the *Kalima* (the basis of Islam)	On the other is Baldev Singh and Khizar Hayat
7.	On the one side is the Consideration of the unity and brotherhood of all Muslims	On the other side is the *Danda* (big stick) of bureaucracy and terror of officialdom
8.	On the one side are the lovers of Muslim League and Pakistan.	On the other are the admirers of Congress and the Unionists.
9.	On the one side is the honour of the Green Banner.	On the other is the Government of Khizar Ministry.[50]

The leaders of the Provicnial Muslim League told the Muslims of Punjab that for the sake of their religion, they have to decide in the light of their strength of faith. Those who opposed the League were denounced as infidels and the copies of the Holy Quran were carried around as an emblem peculiar to the Muslim League.[51] In fact, by its good propaganda work, by educating the masses and making the middle classes realize that their future lay safe not in free India but in Pakistan, the Muslim League had become in the true sense of the term a Muslim nationalist organisation supported by almost all strata of the Muslim society in Punjab.[52]

The Punjab Muslim Students Federation played a dynamic role in mobilizing the Muslim voters in favour of the Muslim League. With the election call, 'now or never', became the slogan of the Punjab Muslim Students Federation. The General Secretary of the Federation Shaikh Rafiq Ahmad, issued the first appeal in this context on August 5, 1945 for collection of funds. The General Secretary directed the District branches of the Federation to hold frequent gatherings exhorting people to send subscriptions directly to the Central League fund.[53]

The Federation framed an 'Election Board' to electrify the election campaign in the province. On October 30, 1945, the Board resolved to issue a series of pamphlets and handbills and outlined a comprehensive programme of rural mass contact campaign to be initiated in the following months.[54] Some of the pamphlets published by the Election Board were entitled as, *'Muslim League and Khaksar', 'Congress and Mussalman', 'Islamic Message of the Quaid-i-Azam', and 'Pakistan and Islamic World'*. All these pamphlets outlined the topics of discussion during the course of election work.[55]

These pamphlets provided basic instructions regarding the mode and subject of the speeches to be delivered to the masses, especially to the villagers. With regard to meetings in the villages, the pamphlets used the term of 'mass attack meetings'. It meant that instead of following a normal pattern of holding meetings, the workers should go from village to village on bicycles, where fiery speeches about the League, Islam and Pakistan be delivered in order to receive immediate response from the rural masses. The pamphlet added that street processions should also be taken out. As regards election campaign in the cities and big towns, the pamphlet used the term, 'Street Corner Meetings'. It stressed the holding of small-scale meetings in the streets of the cities. It also emphasised the propagation of the League cause during railway journeys. The students were further instructed to put up an impressive show of their character and behaviour during the whole campaign and try to say their prayers in mosques where they could get an opportunity to contact the masses.[56]

The Election Board invited names of volunteers to undertake election work for the provincial elections. In response to the Federation's appeals, hundreds of Muslim students enrolled themselves as volunteers and penetrated into the rural areas of Punjab. It was estimated according to a report that during *Id* Holidays about 400 Muslim students had spread all over the province for the election campaign. The report said that they were to undergo a short training course before proceeding to various parts of the province to explain the League's message to the electorate.[57]

On November 11, 1945, Punjab Muslim Students Federation organised a Conference at Sialkot. During this Conference a large number of Muslim students were enrolled as volunteers for the election campaign.[58] Zia-ul-Islam, the President of the Punjab Muslim Students Federation on November 21, 1945, convened an emergent meeting of workers to ponder over the situation and find out ways to intensify the election campaign. While addressing the workers, he observed, 'not only have we to vote for the League now, we must also be prepared to sacrifice our very lives if need be for Islam and the freedom of hundreds of Muslims.'[59]

A deputation of the Federation covered about one hundred villages of the Sargodha district by the end of November 1945. As a result of the propaganda made by the Students Federation this home district of Punjab Premier became a stroghold of the Muslim League.[60] Similarly, another deputation of the Federation covered almost every village of Sheikhupura district. The deputation of Sheikhupura, while recording their impression about the election propaganda, reported that, 'the response to their appeal has been very astonishing in most of the villages in the sense that not only the ordinary villager is prepared to vote for the League, but he can even go to the extent of sacrificing his life for the nation and *Millat*.[61]

Some groups of the students toured various villages of the districts of Lahore, Lyallpur, Gujrat, Sialkot, Montgomery, Attock, Multan, Jhang and Muzaffargarh.[62] By the end of December 1945, various squads of students workers were also able to make whirlwind tours of a number of East Punjab districts, i.e. Amritsar, Hoshiarpur, Jullundur, Ludhiana, Gurdaspur, Rohtak, Ferozepur, Ambala and Hissar.[63] These groups, as reported, addressed several small gatherings, explaining the programme and aims of the Muslim League and deputed a number of local student workers to spread over to certain constituencies.[64]

On December 12, 1945, an Election office had been set up in the Islamia College,. Lahore, which was inaugurated by Nawabzada Liaquat Ali Khan. In his inaugural address, Liaquat Ali Khan advised the Muslim students to work hard and trust in God.[65] Meanwhile, the Muslim students from Aligarh had also joined hands with the Punjab Muslim Students Federation workers and the campaign was carried on with increased vigour and devotion. Qmar Ali Siddiqi, leader of the Aligarh Election Delegation, declared that the battle of the *Karbala* is going to be faught again in this land of five rivers.[66]

Leaders of the Muslim League like Liaquat Ali Khan, Nawab of Mamdot, Mian Mumtaz Daultana and Firoz Khan Noon gave due appreciation to the campaigning programme of the Muslim Students Federation and paid rich tributes to them. Feroz Khan Noon remarked that, 'I am sending out this appeal to Muslim students to sacrifice their Christmas holidays and go out in the villages and convey our message into every corner of the rural areas. Once that is done, I know the victory will be ours.'[67]

With such appeals, the Punjab Muslim Students Federation obviously became more active and devoted to the cause with increased enthusiasm. Some batches of the students now toured the villages of the districts of Rawalpindi, Jhelum, Gujranwala, Dera Ghazi Khan, Shahpur and Mianwali and made profound influence upon the Muslim masses.[68] By mid January 1946, the Punjab Muslim Students Federation workers had already made frequent visits to almost all the constituencies. Now onwards, they intensified their campaign more fervently and until the results of the Provincial Elections, the students workers carried the election work in different batches, touring several constituencies.[69]

Jinnah himself visited Punjab during the last week of January 1946 and addressed the Muslim students in the Habibia Hall, Islamia College, Lahore. Thanking the Punjab Muslim Students Federation for its magnificent work and the sacrifices of the students for the cherished goal of Pakistan, Jinnah said that he was glad to say that all parts of Punjab had been completely revolutionized. Never had such things happened in Punjab.[70] Jinnah further said:

> The students of the Punjab Muslim Students Federation have done wonderful work. I have not adequate words to praise all you have done and the sacrifices you have made. How sincerely and selflessly you have worked, I have no power to give you medals and shields or squares of land. But your reward is that you are serving the nation selflessly and sincerely.[71]

More than 1,500 Muslim students workers combed every village, preaching the message of the League. These students were divided into 160 groups, worked for 134 days during the provincial election and campaigned in about 84 constituencies. Majority of these students, nearly 80 per cent, belonged to the Islamia College, Lahore.[72] A huge number of voters gave a prompt response to these students and pledged vote for the League. The Punjab Muslim Students Federation was able to bring a complete revolution in the outlook of the Muslim masses. Entering each village in groups of twenty to twenty five, these students generally avoided all involvement in local disputes and stressed the importance of Islamic unity and Islamic government. These students of the Federation explained to the villagers the political importance and the religious meaning of the Islamic State i.e. Pakistan.[73]

This vigorous campaigning on the part of the Muslim students profoundly affected the election scenario of the province. Mian Mumtaz Daultana, General-Secretary of the Punjab Provincial Muslim League, declared that in many districts in Multan division, student workers had been able to turn the tide in favour of the League.[74] Chaudhary Moin-ul-Haque, General Secretary of the All-India Muslim Students Federation, with regard to the election work of the Punjab Muslim Students Federation, recorded that, 'These are the people who are carrying the banner of the Muslim League to the remotest corners of the Punjab, and I am confident that ultimately they will give a burial to the Unionist government and it creed for ever.'[75]

Apart from the leaders and workers of the Provincial Muslim League, workers of the Punjab Muslim Students Federation, the religious men i.e. *Sufis* and *Sajjada Nashins* also played crucial role in the provincial elections of 1946. The propaganda and religious appeals made by the *Sufis* and *Sajjada-Nashins* turned the tide in favour of the Muslim League. The Muslim League realised how vital it was to obtain the support of the *Pirs* and *Sajjada-Nashins*. As early as in 1943, the Muslim League at the National level proposed to, 'Respectfully the Muslim religious heads, *Pirs* and *Sufis* to help the Muslim Nation of India in its present life and death struggle, by their sincere prayers and by exhorting their followers to sacrifice their all in the cause of the attainment of a free and independent Muslim India.'[76]

The Punjab Provincial Muslim League, immediately preceding the elections, created a twelve member committee of men of religious influence known as the *Masheikh Committee* in order to marshal *Sufis* and *Pirs* support behind its cause. While some of the members of this committee were men of unquestionable religious authority and power in local and provincial politics, others like the Nawab Iftikhar Husain Khan of Mandot solemnly took the honorific title of the Pir of Mandot Sharif, Shaukat Hayat Khan became *Sajjada-Nashin* of Wah Sharif, Firoz Khan Noon became the *Sajjada-Nashin* of Sargodha Sharif and Ibrahim Ali Chisti, Secretary of the Committee, a worldy figure, was designated as Fazl-i-Hind *Sajjada-Nashin* of Paisa Akbar Sharif.[77] This committee approached individual *Pirs* and asked them to issue *fatwas* in its support. These were disseminated by means of small leaflets and wall posters as well as by publication in such newspapers as *Nawa-e-Waqt*, *Inqilab* and *Eastern Times*.[78]

The *fatwas* issued by the *Pirs* and *Sajjada-Nashins* had wide variations in their content. A *fatwa* issued by Syed Fazal Ahmad Shah, *Sajjada-Nashin* of the shrine of Hazrat Shah Nur Jamal, was couched solely in terms of an appeal to *Piri-Mureedi* relationship. The *fatwa* stated, 'An announcement from the Dargah of Hazrat Shah Nur Jamal. I command all those people who are in my *Silsilah* to do everything possible to help the Muslim League and give their votes to it. All those people who do not act according to this announcement should consider themselves no longer members of my *Silsilah.* Signed Fazal Ahmad Shah, *Sajjada-Nashin* Hazrat Shah Nur Jamal.[79] Some of the *fatwas* threatened the voters that if they did not back the Muslim League they would cease to be Muslims, their marriages would be invalid and if this did not frighten them, then they were told that they would face ex-communication including a refusal to allow their dead to be buried in Muslim graveyards and be debarred from joining in mass Muslim prayers.[80] Pir Samaruddin of Sial Sharif, a Chisti revivalist Shrine, issued an appeal to his Tiwana disciples during a Muslim League meeting held on the outskirts of the Tiwanas' Kalra estate, in Shahpur district, early in January 1946. He declared:

> 'I have never begged for anything in my life before but today I have come out of my home to beg for votes, the Muslim League is a purely religious movement in which all the rich, poor, sufis and scholars are participating. Not as a Pir but even as a Muslim. I have repeatedly advised Nawab Allah Baksh Khan Tiwana who is my murid not to desert the Muslims at this critical time.'[81] Such appeals did much to win support for the Muslim League because of the reverence and fear of the Pirs among the rural population.

A good example of the influence of these *Sajjada-Nashins* in local politics comes from Jhelum District, where the local faction associated with Raja Ghazanfar Ali Khan, the uncle of Pir Fazal Shah of Jalalpur, had shifted to the Muslim League at the time of League-Unionist break in 1944. During the second half of 1945, when the *Pirs* openly entered into the campaigning contest, the Unionist found it impossible to check the growth of the League in this district. Not only did Pir Fazal Shah begin to campaign openly for the League, but other *Sajjada-Nashins* also entered the field. One Unionist worker wrote in December 1945 that, 'The Muslim League has started very intense propaganda on religious lines, Pir M. Husain Shah, son of Pir Jammat Ali Shah, is making a tour of Jhelum Tehsil and issuing *fatwas* that Muslim League is the only Islamic Community and that all the rest are *Kafirs*.'[82] Two weeks later this Unionist worker further wrote that, 'that eighty per cent population of this district is Pir-ridden. They are blind followers of *Pirs*. Pir Jammat Ali Shah's son's personal contacts and *fatwas* have created great obstacles in the way of our workers ... No amount of individual propaganda can convert the blind adherents of the *Pirs*.'[83]

The *Pirs* of the Chishti revivalist shrines were amongst the most active on the Muslim League's behalf. Like *Pir* Qamaruddin of Sial Sharif, *Pir* Fazal Shah of Jalalpur, *Pir* Jammat Ali Shah of Taunsa and Pir Golra were the most influential of the League's Sufi supporters. Pir Fazal Shah toured the Gujar Khan Tehsil of the district of Rawalpindi and tipped the balance in favour of the Muslim League and Pir of Golra did the same in Rawalpindi Tehsil.[84] *Pir* Golra also issued a *firman* in favour of the Muslim League candidate at Gujar Khan.[85] *Pir* Sial also toured the Jhang district and tipped the balance in favour of the Muslim League.[86]

The *Pirs* and *Sajjada-Nashins* of the Chishti revivalist Shrines as suggested by David Gilmartin, supported the Muslim League more due to religious than political considerations. The Muslim League, according to David Gilmartin, offered them to infuse greater religious influence into the politics of the province especially of the rural Punjab. The logic of the support of these religious leaders for Pakistan, as they enters the Muslim League struggle in 1945, was different to that of the religious position of reformist *Ulema*, who had long opposed the idea of Pakistan. The *Ulema* had developed a view of religious solidarity which was itself political and was based on the authority of the *Ulema*, who interpreted the religious law and Muslim public opinion.[87] The thrust of the revivalist *Sajjada-Nashins* concern, however, had always been to influence the political leaders and their followers to regulate their lives according to the religious injuctions.

The leaders of the Provincial Muslim League now provided them such an opportunity. The idea of a state in the hands of such leaders was for them perfectly natural, for in the establishment of such a state based on the Shariat, they could see the projection of their local religious work into a larger political arena. This view explains in large part the attitude of these *Sajjada-Nashins* towards Jinnah, which was in sharp contrast to that of the reformist *Ulema* who generally distrusted Jinnah as a political man with little real awareness of Islam.[88]

The Chishti revivalist shrines had also been influenced to support the Muslim League by the premier shrine of their order at Ajmer. The Dargah of Hazrat Khwaja Moinuddin Chishti at Ajmer had been one of the shrines which during the 1940s become closely connected with the Muslim League. Mirza Abdul Qadir Beg, the Vice-President of the Dargah Committee was the President of the Ajmer Muslim League. League meetings were regularly held at the Dargah.[89] At the time of the *Urs* the Muslim League message was spread amongst the vast number of pilgrims which flocked to the shrine, among whom each year were representatives of all the Punjab's chishti shrines. This leadership from Ajmer was, thus, a major factor in the Chishti Pirs' support for the League in Punjab.[90] Moreover, the already growing popularity of the League on the bases of Islam, also, persuaded the *Pirs* to support the cause of the League and Pakistan.

The Chishti revivalist shrines were, however, not alone to render support in favour of the Muslim League. In some districts, *Pirs* from the *Qadiri* order exerted a far greater influence. The *Sajjada Nashin* of the *Qadiri* shrine of Pir Syed Mohammad Ghaus intervened on the League's behalf in the Shakargarh constituency and thus enabled the Muslim League candidate to defeat the Unionist candidate. A representative of the Qadiri *Pir* family of Pirkot Sidhana was the successful League candidate for the Jhang Central constituency. The shrine of Mian Mir, an influential *Qadiri* shrine of the province, also issued *fatwas* in the League's support.[91] Makhdum Syed Mohammad Nazar Hussain Shah *Sajjada-Nashin* of Koranga in

Multan district issued *firmans* in favour of the Muslim League. The Gilani *Pirs* of Multan did much to counter the influence in support of the Unionist Party throughout the district by the leading Suhrawardi Shrine of Shaikh Bahauddin Zakariya. Sahibzada Syed Mohammad Abbas, *Sajjada-Nashin* of the Shergarh Estate, was the Divisional organizer of the Montgomery Muslim League.[92]

The Muslim League also endeavoured to seek the support of those minority of *Ulema* who showed sympathy to the League cause. Foremost among these was Maulana Shabir Ahmad Usmani, who had once been an active member of the *Jammat-i-Ulema-i-Hind,* and who now was called upon to head the new pro-Pakistan, *Jammat-i-Ulema-i-Islam.* An attempt was made to expand the *Jammat-i-Ulema-i-Islam* to include the rural religions leaders who comprised the bulk of the League's religious support.[93] At the end of January 1946, a provincial Conference of the *Jammat-i-Ulema-i-Islam* was held in Lahore which was attended by leading *Ulema* as throughout India and some rural religious leaders also attended it. After the conclusion of the Conference some of the leading *Ulemas* took up propaganda work, but on the whole the *Ulema's* role in mobilizing support for the League in the countryside remained minimal in comparison with that of the *Pirs.*[94]

The support of the Chishti revivalist shrines and other established shrines proved substantially beneficial for the Muslim League and it achieved greatest success in such areas as Jhang, Multan and Jhelum where it had obtained the support of the leading *Pirs* and *Sajjada-Nashins*. Khalid Saifullah, the editor of the pro-League *Eastern Times* remarked that, 'what are the factors that have brought about the revolution in the Pakistani lands? What has made the great change possible? In my view the greatest praise must be lavished, as far as the Punjab is concerned on the *Pirs* ... who when they saw the Pakistani nation in mortal danger emerged from their cells and enjoined upon their followers to resist evil and vote for the League and Pakistan.'[95]

Moreover, it appears from the working style and socio-cultural and economic conditions of the *Pirs* and *Sajjada-Nashins* that they felt threatened by the League's brand of Islam which went against their grain of localized and personality-based spirituality. They felt that the already growing strength of the League would reduce their influence among their followers, therefore, they supported the League.

The efforts and vigorous propaganda, made by the leaders and workers of the Provincial Muslim League, workers of the Punjab Muslim Students Federation assisted by the students of the Aligarh University and the religions appeals and *fatwas* of the *Pirs* and *Sajjada Nashins* combined together, thus, put the Muslim League in a formidable position.

The Unionist Party, during the elections of 1946, depended much upon the administrative resources, land-grants, war-front funds and propaganda regarding the various agricultural reforms. Faced with the disruption of their support in the countryside, the Unionists increasingly turned to the machinery of government for mobilizing support. Attempts to coerce the village voters proved disastrous. They did irreparable damage to the reputation which the party had achieved during its early years in office. In complete contrast was the Muslim League's identification with the villagers' wartime economic difficulties.[96] The Unionist Party issued its Manifesto which stressed the economic achievement of the ministry including the reduction of the agricultural debt by two crores of rupees. Provincial autonomy, complete independence, free and compulsory primary education for the poor, a reduction in military expenditure were the aims of the Unionist Party.[97]

In response to the Pakistan slogan of the Muslim League, the Unionists put forwarded the slogan of United Punjab and Punjabees. The Unionists argued that the crucial electoral issues for the voters was not Pakistan but the choice was between chaos, disorder and communal bitterness on the one side, which is the only prospect held out by the Muslim League group, and a stable and efficient administration offered by the Unionists in the interests of the masses to which the majority of the Muslims of the province belong.[98] The Unionists during their election campaign stressed the intercommunal cooperation and intercommunal harmony.

However, the economic achievement of the Unionist Party and a call for the inter-communal co-operation, this time, was not responded to by the Muslims of Punjab since the religious appeals and the cry for Pakistan had now become the most successful means of politicizing for the Muslim masses. The religious appeal of Pakistan was admitted by Khizar Hayat Khan himself when he declared that the Unionists were for Pakistan, that Muslims would be voting for Pakistan whether they voted for a Muslim League candidate or a Muslim Unionist.[99] Khizar himself had began to garnish his speeches with verses from the Quran. He would explain the economic benefits given by the Unionist government by using *Quaranic* explanations.[100] Even Sir Chhotu Ram, the prominent Hindu Jat leader of the Unionist Party, shortly before his death, drawn a plan to employ religious preachers to campaign for the Party.[101] The banners flown on the election meeting of the Unionists and League had became an identical green, bearing the Muslim Legend of the crescent.[102]

The Unionist Party, in order to counter the propaganda made by the *Pirs* and *Sajjada Nashins* in favour of the Muslim League, approached the *Ulema* of Ahrar and pro-Congress *Jammat-i-Ulema-i-Hind*. The Unionist had made some organized attempts to win support among the *Sajjada-Nashins*, but among the revivalist they had little success. The Unionist found that the only well-organized groups of religious leaders in opposition to the Muslim League were the reformist *Ulema* who backed the Ahrar and the *Jammat-i-Ulema-i-Hind*, thus they sought their support.[103] Unionist workers in the field in late 1945 and early 1946 were desperate for some sort of religious support to counter the propaganda of the *Pirs*.

The district organiser of the Unionist Party for Jhelum district wrote in December 1945, to the Unionist headquarters, 'Political propaganda was of no use against religious appeals, and *fatwas* in rebuttal are the only antidote now. Either first rate religious speakers should be sent or else *fatwas* against the Muslim League should be obtained from Deoband *Ulema* and circulated in the district.[104] The Unionist leaders in response to such demands sent *Ulema* to the countryside. The Muslim League, however, made fun of this effort by the Unionist to get religious support, charging that they were so desperate that they were sending not trained *maulvis*, but untrained *maulvis* who were paid 30 to 40 rupees a month to do their propaganda. The employment of these untrained *maulvis* only made it clear that the Muslim League had almost completely taken over the rural religious base on which the Unionist Party itself had once relied.[105]

Sir Chhotu Ram, senior most leader of the Unionist Party, did his best to maintain the rural base of his party in the Eastern Punjab. He consoled the workers of the Unionist Party who were disheartened by the rising tide of communalism with verses from Iqbal and advised the voters to keep their religious beliefs strictly outside the politics.[106] The constant round of speaking engagements on top of Ministerial duties undermined the health of Sir Chhotu Ram and he died on January 9, 1945.[107] The sudden death of Sir Chhotu Ram was a great blow to the Unionist Party. Khizar Hayat Khan Tiwana[108] as well as Wavell[109] also mourned the death of this prominent Jat Leader at this crucial juncture.

The Congress, was another important political party to take part in the provincial election of 1946. The Punjab Congress at this time, however, was structurally weak, disorganized, divided and faction ridden. The resignation of Mian Iftikhar-ud-Din, President of the Punjab Provincial Congress Committee, from the Congress to join the Muslim League at this juncture, came as a big blow to the Congress.[110] Moreover the factional struggle between the groups of Gopi Chand Bhargawa and Satyapal further deterioted the position of the Punjab Congress. Maulana Abul Kalam Azad, President of the Indian National Congress, came to Punjab, talked to the various groups of the Congress and to a large extent succeeded in effecting a compromise among the various groups and appointed Maulana Daud Ghaznavi as president of the Punjab Provincial Congress Committee.[111] However, the Punjab Congress was again divided on the issue of its attitude towards the Akalis, some of the leaders of the Provincial Congress wanted an election compromise with the Akalis whereas others were against any compromise.[112]

The dominant features of the Congress election propaganda in Punjab were the demand for the release of the Indian National Army personnels and a slogan of complete Independence. The Congress formed Indian National Army defence committees and observed an Indian National Army week from October 21, 1945 to October 28, 1945. The campaign consisted of numerous meetings, processions and the submission of a charter to the Viceroy and the commander-in-chief in which the signatories demanded amnesty for the Indian National Army personnel.[113] In Amritsar, an Azad Hind Volunteer Corps was organised by the district Congress Committee.[114] The Punjab Congress collected funds in the name of the Indian National Army, demanded regular employment for the Indian National Army personnel and appealed to the business concerns to give employment to Indian National Army men.[115] This attitude of the Congress strengthened its position especially in the Eastern Punjab.

The sudden death of Sir Chhotu Ram in January 1945, may be called a blessing in disguise for the Provincial Congress, since it removed the last breakwater against the incoming Congress tide in the Eastern Punjab.[116] Prem Choudhary has argued that the war time grievances of the people of this region, high prices, shortage and economic controls alienated the Unionists' traditional supporters in this region and led to the consolidation of the Congress. The Congress cashed by cleverly linking complete independence with a period of abundance in essential commodities, as did the Muslim League in the West Punjab.[117]

The Akalis and the nationalist Sikhs were also divided into different factions on the eve of the elections of 1946. Master Tara Singh, Giani Kartar Singh, Baba Kharak Singh, Udham Singh Nagoke and Sardar Baldev Singh were the leaders of different factions of the Akalis and nationalist Sikhs. However, the anti-Pakistan feelings and the opposition of the Muslim League brought the different Sikh leaders together and they decided to contest the elections under the banner of the Panthic Sikhs.[118]

The Akali electioneering campaign was marked by an anti-Pakistan and anti-Muslim League slant. The Akalis, like the Congress, fully utilised the issue of the Indian National Army personnel during their election campaigns.[119] Thus, the Panthic Sikhs consolidated their position in the Central Punjab. Other political parties like the communists, the Ahrars, the Khaksars and the Hindu Mahasabha also contested the elections but with little success.

Out of a total of 175 seats in Punjab Legislative Assembly, 14 candidates were elected unopposed including nine of the

Congress, three Unionists and two Leaguers.[120] Of the remaining 161, as many as 461 candidates contested the elections. Party wise distribution of these candidates was, Congress-82, Muslim League-85, Unionist Party-99, Communists-24, Panthic Sikhs-28, The Ahrars-17, Khaksars-04, Hindu Mahasabha-02 and independents and others-120.[121] Polling was held from February 1, 1946 to February 15, 1946. After a week of the commencement of the polling results started coming.[122] The Unionist Party, after the results, was reduced to a rump of 21 members in the Provincial Assembly. The Muslim League had captured seventy-five of the eighty-six Muslim seats, winning all eleven of the urban and sixty-four of the seventy-five rural constituencies. The party-wise position in the Assembly was as shown in Table 5.1.

Table 5.1

Results of the Provincial Elections, 1946[123]

Party Number	*Number of Votes Polled*	*Percentage of Votes Polled*	*Total of Seats*
1. Muslim League	6,80,823	32.8	75
2. Congress	4,77,765	23.1	51
3. Unionist Party	4,19,231	20.2	21
4. Panthic Sikhs	1,60,763	7.8	21
5. Communists	39,576	1.9	—
6. Others and Independents	2,95,238	14.2	07
Total	20,73,336	100.0	175

The grand victory of the Muslim League in Punjab, gave a decisive turn to the movement for Pakistan, though it was a severe blow to the concept of an united India. Jinnah was overjoyed with the success of Punjab Muslim League and he sent a congratulatory message to Nawab of Mamdot, the President of the Punjab Provincial Muslim League. Jinnah wrote:

> *Accept hearty congratulations. The Musalmans of Punjab have proved that the Punjab is the foundation stone of Pakistan. In spite of so many hurdles 90 per cent success is a resounding*

victory which the entire Indian Muslim population can be proud of—it is the fatwa *of the Muslims of Punjab that the Muslim League is the only representative party of Muslims of India.*[124]

In an interview on March 7, 1946. Jinnah again said, 'I am more than happy that we have already won the battle for Pakistan in the Punjab by carrying away 90 per cent of the Muslim seats.'[125] *S.E. Abbott, then Secretary to Khizar Hayat Khan, attributed the League's victory to the Muslim belief is the inevitability of Pakistan.*[126]

The election results also revealed the consolidation of anti-Pakistan opinion among the minority communities of Punjab. The success of the Congress in this election was unprecedented, it had eclipsed all competitors for the *Hindu* vote and captured 56.18 per cent votes in the general constituencies and 41.14 per cent votes in the Sikh constituencies. The Panthic Sikh also consolidated its position in the Central Punjab and captured 40.73 per cent votes in the Sikh constituencies, in the face of the threat of Pakistan.[127]

It is obvious from the above discussions that the period from July 1945 to March 1946 was a landmark not only in the history of Punjab Provincial Muslim League but also in the history of Punjab. During this period the Provincial Muslim League successfully popularized the demand of Pakistan in to the every nook and corner of the Muslim Punjab and achieved grand victory in the provincial elections of 1946. The vigorous propaganda conducted by the leaders and workers of the provincial Muslim League, the relentless struggle undertaken by the workers of the Punjab Muslim students federation in the countryside of Punjab based on Islamic appeals and religious symbols and the *fatmass* issued by the *Pirs* and *Sajjada Nashins* of the Province, in the name of Islam, in fact, consolidated the position of the Muslim League and the cause of the Pakistan which in turn led to its victory in the provincial elections of 1946.

Foot Notes

1. Government of India to Secretary of State, August 1, 1945, N. Mansergh and Penderel Moon (ed.), *op.cit.*, Vol. VI, p. 1.
2. Governors Conference, August 1, 1945, *Ibid.*, p. 6.

3. *Ibid.*, p. 23.
4. Wavell to Pethick-Lawrence, August 21, 1945, *Ibid.*, p. 113.
5. Prime Minister, Attlee's Statement in the Parliament, September 11, 1945, *Ibid.*, p. 230.
6. Pethick-Lawrence to Wavell, September 18, 1945, *Ibid.*, pp. 270-71.
7. Wavell to Pethick-Lawrence, October 5, 1945, *Ibid.*, p. 342.
8. *The Dawn*, Delhi, October 2, 1945.
9. *Ibid*, July 21, 1945.
10. Punjab Forthightly Report for the Second half of July 1945, *Home Political*, File No. 18/7/1945.
11. Jinnah to Mian Mumtaz Daultana, July 31, 1945, *Shamsul Hasan Collection*, Punjab, Vol. III, p. 36.
12. Firoz Khan Noon to Khizar Hayat Khan Tiwana, August 21, 1945, *Shamsul Hasan Collection*, Punjab, Vol. IV, p. 15.
13. *Eastern Times*, Lahore, September 16, 1945.
14. *Ibid.*, September 26, 1945.
15. *Ibid.*, October 4, 1945.
16. *Ibid.*, September 24, 1945.
17. Ghulam Bhik Nairang to Jinnah, August 28, 1945, *Shamsul Hasan Collection*, Punjab, Vol. III, p. 59.
18. *The Dawn*, Delhi, September 2, 1945.
19. Vicky Noon to Jinnah, October 10, 1945, *Shamsul Hasan Collection*, Punjab, Vol. IV, p. 19.
20. Wavell to Pethick-Lawrence, October 16, 1945, N. Mansergh and Penderel Noon (ed.), *op.cit.*, Vol. VI, p. 348.
21. Vicky Noon to Jinnah, October 10, 1945, *Shamsul Hasan Collection*, Punjab, Vol. IV, p. 19.
22. Mian Bashir Ahmad to Jinnah, November 14, 1945, *Ibid.*, Vol. III, p. 22.
23. *Ibid.*
24. *The Statesman*, Delhi, October 27, 1945.
25. Mian Bashir Ahmad to Jinnah, November 14, 1945, *Shamsul Hasan Collection*, Punjab, Vol. III, p. 21.
26. *The Tribune*, Lahore, October 3, 1945.
27. Ian Talbot, 'The 1946 Punjab Elections,' *Modern Asian Studies*, 14, J, 1980, p. 75.
28. *Ibid.*
29. *Ibid.*, pp. 75-76.
30. Ian Talbot, 'The Growth of the Muslim League in the Punjab 1937-1946', *Journal of Commonwealth and Comparative Politics*, March, 1982, pp. 22-23.
31. Ayesha Jalal, *op.cit.*, p. 142 .
32. *Eastern Times*, Lahore, October 20, 1945.

33. Ian Talbot, 'The 1946 Punjab Elections,' *Modern Asian Studies*, 14. I, 1980, p. 76.
34. This decision was the result of pressure from local League branches in the major recruiting areas, for example, the Montgomery District Muslim League on 10.2.1946 passed a resolution condemning the attitude of the British Raj against the I.N.A. Personnel, *Shamsul Hasan Collection*, Punjab, Vol. II, p. 18.
35. Prem Chowdhary, 'The Congress Triumph in South-East Punjab: Elections of 1946', *Studies in History*, 2.2.1980, pp. 98-105.
36. Mohammad Zafarullah to Jinnah, October 29, 1945, *Shamsul Hasan Collection*, Punjab, Vol. I , p. 62.
37. *Civil and Military Gazettee*, Lahore, December 2, 1945
38. *Ibid.*, Lahore, December 11, 1945.
39. Statement of Jinnah at a Press Conference at Lahore on January, 29, 1946. *Shamsul Hasan Collection*, Punjab, Vol. I, p. 100.
40. Ghulam Bhik Nairang to Jinnah, August 28, 1945, *Shamsul Hasan Collection*, Punjab, Vol. III, p. 59.
41. President, Amritsar District Muslim League to Jinnah, January 18, 1946, *Ibid.*, Vol. I, p. 101.
42. Mumtaz Daultana to Jinnah, January 17, 1946, *Ibid.*, Vol. II, p. 21.
43. Mian Amiruddin to Jinnah, January 28, 1946, S.Q. Hussain Jafari (ed.), *op.cit.*, pp. 36-37.
44. Jinnah to Mumtaz Daultana, January 17, 1946. *Shamsul Hasan Collection*, Punjab, Vol. II, p. 22.
45. Jinnah to Mian Amiruddin, January 28, 1946, S.Q. Hussain Jafari (ed.), *op.cit.*, p. 38.
46. Statement of Jinnah at a Press Conference at Lahore on January 29, 1946, *Shamsul Hasan Collection*, Punjab, Vol. I, p. 100.
47. *The Dawn*, Delhi, November 24, 1945.
48. *Ibid.*, December 2, 1946.
49. *Ibid.*, December 27, 1946.
50. Glancy to Wavell, February 28, 1946, see Anita Inder Singh, *op.cit.*, pp. 133-34.
51. Glancy to Wavell, February 2, 1946, *Ibid.*, p. 134.
52. See W.C. Smith, *op.cit.*, p. 331.
53. Sarfaraz Hussain Mirza, *op.cit.*, p. 304.
54. *Ibid.*
55. *Ibid.*
56. *Ibid.*, pp. 304-05.
57. *Eastern Times*, Lahore, October 23, 1945.
58. *Ibid.*, November 12, 1945.
59. *Ibid.*, November 22, 1945.
60. *Ibid.*, November 24, 1945.

61. *Ibid.*, November 27, 1945.
62. Sarfaraz Hussain Mirza, *op.cit.*, pp. 308-12.
63. *Ibid.*, pp. 308-15.
64. *Ibid.*, p. 309.
65. *Eastern Times*, Lahore, December 16, 1945.
66. *The Dawn*, Delhi, December 19, 1945.
67. *Ibid.*, December 22, 1945.
68. Sarfaraz Hussain Mirza, *op.cit.*, pp. 314-22.
69. *Ibid.*, pp. 321-34.
70. *Eastern Times*, January 28, 1946.
71. *Ibid.*
72. Sarfaraz Hussain Mirza, *op.cit.*, pp. 336-38.
73. Report of Abdul Razzaq, General Secretary, Muslim Students Federation, Lahore, January 25, 1946, *Shamsul Hasan Collection*, Punjab, Vol. II, p. 30.
74. *Eastern Times*, January 4, 1946.
75. *Ibid.*, January 27, 1946.
76. Ian Talbot, 'The 1946 Punjab Elections', *Modern Asian Studies*, 14, I, 1980, p. 82.
77. See, Ayesha Jalal, *op.cit.*, p. 147.
78. Ian Talbot, *Punjab and the Raj 1849-1947*, p. 211.
79. Ian Talbot, 'The 1946 Punjab Elections', *Modern Asian Studies*, 14, I, 1980, p. 82.
80. Glancy to Wavell, January 16, 1946, See Ayesha Jalal, *op.cit.*, p. 147.
81. Ian Talbot, 'Deserted Collaborators: The Political Background to the Rise and Fall of the Punjab Unionist Party 1923-1947, *The Journal of Imperial and Commonwealth History*, October 1982, p. 87.
82. David Gilmartin, 'Religious Leadership and the Pakistan, Movement in the Punjab', *Modern Asian Studies*, 13, 3, 1979, pp. 514-15.
83. *Ibid.*, p. 515.
84. *Ibid.*
85. *Eastern Times*, Lahore, January 19, 1946.
86. *Ibid.*, January 23, 1946.
87. David Gilmartin, 'Religious Leadership and the Pakistan Movement in the Punjab', *Modern Asian Studies*, 13.3.1979, p. 509.
88. *Ibid.*, pp. 509-10.
89. Ian Talbot, 'The 1946 Punjab Elections', *Modern Asian Studies*, 14, I, 1980, p. 86.
90. *Ibid.*
91. *Ibid.*

92. *Ibid.*, pp. 86-87.
93. David Gilmartin, 'Religious Leadership and the Pakistan Movement in the Punjab', *Modern Asian Studies*, 13.3.1979, pp. 510-11
94. Ian Talbot, 'The 1946 Punjab Elections', *Modern Asian Studies*, 14, I. 1980, p. 79.
95. Ian Talbot, 'The Growth of the Muslim League in the Punjab 1937-46,' *Journal of Commonwealth and Comparative Politics*, 13, I, 1982, p. 26.
96. Ian Talbot, 'The 1946 Punjab Elections', *Modern Asian Studies*, 13.3.1979, p. 90.
97. *Civil and Military Gazette*, November 29, 1945.
98. *The Tribune*, October 28, 1945.
99. *Civil and Military Gazette*, Lahore, October 29, 1945.
100. *Ibid.*, December 28, 1945.
101. Madan Gopal, *Sir Chhotu Ram a Political Biography*, New Delhi, 1977, p. 146 .
102. *Civil and Military Gazette*, February 8, 1946.
103. David Gilmartin, 'Religious Leadership and the Pakistan Movement in the Punjab,' *Modern Asian Studies*, 13.3.1979, p. 515.
104. *Ibid.*, pp. 515-16.
105. *Ibid.*, p. 516.
106. D.C. Verma, *Sir Chhotu Ram: Life and Times*, New Delhi, 1981, pp. 174-75.
107. Madan Gopal, *op.cit.*, p. 150 .
108. Ian Talbot, *Khizar Tiwana: The Punjab Unionist Party and the Partition of India*, Richmond, 1996, pp. 135-36.
109. Wavell to Amery, January 30, 1945, N. Mansergh and Penderel Moon (ed.), *op.cit.*, Vol. V, p. 489.
110. Punjab Fortnightly Report for the Second half of September 1945, *Home Political*, File No. 18/9/1945.
111. *Ibid.*, Second half of October 1945, *Home Political*, File No. 18/10/1945.
112. *Ibid.*, Second half of December 1945, *Home Political*, File No. 18/12/1945.
113. *Ibid.*, Second half of November 1945, *Home Political*, File No. 18/11/1945.
114. *Ibid.*, Second half of December 1945, *Home Political*, File No. 18/12/45.
115. *Ibid.*, Second half of January 1946, *Home Political*, File No. 18/1/1946.
116. Madan Gopal, *op.cit.*, p. 151.
117. Prem Choudhary, 'The Congress Triumph in the South East Punjab: Elections of 1946; *Studies in History*, 2.2.1980, pp. 103-05.

118. Wavell to Pethick-Lawrence, September 19, 1945, N., Mansergh and Penderel Moon (ed.), *op.cit.*, Vol. VI, p. 93.
119. Punjab Fortnightly Report for the Second Half of November 1945, *Home Political*, File No. 18/11/1995.
120. *The Tribune*, February 1, 1946.
121. *Home Political*, File No. 79/46, Part-I, 1946, pp. 202-05.
122. On February 21, 1946, the Presidents of the four major provincial political parties, declared elected from their respective constituencies. *The Tribune*, February 22, 1946.
123. *Return Showing the Results of Elections to the Central Legistlative Assembly and the Provincial Legislatures 1945-46*, New Delhi, 1948, p. 73.
124. Ikram Ali Malik, *op.cit.*, p. 590.
125. *Indian Annual Register*, 1946, Vol. 1, p. 42.
126. Anita Inder Singh, *op.cit.*, p. 136.
127. *Home Political*, File No. 79/46, Part-I, 1946, pp. 210-11.

6

Partition of Punjab

The period from March 1947 to August 1947 was a landmark in the history of Punjab Provincial Muslim League and it also affected very profoundly the courses of national history. The Muslim League considered its victory in the elections of 1946 a sort of *fatwa* issued by the Muslim Punjab in favour of Pakistan and therefore it was no more in need of a plebiscite in order to prove its strength and to justify the demand of Pakistan. The attitude of the British and the deteriorating relationship between the Congress and the Muslim League further strengthen the cause of the League. Thus, the Muslim League started a sort of *Jehad* in the province and ultimately achieved its cherished goal of the establishment of Pakistan in the name of Islam.

Although the Muslim League was the single largest party in the Punjab Assembly, but it was not in a position to form the ministry. Attempts were made to form a Congress-League ministry, with half the members representing the Muslim League and others half from the Congress. The negotiations, however, broke down as the League objected to the inclusion of non-League Muslim in the ministry. The League wanted the Congress to join the coalition as a representative of the Hindus alone—a position the Congress was not prepared to accept.[1]

Maulana Abul Kalam Azad, at this juncture, visited Punjab and hold negotiations with the Unionists and Panthic Sikhs and succeeded in organising a Congress-Akali-Unionist coalition under the leadership of Khizar Hayat Khan.[2] Since no one was willing to ally with the League, so in the end the Governor, Glancy, invited Khizar Hayat Khan to form the ministry and he managed to do so with the help of the Congress and the Panthic Sikhs.[3] The Muslim League now declared its determination to establish undiluted Muslim rule in Punjab and directed all its energies towards overthrowing the new coalition.[4]

Glancy's decision to invite Khizar Hayat to form a coalition ministry was severely criticised by the Muslim League. Nawabzada Liaquat Ali Khan and Nawab of Mamdot complained to the Viceroy. Nawabzada Liaquat Ali Khan retorted, 'By accepting the so-called coalition , the Governor is either blind or dishonest ... I want to make it plain to the Governor and the people of this province that here only the Muslims have the right to form a government. No other power has a right to impose any government on the Musalmans against their wishes.'[5]

Nothing could have enraged Jinnah more than the sight of a Muslim collaborating with the Hindus and Sikhs and destroying the prospects of a Muslim state. If the Punjab slipped out of his hand, his Pakistan might recede into political oblivion. The Punjab was central to his Pakistan and Jinnah could hardly afford to lose it without losing Pakistan itself.[6] Jinnah quickly began organising a Muslim mass-movement against the coalition in order to prevent his enemies from consolidating their power. The formation of a coalition ministry on March 11, 1946 was preceded by a Muslim League organised *hartal* on March 7, 1946 throughout the province and the celebration of 'Traitors Day' on March 9, 1946.[7] There were noisy and abusive demonstrations outside the Premier's house, which led to communal clashes before the Sanatan Dharma College, Lahore, on March 9, 1946.[8] The government reacted and promulgated Section 144 IPC in Lahore and Amritsar, banned meetings and processions, League activists who preached violence and communal hatred were apprehended. The houses of those possessing illegal arms were searched.[9]

These measures did not dampen the violent spirit of the Leaguers. They started a campaign for civic rights for all Panjabis, and for the repeal of repressive laws. The Budget session of the Punjab Assembly, which was held from March 21 to March 30, 1946, witnessed unruly scenes and was marked by frequent interruptions, uproars and comments by the Muslim League members. The League members shouted slogans like *'Allah-o-Akbar'*, *'Pakistan Zindabad'*, *'Muslim League Zindabad'*, *'Quaid-i-Azam Zindabad'*, etc. The visitors sitting in the gallery also joined them. There was pandemonium which was brought under control with great effort.[10]

This occasion of the Budget session was utilised by the Muslim League members to direct their criticism against Khizar Hayat Khan and the coalition government. Chaudhary Mohammad Hasan addressed the Premier as 'Malik Sir Gaddar Hayat Khan', Shaukat Hayat Khan called him a Quisling.[11] The Muslim League members called the coalition a 'fraud' and criticised the Governor, Sir Bertarnd Glancy, for his connivance in creating this unnatural alliance.[12] Raja Ghazanfar Ali Khan thought that the coalition was only a combination of heterogeneous elements united only in their hatred of the Muslim League.[13] He appealed to Khizar Hayat Khan and other Muslim members of the Unionist Party, in the name of Islam to join the Muslim League. He also expressed surprise at the Congress alliance with the reactionary and pro-British Unionist Party.[14] Begum Jahan Ara Shah Nawaz of the Muslim League asked the nationalist Muslims to withdraw and facilitate a compromise between the Muslim members of the Congress and the Muslim League.[15]

The Muslim League Assembly Party, however, failed to break up the coalition ministry during the Budget session neither the Muslim Unionist crossed floor to join them. However, one fallout of this Budget session was that the Akalis intensified their attempts at popularising the demand for a separate Sikh state as a counter move to the Muslim League's demand for Pakistan.[16]

Meanwhile in March 1946, the British Government sent a three member Cabinet Mission to India to finalise the mode of transfer of power. The Cabinet Mission, consisting of Lord Pethic Lawrence, Sir Stafford Cripps and Sir A.V. Alexender, arrived in India on March 24, 1946. For about a fortnight, the Mission exchanged notes with political parties, provincial Chief Ministers, opposition leaders, spokesmen of minorities and others. Khizar Hayat Khan met with Wavell and the three-man team of the Cabinet Mission, when the same had arrived in Karachi. Mamdot had already informed the Mission that an undivided Punjab should be included in Pakistan. Khizar minced no words when he maintained that the Pakistan issue would never have arisen in its present shape, if Jinnah had been officially asked to define what he wanted. Even now it was not too late.[17] When Cripps, however, pressed him concerning the effects of the establishment of Pakistan on the Punjab, Khizar explained that Muslims would be pleased, if it included the whole of the province as now existed. The Sikhs' relations with the new government, however, would be very difficult and they might not be dealt with peacefully.[18]

The Akalis also met the members of the Cabinet Mission and told them that if the demand for Pakistan was accepted then the Sikhs must be given a separate State of their own in Punjab.[19] When the Cabinet Mission had submitted its plan on May 16, 1946, suggesting the formation of a Constituent Assembly and constituting an Interim government, Khizar further elaborated to Sir Evan Jenkins, the new Governor of Punjab, his solution to the constitutional deadlock. Khizar suggested a provincial autonomy to Punjab and a weak federal centre.[20] The scheme, however, ran into the sand when Nehru maintained that the Congress would not be bound by its safeguards for the Muslim majority areas. Jinnah responded by calling for *Direct Action.* This precipitated the communal breakdown which led to the final depart between the communities.[21]

Meanwhile, the Muslim League Legislators' convention was held in Delhi from April 7, 1946 to April 9, 1946. It was resolved in the convention that the Muslims will never submit to any constitution for a United India.[22] Nawab of Mamdot[23] and Sardar Shaukat Hayat Khan[24] declared that the Muslims will fight unto death if any attempt is made to submit their nation to the domination of anyone else. Finally, the League Legislators pledged to undergo any sacrifice for the attainment of Pakistan.[25]

At the All-India Muslim League Council meeting held in Bombay on July 29, 1946, the Muslim League withdrew its acceptance of Cabinet Mission plan and passed the historic

'Direct Action' resolution, the resolution stated, 'The Council of the All-India Muslim League is convinced that now the time has come for the Muslim Nation to resort to Direct Action to achieve Pakistan to assert their just rights, to indicate their honour and get rid of the present British slavery and the contemplated future caste, Hindu domination.[26] The Working Committee of the All-India Muslim League was authorised to chalk out 'Direct Action' programme and as such August 16, 1946 was fixed as the 'Direct Action Day' and the Provincial Leagues were also directed to observe 'Direct Action Day' on the same day.[27]

The Punjab Provincial Muslim League chalked out a programme so as to educate the Muslim public in the light of the decision of the League. Special messengers were dispatched to all parts of the Province to carry the League message. Circulars explaining the decision of the League were issued which called for holding meetings all over Punjab. A number of volunteer squads went round the towns, carrying playcards and flag of the League. The Provincial League deputed Nawab of Mamdot, Sardar Shaukat Hayat Khan, Mian Mumtaz Daultana, Mian Iftikharuddin, Shaikh Karamat Ali and Raja Ghazhafar-Ali Khan to supervise the deliberations of the Direct Action Day.[28] Meanwhile, the Muslim League's slogan 'Islam in Danger', was arousing strong religious sentiments among the Muslims of the Province. The defection of Maulana Daud Ghaznavi, President of the Punjab Provincial Congress Committee, from the Congress to the Muslim League, at this crucial juncture, was an illustrated sign of the religious sentiments of the Muslims.[29]

The Punjab Muslim Students Federation, at this occasion exerted itself with a prompt response and chalked out a programme which included holding of meetings and passing of resolutions in support of the Direct Action Day. Zia-ul-Islam, the President of the Punjab Muslim Students Federation issued a lengthy statement exhorting the Muslim students of Punjab to prepare themselves for any sacrifice for the nation. He directed the students to hold meetings at their places—towns, villages and even remote areas of the province to explain the League policy and its programme for the achievement of Pakistan.[30] Zia-ul-Islam also instructed the students that the flag hoisting ceremony should be observed in all the wards of the Federation's branches on the eve of Direct Action Day.[31]

On August 16, 1946, the *Direct Action Day* was observed throughout the Province. Complete strike was observed in various towns and cities. Public meetings were held and resolutions were passed criticising the dishonest methods of the British imperialism and the fascist techniques of the Hindu Congress.[32] According to a report, ten million audience attended hundreds of meetings held throughout the province and no untoward incident was reported from any place.[33] At Lahore, total strike was observed on that day which was unprecedented in the history of this city.[34] Huge gatherings were held in Barkat Ali Hall, the Habibia Hall and all mosques of the city. Vicky Noon addressed an exclusively women's gathering in Lahore and asked Muslim women to be ready for making all sacrifices to achieve Pakistan. She further said, "the time has come when we will not hesitate to sacrifice our property, our rest, our lives and even our children's lives in the struggle to obtain our objective".[35]

The workers of the Punjab Muslim Students Federation propagated the message of the League throughout the province on the Direct Action Day and the Federation declared that the Muslim youth would sacrifice their everything and would lay their lives for the cause of Pakistan.[36] The Provincial Muslim League appealed to the Muslims of the Province to denounce their titles for the cause of Pakistan and Islam. The appeal stated, 'You are a Muslim, do your duty to Islam, cast off that yoke of slavery, bestowed by British Imperialism, joyfully renounce your Title, your Nation demands it, honour conferred by Millat is more Glorious'.[37]

The Direct Action Day was converted into Direct Action Movement in Punjab, since Jinnah and Provincial Muslim League, at any cost, wanted to overthrow the coalition government of Khizar Hayat Khan. Workers of the Provincial Muslim League and Punjab Muslim Students Federation spread throughout the Province and propagated the cause of Pakistan and Islam and vehemently attacked the coalition government of Khizar. Nawab of Mamdot, appealed to students to be prepared for the last attack.[38] He said:

> In the name of Islam and Pakistan, I appeal to the Muslim students to stand resolute and prepared. Let us once again spread out in the countryside and during what remains of the vacations recreate and improve upon the atmosphere of which they alone were responsible during the past winter months. I say to them, reach your people and lead them, to Pakistan. You did not fail six months ago, by God's grace you will not fail now.[39]

The League campaign in the Province assumed the threat of *Jehad*, and there was increasing response to its religious exhortation. The Lahore action committee decided to organise a Conference of *Ulema* and *Pirs* who were to be persuaded to issue a *fatwa* in favour of *Jehad*.[40] It was reported in the *Eastern Times* that the Conference of *Pirs* and *Ulema* was held in the second half of October 1946 and all the prominent religious leaders were invited and participated in the Conference in order that the Direct Action Movement of the Muslim League may get their sanction. It seems that the Direct Action Movement, by this step, may take the form of *Jehad* against Islam enemies in India.[41] Raja Ghazanfar Ali Khan, the spokesman of the Provincial Muslim League, claimed that 'Direct Action' meant *Jehad* with all its implications.[42]

The Working Committee of the Provincial Muslim League chalked out a programme, of Civil Disobedience, which included non-payment of taxes and revenue, deliberate violation of Central measures and laws and boycott of non-Muslim traders and goods. The Working Committee also invested the Provincial League President with dictatorial authority, including the power of naming his successor.[43] The Punjab Muslim Student Federation' Muslim League also drew up a plan of action and decided to set up centres for the recruitment of cadres with a view to giving them training to meet the worsening communal situation. The League propaganda, thus, became increasingly bitter.[44]

Consequently, there was marked deterioration in the communal harmony in the province. Communal disorders occurred in the different parts of the province.[45] In the prevailing atmosphere both the *Muslim League National Guards* and the *Rashtriya Swam Sevak Sangh*, became increasingly popular with their co-religionists. According to an official estimate, the number of Muslim League National Guards rose from 1,500 in December 1945 to approximately 22,000 a year later and the strength of the RSS volunteers increased from 14,000 to nearly 16,000 during the same period.[46] To check the growing communal tendencies, the Punjab Government promulgated the Punjab Public Safety Ordinances and issued orders prohibiting drilling, processions, demonstrations, public meetings and the possession of any offensive weapons.[47] The Provincial Muslim League, however, strongly protested against the promulgation of the Punjab Public Safety Ordinances and other repressive measures taken by the government. Sadiq Hussain, the Vice-President of the Punjab Muslim League, declared that the League workers will boldly defy these ordinances.[48]

In the meantime, the communal situation in Panjab had taken a turn for the worse. Serious violent riots had occured in different parts of the province especially in the districts of Multan, Rawalpindi and Rohtak. Hindus and Sikhs felt alarmed and insecure and they were unable to give sufficient support to the Khizar Government. The intelligence reports had revealed that the Muslim League National Guards and the *Rashtriya Swam Sevak Sangh* were clandestinely training for armed combat with knives and lathis. Khizar consequently decided to take action against them, with the full approval of Sir Evan Jenkins, the Governor of Punjab.[49] On January 24, 1947 under the Criminal Law Amendment Act, orders were issued by the Punjab Government banning the Muslim National Guards and the RSS.

The office of the Muslim League National Guards was searched and houses of the leaders of the Provincial League were raided. Prominent League leaders like Mian Iftikhar-ud-Din, Begam Shah Nawaz, Nawab of Mamdot, Mian Mumtaz Daultana, Sardar Shaukat Hayat Khan, Raja Ghazhafar Ali Khan and Malik Firoz Khan Noon were arrested.[50] This action of the Punjab Government created immediate and furious reaction amongst the Muslims, who were already in a bellicose mood against the coalition Government. The Punjab Muslim Students Federation called an emergent meeting on January 24, 1947 and decided to launch a forceful movement in defiance of the

Government ban and the arrest of the League Leaders.[51] The students took out a procession in Lahore, marched in the streets and on the roads of the city with shouts of 'Release our Leaders', 'Down with Governor-Jenkins', and '*Lay Key Rahain Gay Pakistan*', etc., the processionists reached Anarkali Bazar where about thirty of them offered arrests. The students, on January 25, 1947, also took out a procession and about eighty-six of them offered arrests. The movement of the students further roused the sentiments of the Muslims of Punjab.[52]

The echoes of the movement were soon heard from all over the Muslim Punjab. Complete strike was observed and processions were taken out in different towns and cities of the province on January 25-26, 1947 by the League workers including women.[53] The League Assembly Party met on January 25, 1947 in the Punjab Assembly chambers and passed a resolution condemning the action taken against the Muslim League National Guards in the Province and banning the legal activities of the League in Punjab.[54] Soon after the meeting, seven members of the League Assembly Party were arrested since they had deliberately defied a ban on the meetings. They were joined by eight of their colleagues after police had been called to a demonstration in the late afternoon at the Mochi Gate, Lahore. The police used tear gas to disperse the crowds and also arrested a number of female protesters.[55]

However, after watching the whole situation carefully and in order to check the communal consequences of the agitation, with the advise of Sir Evan Jenkins, the Khizar Government released all the prominent leaders of the Muslim League at late night on January 27, 1947.[56] Khizar Hayat Khan called a cabinet meeting on the morning of January 28, 1947. In the meeting, it was decided to withdraw the ban on the Muslim League National Guards and the RSS, whilst reemphasising the Ministry's commitment to maintaining law and order.[57] The Muslim League's initial grievance had been fully met. However, the desire of the Provincial League and Jinnah was to see downfall of Khizar Government. Shaukat Hayat Khan uncompromisingly declared that, 'The Khizar Ministry must be made to go whatever the cost to the Muslim League'. He boosted that the opposition would put out 15 million Muslims to break the law.'[58] Khizar now had no alternative but to tough things out. Following a day of great tension, he ordered the police to strike during the night of January 28-29, 1947. All the important leaders of the League in Lahore, including the Nawab of Mamdot and Malik Feroz Khan Noon were arrested and detained outside the city. A rigid censorship was introduced.[59]

This action, however, brought only a temporary halt of demonstration in Lahore. The agitation now also spread to the other districts. This agitation which had began as a movement of the students, politicians and their wives who had for the first time taken to the streets, now attracted the attention of the wider sections of the Muslim population and they were increasingly drawn into the movement.[60] There was a ten thousand strong procession in Lahore on January 30, 1947. A procession of thirty thousands moved through the streets of Muzzaffargarh. Strikes became an important feature in the Muslim League agitation. Complete strike was observed for a number of times in Lahore, Muzzaffargarh, Gujrat, Rawalpindi, Sargodha, Multan, Kasur, Firozpur, Amritsar, Jullundur, Attock, Lyallpur and Rohtak and processions were also taken out.[61] Clashes between the police and demonstrators became increasingly violent. In one incident in Lahore, five hundred rounds of tear gas were fired.[62]

Sir Evan Jenkins, Governor of Punjab, remarked that, 'the Agitation has convinced Hindus and Sikhs that the League wants undiluted Muslim Raj'.[63] Master Tara Singh issued a statement that the Sikhs were in danger and must revive their army under his command.[64] Khizar Hayat Khan and his family especially became the target of the anger of the Muslim League. Mock mourning was enacted outside Khizar's residence on a number of occasions.[65] All sort of Punjabi invectives and humiliating slogans were raised against Khizar and his family. One of the slogans raised against Khizar was, *'Pola Ek Juti Da, Khizar Putar Kutti Da'*, (Khizar a son of bitch, should be beaten with a shoe).[66] He had been depicted as a *Kafir* and the main impediment in the way of the establishment of Pakistan. He had been compelled to move from house to house each night to avoid the threat of assassination at the hands of the Muslim League.[67]

After Attlee's announcement of February 20, 1947, that His Majesty Government intended to transfer power by a date no later than June 1948, Khizar became increasingly gloomy.[68] Just six days after Attlee's announcement, a compromise was secured between the Government and the League. Khizar agreed to introduce new legislation to replace the Punjab Public Safety Ordinance. He also lifted the ban on public meetings and agreed to release all political prisoners except those convicted for offences under section 325 of the Indian Penal Code. However, the ban on processions was not removed.[69]

However, Jinnah, more than even before, now could not permit the coalition to stay in office. Khizar was also advised by his friends that he should no longer act as a buffer between the Muslim League and the minorities.[70] Unable to face the situation, Khizar Hayat Khan, without consulting his cabinet colleagues, finally submitted the resignation of his Government on March 2, 1947.[71] In a press statement Khizar said that the transfer of power was now a reality confronting the people of the Punjab. The Muslim League should face this on behalf of the Muslim majority and make arrangements on the future with the minority representatives as it saw fit. This would only be possible if the Muslim Unionists were no longer in the middle. The statement concluded that Khizar would be willing to assist the Muslim League in any way possible. It also, however, reiterates his long held view that Punjabis would suffer a great loss if the province was divided and that his utmost desire was to maintain the integrity of Punjab.[72]

The fall of the Khizar Government came as severe blow to the non-Muslims of the Province. League's demand of Pakistan was at the zenith. Communal frenzy gripped all sections of people. Fearing terrible consequences from a Muslim League Ministry, discontent was widespread among the Hindus and the Sikhs. Violating a ban order on processions, the erstwhile Finance Minister in the Khizar Ministry, Bhim Sen Sachar, led a procession to the Assembly House in Lahore only a day after its fall, and addressed the demonstrating crowds, 'I as a member of the Government, hereby declare that you have every right to take out processions.'[73] This was intended as a reminder to the prospective League Government that if the Muslims could break the law under the coalition

Government, the non-Muslims had the same power when a League Government took over. An inflamed Master Tara Singh unsheathed his *Kirpan* before the crowd assembled in front of the Punjab Assembly and shouted *'Pakistan Murdabad'*, and *'Raj Karega Khalsa, Aaki rahe na koi'*. (The pure will rule, none will remain deprived).[74]

Sir Evan Jenkins saw the Nawab of Mamdot, President of the Punjab Provincial Muslim League, late in the morning of March 3, 1947. He gave him an absolutely free hand to form a Ministry in the expectation that the Muslim League President would be able to report positive progress by March 8, 1947 at the latest. However, the installation of a Muslim League led coalition Ministry proved impossible since neither the Congress, Akali Dal, Unionists nor any independent was willing to support the Muslim League Ministry. The Punjab, therefore, was brought under Governor rule under section 93 of the Act of 1935.[75]

Within less than a week of the fall of the coalition Government, communal violence has reached alarming proportions and the Congress had demanded the partition of the Province.[76] The violence spread from the cities to the countryside and the villages of the districts of Lahore, Amritsar, Jhelum, Gujrat, Attock, Multan and Rawalpindi became the worst victim of the violence and the riots. About 40,000 people, mainly Sikhs, had taken refuge in hurridly established camps.[77] Master Tara Singh, expressed grave concern about the future of the Sikh areas, and welcomed the decision of the Congress regarding the partition of the Province. Master Tara Singh announced that:

> The Congress had not defined the Scheme of the partition. The Sikhs will be glad if the Muslim League accept the principle and concede the Sikh demand of forming districts into a separate province in which the Sikhs and Hindus are given as much land as they possess at present. We cannot tolerate a division in which predominantly Sikh districts were partitioned.[78]

It is here important to discuss the relationship between the Congress and the Muslim League at the national level which was deteriorating to the worst ever since their differences regarding the Cabinet Mission Plan and which in turn affected the provincial politics. When the Indian National Congress and the All India Muslim League had failed to agree on the issues of Constituent Assembly and the Interim Government, the Cabinet Mission, then put forward its own proposals in its statement of 16 May 1946. The cabinet Mission envisaged a Federal Union controlling Defence, Foreign Affairs and Communications, with residuary subjects vested in the provinces. The Union had the power to raise its own revenue. There would be an executive and Muslim provinces. The provinces were free to form groups with executives and legislatures and each group could determine the provincial subjects to be taken in common.[79]

The plan further laid down in paragraph 19, the procedure for the election and working of the Constituent Assembly to draw up the Union, Group and Provincial constitutions. The Plan contemplated that after the election the provincial representatives were to divide into three sections, Section-A comprising Bombay, Madras, UP, C.P., Bihar and Orissa, Section B comprising Punjab, Sind, N.W.F.P. and British Baluchistan and Section-C comprising Bengal and Assam. These three sections were to settle Provincial Constitutions and also to decide a Group Constitution. After the constitutional arrangement had come into operation, it was to be open to any province to effect to come out of the group in which it had been placed by these deliberations. The Cabinet Mission avoided any reference to Pakistan by name and sovereignty of Pakistan was ruled out, but the three tier structure would ensure the autonomy of Muslim majority provinces.[80]

In an effort to lure both the Congress and the League to participate in the Constituent Assembly, the Cabinet Mission delegates gave different assurance to both the parties. Cripps and Pethick-Lawrence confirmed to the League delegates that meetings of the sections were necessary and sections would proceed to make Constitutions for the provinces within the groups. This clearly meant that grouping in practise would be compulsory and sovereignty would not be given until the Constitution had been framed.[81] On the other hand, Nehru and Azad were assured by Wavell that the Constituent Assembly might be regarded as a sovereign body for the purpose of the constitution making.[82] In fact, the grouping provisions in the Cabinet Mission Plan kept the idea of the Pakistan very much alive.

There .were vital differences between the Congress and the Muslim League regarding the Cabinet Mission Plan. The Congress apparently felt that when it came to forming zonal Government, a province or a part of the province could opt out of the zone. It had not really accepted the either the three-tier Government or limitations on the power of the Constituent Assembly laid down in the plan.[83] After the elections of the Constituent Assembly, the Congress insisted on its functioning. As the Congress had a predominant majority, naturally it was likely to insist on its own interpretations of the Plan and secure that the Constituent Assembly went its way.[84] Jinnah described this as a blunder of a very grave and serious character.[85] The Constituent Assembly started its working on December 9, 1946. The Muslim League boycotted it and stated that the election to and thereafter summoning of the Constituent Assembly in spite of strong protests and most emphatic objections on the part of the League, were void, in valid and illegal.[86]

Apart from the fundamental differences regarding the election and functioning of the Constituent Assembly, there were vital differences between the Congress and the League regarding the formation of the Interim Government, on the basis of the parity. Since no agreement reached between the parties on this issue, the Cabinet Mission on its own issued a statement regarding the formation of the Interim Government composed of six Congress representative (including one Schedule Caste), five Muslim Leagues, one Sikh, one Parsi and one Christian.[87] The Muslim League had at first refused to join the Interim Government in the hope that this would keep out the Congress. However, when the Interim Government began functioning since September 1946 without the League, then it became greatly upset. In November 1946, the Muslim League also decided to join the Interim Government.[88]

The object of the Congress members in the Interim Government was to bring into existence healthy convention of non-interference by the Viceroy and the Interim Government working as a team. so that it may be replaced by the National Government in due course. The Muslim League members, however, had entered the Government with the allowed object of holding Congress to ransom, best anything should be done which might prejudice its claim for Pakistan. In this campaign, their chief weapon was the emphasis on legality preventing the Government from functioning as a cabinet and to increase the power and influence of the Viceroy in order to save themselves from being overriden by the Congress majority.[89] To the Congress members that attitude seemed reactionary, it insisted on keeping the status quo and forbade any progress by conventions. There was continual friction between the League and the Congress in the Interim Government. Liaquat Ali Khan, who was the Finance Member of the Interim Government, seldom agreed to the proposals coming from the Congress members.[90]

The Congress members, in February 1947, demanded that as a consequence of the Muslim League attitude it is no longer possible for members of the Muslim League to continue in the Interim Government.[91] In a press interview, Sardar Patel made it clear that Congress would withdraw from the Interim Government if the League was allowed to remain in it.[92] Rajender Prasad, however, confessed privately that there was very little chance of the Muslim League being asked to quit.[93] Attlee, the Prime Minister, however, advised the Viceroy to play for the time since withdrawal of the either party will lead to a dangerous situation.[94] The situation, however, remained the same. Lord Clydesmuir, who officiated as Governor General during the absence of Lord Mountbatten in May 1947, observed, 'At that time relations between the Hindus and Muslims, members of the Government, had almost reached breaking point. At the centre there was a joint Cabinet in name only.'[95]

As discussed earlier, Attlee, the Prime Minister on February 20, 1947, announced in the Parliament that the His Majesty's Government wish to make it clear that it is their definite intention to take the necessary steps to effect the transference of power into responsible Indian hands by a date not latter than June 1948. His Majesty's Government will have to consider to whom the powers of the Central Government in British India should be handed over, on the due date, whether as a whole to some form of Central Government for British

India or some areas to the existing Provincial Governments or in such other way as may seem most reasonable and in the best interests of the Indian people.'[96] This statement of the British Minister further deteriorated the relationship between the Congress and the Muslim League. This statement altered the course of history. The echoes of this momentous announcement reverberated throughout the subcontinent. For the first time, the Indians felt that the British irrevocably intended to leave. It paved the way for partition and even represented an indirect concession to the League demand for Pakistan.[97]

Gandhi rightly perceived this statement when he said that this may lead to Pakistan for those provinces or portions which may want.[98] This statement together with the Muslim League's policy of obstruction prepared the Congress leaders to accept partition, as they were fed up with the Muslim League's tactics. Nehru subsequently said that there was an overwhelming sense of conflict during the Interim Government days by pulls in different directions by the Muslim League. It was felt that if some arrangement could be arrived at to prevent partition, these conflicts and disruptions would continue and might come in the way of any marked progress in the economic and other planning later. It would have left the Federal Government weak.[99]

Meanwhile, as discussed earlier, communal violence brokeout in different parts of Punjab. A large section of Hindus in the context of triumphant assertion of Muslim communalism tended to wear round to a Hindu communalist perspective posting the idea of community as a nation. The Punjab Provincial Congress leadership also realised that now it was unable to check the growth of Muslim Communalism and the demand of Pakistan. In such conditions, some Hindu Congressmen with Hinduized consciousness tended to move towards communalism viewing Muslims as an enemy. This created possibilities of active collaboration of these Congressmen with the volunteers of the RSS in building a combined force against the Muslims. As soon as the Congress leadership at the national level came to know about this collaboration, it wrote to the Punjab Congress Committee not to allow the RSS workers to participate in its activities.[100] However, for a common Hindu, there was no difference between the RSS and the Congress because both were adopting the same attitude against the Muslim League.

Thus, the communal violence in the province vitiated the political atmosphere. Jawaharlal Nehru, after visiting the riot-affected areas in Punjab, said at a press conference at Lahore that all that has happened is intimately connected with political affairs. I propose to say nothing about that aspect, except this that if politics is to be conducted in this way, then it cease to be politics and become some kind of jungle warfare which reduces human habitation to the state of a desert.[101] It was in these circumstances that on March 8, 1947, the Congress resolved that these tragic events, the communal riots in Punjab, have demonstrated that there can be no settlement of the problem of Punjab by violence and coercion and no arrangement based on coercion can last. Therefore it is necessary to find a way out which involves the least amount of compulsion. This would necessitate the division of Punjab into two provinces, so that the predominant Muslim parts may be separated from the predominantly non-Muslim parts.[102]

It was at this juncture, when Punjab was facing a great amount of communal violence, that Mountbatten was appointed as new Viceroy of India and he arrived in Delhi on March 22, 1947. Sir Evan Jenkins informed Mountbatten regarding the communal situation of the Province. It was told to the Viceroy that in the predominately Muslim regions of Rawalpindi and Multan, the minority communities, particularly the Sikhs, faced daily risk to their lives, property, houses and lands. Hundreds were killed, and thousands more fled to the towns to escape slaughter.[103] The most serious threat to the security of Punjab came from the attitude of Jinnah, who relentlessly continued his efforts for a League Government, unmindful of the reactions of the non-Muslims. The Sikh preparation to counter Jinnah's stand on Punjab posed a troublesome problem for Mountbatten. His first step was to ascertain from the army generals and the Governor, their views on the situation. General Messervy told the Viceroy that, 'The atmosphere was eclectic and it was common knowledge that the Sikhs and the Muslims were arming for a more serious clash which he felt was inevitable.'[104]

Meanwhile, the Hindus of Punjab were now bent on partition. Some Hindu members of the Central Legislative Assembly from Punjab like Pandit Thakur Das Bhargawa, Raizada Hans Raj, Diwan Chaman Lal, Chaudhry Sri Chand and Diwan Rup Chand, pressed upon Jawaharlal Nehru to carry their decision to the Interim Government that, 'We have come to the conclusion that the only way out of the present deadlock is to partition the Punjab into two provinces. That and that alone, in our views, can cease the tension in the Province which may increase at any moment. Effective steps may, therefore, be taken forthwith to constitute two provinces out of the present Punjab and we are fully convinced that partition is the only solution of this vexed problem.'[105] On April 16, 1947, the Working Committee of the Shiromani Akali Dal also adopted the resolution of the partition of the province.[106]

The Sikhs were much more disturbed over the issue of partition than the Hindus. The latter had overwhelming majority in two divisions out of the total of five in Punjab, and these would obviously have to merge with Hindustan. But the Sikhs were distributed all over the province and as a matter of fact there was not a single district in which the Sikhs were in the majority and they had a large number of historic Gurdwaras in Punjab scattered over the whole province. All these would be adversely affected by partition. Master Tara Singh, Giani Kartar Singh and Sardar Baldev Singh met the Viceroy on April 18, 1947 to present their case. Mountbatten discussed with them the prospect and problems of partition. The unhappy leaders admitted that the Sikhs would not be in a majority in any part of the Punjab, but they were now so bitterly anti-Muslim that they would not mind forming a Hindu-Sikh Province.[107]

In the course of their discussions, the Sikh leaders made rather an unusual request to the Viceroy that if he decided upon Pakistan and a partition of Punjab, he should publicly give the Sikhs the choice of joining either Pakistan or Hindustan, so that they might have some bargaining power to gain the best terms. The Viceroy fairly agreed to this proposal. Although the Sikhs had already decided not to live with the Muslims but by concealing their wish they wanted to negotiate with the Congress to get best out of the bargain.[108]

On April 21, 1947, Jawaharlal Nehru and Sir Evan Jenkins received a statement jointly issued by Bhim Sen Sachar and Sardar Swaran Singh representing the opinions of Punjab Congress Assembly Party and the Panthic Sikh Assembly Party of Punjab regarding the partition of the province. The statement uttered, 'We cannot submit to be ruled by those who have committed or caused to be committed the inhuman atrocities in the Punjab and therefore demand that immediate steps be taken to divide the Punjab into two and if necessary three autonomous provinces'. Bhim Sen Sachar and Swaran Singh suggested that the Lahore division, temporarily, will be governed by Muslims, Hindus and Sikhs. 'This central province could ultimately be partitioned between Muslim and Hindu-Sikh Punjab after a Boundary Commission went into its details.'[109]

Jinnah, however, was still hopeful of acquiring the whole of Punjab for Pakistan despite the concerted non-Muslim demand for partition. He informed Mountbatten that the Sikhs liked him personally and had always trusted him and would join Pakistan.[110] Meanwhile, Nawab of Mamdot, claimed 93 members supported him out of the total of 175 in the Legislative Assembly, and Jinnah immediately pressed for a League Ministry. Mountbatten, however, told Jinnah that such a move would led to the communal violence in the province and also told him that since a decision would be made within a month, which would probably involve the partition of Punjab, it seemed futile to put in a ministry for such a short period.[111] At this, Jinnah became quite frustrated as the whole of Punjab was in his long standing scheme of Pakistan. Liaquat Ali Khan gave vent to his frustration by charging the Sikhs of an uncompromising attitude towards Muslims.[112] Thus, by the end of April 1947 partition had become almost a certainty.

While the partition of the province had become a reality Khizar Hayat Khan, the former Premier, was still hopeful of the unity and issued a statement from Delhi on May 2, 1947, saying, 'I am convinced that a division of the province would prove extremely detrimental to the interests of all the communities and classes in the province, and would reverse the process of progressive, beneficent development which had been carried on in the province during the last quarter of a century.'[113] Jinnah immediately took advantage of this statement and announced that such a united Punjab must be a part of Pakistan. This in turn provoked Hindu-Sikh insistence that Muslims should not get more than two-fifths of the province. Sir Evan Jenkins, because of such developments, feared large scale and serious communal violence in the province.[114]

On the other hand, Mountbatten and his senior staff, in the first half of May 1947, was seriously preparing a partition plan. On behalf of the Viceroy, Lord Ismay and Abell were working in London on the details of the plan. Mountbatten warned the different communities of Punjab not to take part in the communal violence. The Viceroy said, 'If the Sikhs made trouble it was my intention to warn them that they would have to fight the army and air force, in exactly the same way as the Muslim League would be faced with army and air force if they made any further trouble.'[115] On May 18, 1947, Mountbatten left for London to finalise the partition plan and before leaving Delhi he instructed Arthur Smith, the Deputy Commander-in-Chief to position an additional infantry division in Punjab.[116] Indian leaders accepted Mountbatten's partition plan within three days of his return and it was announced on June 3, 1947.[117] On June 4, 1947, in a press conference Mountbatten told that the transfer of power would take place on August 15, 1947.

While accepting the Mountbatten plan of June 3, 1947, Jinnah announced that, 'It is clear that the plan does not meet in some important aspect of our point of view, and we cannot say or feel that we are satisfied or that we agree with some of the matters dealt with by the plan. It is for us now to consider whether the plan, as presented to us by His Majesty's Government, should be accepted by us a compromise or a settlement'.[118] The All India Muslim League Council in its meeting held in Delhi on June 9-10, 1947 also resolved that:

> The Council of the All-India Muslim League is of the opinion that the only solution of India's problem is to divide India into two—Pakistan and Hindustan. The Council is of the opinion that although it cannot agree to the partition of Bengal and the Punjab, or gives its consent to such partition, it has to consider His Majesty

> Government's plan for the transfer of power as a whole. The Council, therefore, hereby resolves to give full authority to the President of the All-India Muslim League, Quaid-i-Azam M.A. Jinnah, to accept the fundamental principles of the plan as a compromise, and to leave it to him, with full authority, to work out all the details of the plan.[119]

The partition plan of Mountbatten of June, 3, 1947, contained following clauses regarding the Punjab:

1. The Provincial Legislative Assemblies of Bengal and Punjab (excluding the European members) will, therefore, each be asked to meet in two parts, one representing the Muslim majority districts and the other the rest of the Province. For the purpose of determining the population of the districts, the 1941 census figures will be taken as authoritative.
2. The members of the two parts of each Legislative Assembly sitting separately will be empowered to vote whether or not the province should be partitioned. If a simple majority of either part decided in favour of partition, division will take place and arrangements will be made accordingly.
3. Before the question as to the partition is decided it is desirable that the representatives of each part should know in advance which Constituent Assembly the two parts subsequently decided to remain united.
4. As soon as a decision involving partition has been taken for either province, a boundary commission will be set up by the Governor-General, the membership and terms of reference of which will be settled in consultation with those concerned. It will be instructed to demarcate the boundaries of the two parts of the Punjab on the basis of ascertaining the contiguous majority areas of Muslims and non-Muslims.[120]

In accordance with the partition plan of June 3, 1947, the two sections of the Punjab Legislative Assembly—western and eastern—met separately on June 23, 1947. The Eastern Punjab decided in favour of Partition by 50 votes against 22 votes. The western Punjab decided in keeping a United Punjab by 69 votes against 27. Thus the western Punjab decided to join the new Constituent Assembly envisaged for Pakistan and the Eastern Punjab gave their decision in favour of joining the existing Constituent Assembly for India. Before meeting separately a joint session of both the sections was also conducted where 91 members voted for joining the new Constituent Assembly whereas 77 voted in favour of joining existing Constituent Assembly. Dewan Bahadur S.P. Singha presided over the joint session and separate section of the West Punjab whereas Sardar Kapur Singh was in Chair in the Eastern Section meeting.[121]

Punjab Partition Committee was appointed on June 30, 1947 under the chairmanship of Sir Evan Jenkins. The other members of the committee were, Zahid Husain, Mian Mumtaz Daultana, Gopi Chand Bhargawa and Sardar Swaran Singh. The task of the Committee was to ensure a smooth transfer of power by determining the division of assets, personnel and liabilities before partition.[122]

On June 30, 1947, itself a Boundary Commission for Punjab also appointed and the Commission was instructed to demarcate the boundaries of the two parts of Punjab on the basis of ascertaining the contiguous majority areas of Muslims and non-Muslims. In doing so it will also take into account other factors. The members of the commission were Justice Din Mohammad, Justice Muhammad Munir, Justice Mehar Chand Mahajan and Justice Teja Singh.[123] The Chairman of the Boundary Commission, Sir Cyril Radcliffe, a Vice-Chairman of the General Council of the English Bar, however, was appointed on July 5, 1947.[124] On July 17, 1947, a Punjab Boundary Force, under the commandership of Major General Rees, was established to maintain law and order during partition.[125]

While these activities were going on, the Punjab was in flames. Killing, slaughters, arson, rape, abduction, rioting and total lawlessness was reigning the Punjab. Mutual trust and goodwill absolutely disappeared at all levels of Punjabi society as British rule drew to a close. Stabbings, killings and fires were now became the facts of Punjabi life. The Governor in a gross understatement of the fact declared that communal hostility is now universal.[126] The continued growth of the para-military organisations within the province further added to the large scale communal violence. By June 1947, the strength of the RSS and Muslim League National Guards had increased enormously.[127] The worst affected areas were Multan and Rawalpindi divisions, where the Sikhs and Hindus were in minority. In Eastern Punjab the armed bands of Sikhs and Hindus were sacking Muslim villages in the district of Gurgaon.[128]

Once the decision to divide the Punjab was taken, communal violence flared up with greater intensity in almost every part of the province. Even the civil administration and the police, also, became a party to the communal violence. Muslims had the support of Punjab police whereas Sikhs and Hindus were backed by Hindu big-business and personal armed police of the Rajas of Patiala, Faridkot, Nabha and others in addition to the Hindu civil and police personnel. Large scale disturbances occurred in the districts of Sialkot, Gujranwala, Sheikhupura, Lyallpur, Montgomery, Lahore, Jhang, Amritsar, Gurdaspur, Hoshiarpur, Jullundur, Ferozepur, Ludhiana, Multan, Jhelum, Sargodha and Rawalpindi.[129]

Meanwhile, the Punjab Boundary Commission was busy in the task of fixing a boundary between the west Punjab and East Punjab. Later on, an amendment was introduced in the Punjab Boundary Commission Award which practically reduced the Commission to a one-man commission, in a way it helped the smooth working of the Boundary Commission.[130] The Commission adopted the judicial procedure for the completion of its task. All the parties were allowed to present their case to the commission. The Muslim League, Congress and the Panthic Sikhs, all the three presented their respective memorandum to the Punjab Boundary Commission and respectively demanded that the boundary between West and East Punjab should be fixed on river Sutlej, river Ravi and river Chenab.[131] The Punjab Boundary Commission held public sittings from July 21, 1947 to July 31, 1947 and after July 31, 1947 the Commission retired to Simla. The Punjab Boundary Commission Award was submitted on August 13, 1947 and was announced only on the afternoon of August 16, 1947.[132]

The Radcliffe Award gave to the East Punjab, the whole of Jullundur and Ambala divisions, besides the Amritsar district, three *tehsils* of Gurdaspur district and a portion of the Lahore district of the Lahore division. East Punjab obtained control over three of the five rivers of the United Punjab, the Beas, the Sutlej and the Upper water of the Ravi. About thirty-eight per cent of the area and forty-five per cent of the population were assigned to East Punjab. West Punjab, on the other hand, obtained the whole of Multan and Rawalpindi divisions and the districts of Sheikhupura, Sialkot, Gujranwala, and Lahore and the Shakargarh tehsil of the Gurdaspur district of the Lahore division. The West Punjab obtained about sixty-two per cent of the area and fifty-five per cent of the population, together with a major share of the sources of income of the united Punjab.[133] However, there was widespread resentment among all the major communities of Punjab against the Radcliffe Award. The division of the territories and boundary line between the West Punjab and the East Punjab is shown in Map 6.1.

The British divided and quit on August 15, 1947. While New Delhi and Karachi, joyfully celebrated the Independence Day, the cities, towns and countryside of the Punjab groaned under the fury of fire and sword amidest blood and tears. Over the next several weeks a large number of people migrated from the west Punjab to the East Punjab and from the East Punjab to the west Punjab and it was one of the greatest migration in the history of modern times. According to an estimate about five million people fled their homes on either side and suffered the hardship and agony of becoming refugees. Large scale communal violence, arson, abduction and massacre occurred during this process of migration and as a result nearly half a million people lost their lives.[134] The Punjab Boundary Force proved inadequate to control the law and order situation. The Civil and Military Gazette of Lahore commented that the situation had been so grave that had the entire force of India and Pakistan been employed it could not have brought it under control.[135] The disintegration of the police force of Punjab and its indifferent attitude further made the task impossible. Thus the land of five rivers paid a heavy price to achieve freedom from the yoke of foreign rule.

It is obvious from the foregone discussions that Jinnah and Punjab Muslim League considered its victory in the election of 1946 as a *fatwa* in favour of Pakistan. Thus the Muslim

Map 6.1: The Boundary Line Between the East Punjab and the West Punjab

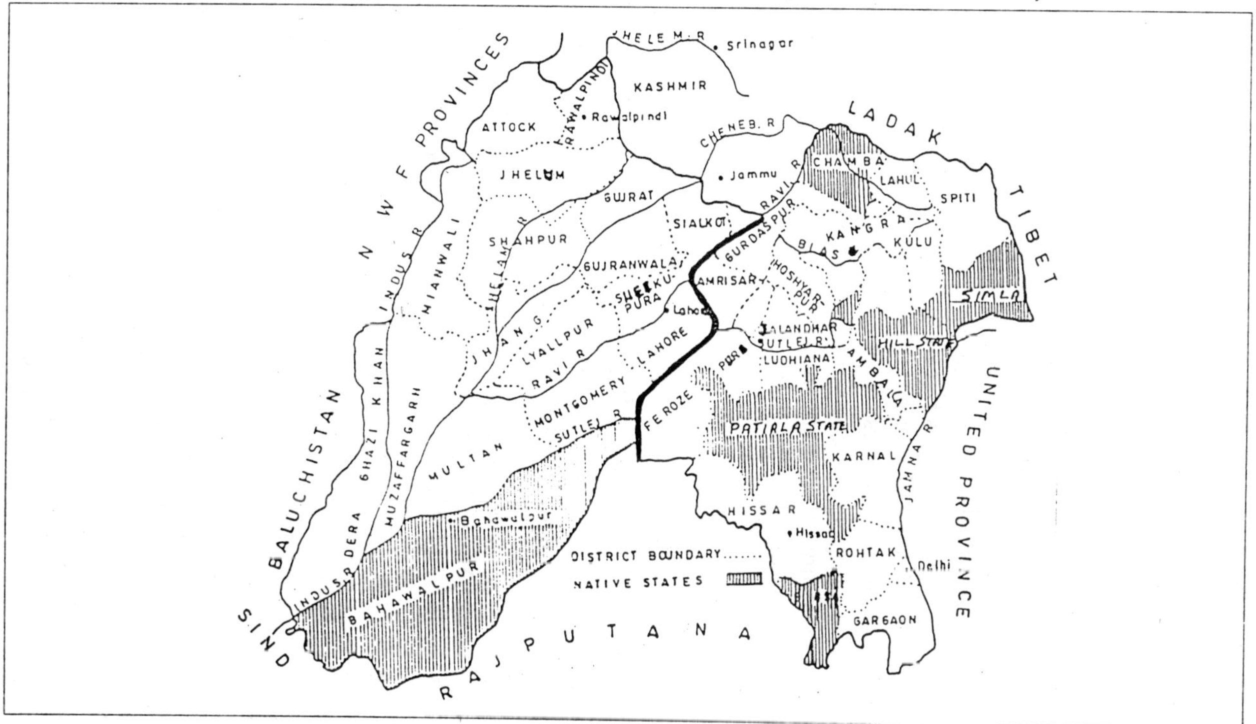

Source: Kirpal Singh, *Partition of Punjab*, Patiala, 1972, p. 87.

League started a sort of *Jehad* against the Coalition ministry when it failed to install a ministry of its own. All sorts of humiliating slogans and Punjabi invectives were used against the inter-communal government and against those Muslims who were not supporting the cause of the Pakistan. Such kind of activities on the part of the Muslim League created tension and fear among the Hindus and Sikhs of the province which led to the communal disturbances in the province and subsequently raised the demand of partition of the province. The attitude of the British towards the League and the deteriorating relationship between the Congress and the League at the national level also strengthened the cause of the Muslim League. Thus, the politics of the Provincial Muslim League and its specific political goals ultimately led to the partition of the province and the establishment of a new nation state i.e. Pakistan, although it was maimed and mutilated.

Foot Notes

1. *Punjab Legislative Assembly Debates,* 1946, Vol. XXV, pp. 44-45.
2. Punjab Fortnightly Report for the First half of March, 1946, *Home Political,* File No. 18/3/1946.
3. *The Tribune,* Lahore, March 9, 1946.
4. Punjab Fortnightly Report for the First half of March 1946, *Home Political,* File No. 18/3/1946.
5. Ikram Ali Malik, *op.cit.,* p. 593.
6. Penderel Moon, *Divide and Quit,* London, 1961, p. 72.
7. *Civil and Military Gazette,* Lahore, March 11, 1946.
8. *Ibid.*
9. *Ibid.,* March 13, 1946.
10. Imran Ali, 'Relations Between the Muslim League and the Punjab National Unionist Party 1935-47', *Journal of South Asea,* VII, II, p. 63.
11. *Punjab Legislative Assembly Debates,* 1946, Vol. XXV, pp. 43-44.
12. *Ibid.,* p. 76.
13. *Ibid.,* p. 44.
14. Punjab Fortnightly Report for the Second half of March 1946, *Home Political,* File No. 18/3/1946.
15. *Punjab Legislative Assembly Debates,* 1946, Vol. XXV, p. 64.
16. Satya M. Rai, *Legislative Politics and the Freedom Struggle in the Punjab 1897-1947,* Delhi, 1984, pp. 320-21.
17. Khizar's meeting with the Cabinet Mission on April 5, 1946, N. Mansergh and Penderel Moon (ed.), *op.cit.,* Vol. VII, p. 148.

18. *Ibid.*, pp. 149-50.
19. Akalis' meeting with the Cabinet Mission on April 9, 1946, *Ibid.*, pp. 170-71.
20. Sir Evan Jenkins to Wavell, May 17, 1946, N. Mansergh and Penderel Moon (ed.), *op.cit.*, Vol. VII, p. 604.
21. Ian Talbot, *Khizar Tiwana: The Punjab Unionist Party and the Partition of India*, p. 151.
22. S.S. Pirzada (ed.), *op.cit.*, Vol. II, p. 513.
23. *Ibid.*, p. 518.
24. *Ibid.*, p. 520.
25. *Eastern Times*, Lahore, April 11, 1946.
26. S.S. Pirzada (ed.), *op.cit.*, p. 558.
27. Punjab Fortnightly Report for the First half of August 1946, *Home Political*, File No. 18/8/1946.
28. *Eastern Times*, Lahore, August 12, 1946.
29. Punjab fortnightly Report for the First half of August 1946, *Home Political*, File No. 18/8/1946.
30. *Eastern Times*, August 10, 1946.
31. *Ibid.*, August 11, 1946.
32. *Ibid.*, August 19, 1946.
33. *Ibid.*, August 20, 1946.
34. *Ibid.*, August 21, 1946.
35. *Ibid.*, August 22, 1946.
36. *The Dawn*, Delhi, August 22, 1946.
37. *Eastern Times*, August 16, 1946.
38. Sarfaraz Hussain Mirza (ed.), *op.cit.*, p. 361.
39. *The Dawn*, September 5, 1946.
40. Punjab Fortnightly Report for the Second half of September 1946, *Home Political*, File No. 18/8/1946.
41. *Eastern Times*, October 26, 1946.
42. Punjab Fortnightly Report for the First half of September 1946, *Home Political*, File No. 18/11/1946.
43. *Ibid.*, First half of September 1946, *Home Political*, File No. 18/9/1946.
44. *Ibid.*, First half of October 1946, *Home Political*, File No. 18/10/1946.
45. *Ibid.*, First half of November 1946, *Home Political*, File No. 18/11/1946.
46. *Ibid.*, Second half of December 1946, *Home Political*, File No. 18/12/1946.
47. *Ibid.*, Second half of November 1946, *Home Political*, File No. 18/11/1946.
48. *Eastern Times*, December 14, 1946.
49. Ian Talbot, *Khizar Tiwana: The Punjab Unionist Party and the Partition of India*, p. 155.

50. Jenkins to Wavell, January 26, 1947, N. Mansergh and Penderel Moon (ed.), 1, *op.cit.*, Vol. IX, p. 556.
51. Sarfaraz Hussain Mirza, *op.cit.*, p. 368.
52. *Eastern Times*, January 26, 1947.
53. *Ibid.*
54. *Ibid.*, January 27, 1947.
55. Jenkins to Wavell, January 26, 1947, N. Mansergh and Penderel Moon (ed.), *op.cit.* Vol. IX, p. 559.
56. Jenkins to Pethic-Lawrence, January 27, 1947, *Ibid.*, p. 505.
57. Jenkins to Pethic-Lawrence, January 29, 1947, *Ibid.*, p. 571.
58. *Ibid.*
59. *Ibid.*
60. See for details, Ian Talbot, 'The Role of the Crowd in the Muslim League Struggle for Pakistan', *The Journal of Emperial and Commonwealth History*, 21, 2, 1993, pp. 315-32.
61. *Ibid.*, pp. 325-32.
62. *Eastern Times*, February 11, 1947.
63. Jenkins to Wavell, February 3, 1947, N. Mansergh and Penderel Moon (ed.), *op.cit.*, Vol. IX, p. 655.
64. Jenkins to Wavell, February 12, 1947, *Ibid.*, p. 680.
65. *Eastern Times*, February 13, 1947.
66. An interview held with Late Dr. S.R. Raheja (my maternal grand father, who was a resident of District Multan, till August, 1947), on 20.10.1996.
67. Penderel Moon, *Divide and Quit*, p. 77.
68. Jenkins to Wavell, March 3, 1947, N. Mansergh and Penderel Moon (ed.), *op.cit.*, Vol. IX, p. 829.
69. *Eastern Times*, February 27, 1947.
70. Jenkins to Wavell, March 3, 1947, N. Mansergh and Penderel Moon (ed.), *op.cit.*, Vol. IX, p. 830.
71. *Ibid.*
72. Ian Talbot, *Khizar Tiwana: The Punjab Unionist Party and the Partition of India*, pp. 160-61.
73. *Civil and Military Gazette*, Lahore, March 4, 1947 and Penderel Moon, *op.cit.*, p. 77.
74. *Ibid.*
75. Jenkins to Wavell, March 5, 1947, N. Mansergh and Penderel Moon (ed.), *op.cit.*, p. 868.
76. Resolution of the Congress Working Committee, March 8, 1947, *All India Congress Committee Papers*.
77. Penderel Moon, *Divide and Quit*, pp. 79-80.
78. *The Statesman*, Delhi, March 11, 1947.
79. N. Mansergh and Penderel Moon (ed.), *op.cit.*, Vol. VII, pp. 582-85.

80. *Ibid.*, pp. 586-97.
81. *Ibid.*, pp. 577-78.
82. *Ibid.*, pp. 581-82.
83. Pattabhi Sitaramayya, *op.cit.*, Vol. III, pp. 801-03.
84. *Ibid.*, pp. 805-06.
85. Penderel Moon (ed.), *op.cit.*, p. 273.
86. *Ibid.*, p. 275.
87. M. Mansergh and Penderel Moon (ed)., *op.cit.*, Vol. VII, p. 955.
88. *Ibid.*, p. 980.
89. H.V. Hodson, *The Great Divide*, pp. 182-83.
90. Maulana Abul Kalam Azad, *India Wins Freedom*, p. 16.
91. P. Sitaramayya, *op.cit.*, Vol. III, p. 848.
92. *The Statesman*, February 7, 1947.
93. *The Dawn*, February 12, 1947.
94. N. Mansergh and P. Moon (ed.), *op.cit.*, Vol. IX, p. 690.
95. H.V. Hodson, *op.cit.*, p. 193.
96. N. Mansergh and Penderel Moon (ed.), *op.cit.*, Vol. IX, p. 920.
97. H.V. Hodson, *op.cit.*, pp. 201-03.
98. P. Sitaramayya, *op.cit.*, pp. 201-03.
99. *The Tribune*, February 8, 1959.
100. *All India Congress Committee Papers.*
101. N.N. Mitra, *Indian Annual Register*, 1947, Vol. I, pp. 111-12.
102. *All India Congress Committee Papers* and N.N. Mitra, *op.cit.*, 1947, Vol. I, pp. 118-19.
103. Sir Evan Jenkins to Lord Mountbatten, March 26, 1947, *Mountbatten Papers.*
104. Staff Meeting of Mountbatten, March 27, 1947, *Ibid.*
105. Jawaharlal Nehru to Mountbatten, April 9, 1947, *Ibid.*
106. Resolution of the Working Committee of Shiromani Akali Dal passed on April 16, 1947 and sent to the Viceroy, *Ibid.*
107. Master Tara Singh, Giani Kartar Singh and Sardar Baldev Singh Interview with Mountbatten, Interview No. 76, April 18, 1947, *Ibid.*
108. *Ibid.*
109. Sir Evan Jenkins to Lord Mountbatten, April 30, 1947, *Ibid.*
110. Jinnah's Interview with Mountbatten, Interview No. 100, April 26, 1947, *Ibid.*
111. Jinnah's Interview with Mountbatten, Interview No. 101, April 27, 1947, *Ibid.*
112. Sir Evan Jenkins to Mountbatten, April 29, 1947, *Ibid.*
113. *The Statesman*, Delhi, May 2, 1947.
114. Sir Evan Jenkins to Mountbatten, May 3, 1947, *Ibid.*
115. Mohammad Ismail Chundrigar Interview with Mountbatten, Interview No. 107, May 3, 1947, *Ibid.*

116. Arthur Smith Interview with Mountbatten, Interview No. 137, May 15, 1947, *Ibid.*
117. *Indian Annual Register*, 1947, Vol. I, pp. 110-11.
118. S.S. Pirzada (ed.), *op.cit.*, Vol II, p. 564.
119. *Ibid.*, p. 568.
120. Partition Proceedings, Vol. VI, pp. 1-6, See Kirpal Singh (ed.), *Select Documents on Partition of Punjab 1947: India and Pakistan*, New Delhi, 1991, pp. 94-95.
121. *The Tribune*, Lahore, June 24, 1947.
122. Sir Evan Jenkins to Mountbatten, June 30, 1947, *Mountbatten Papers*.
123. Partition Proceedings, Vol. VI, p. 89, See Kirpal Singh (ed.) *op.cit.*, pp. 120-21.
124. *The Statesman*, Delhi, July 5, 1947.
125. Partition Proceedings, Vol. IV, p. 169, See Kirpal Singh (ed.), *op.cit.*, pp. 172-73.
126. Sir Evan Jenkins to Mountbatten, May 25, 1947, N. Mansergh and Penderel Moon (ed.), *op.cit.*, Vol. X, p. 985.
127. Punjab Fortnightly Report for the First half of June 1947, *Home Political*, File No. 18/6/1947.
128. Liaquat Ali Khan to Mountbatten, May 30, 1947, N. Mansergh and Penderel Moon (ed.), *op.cit.*, Vol. X, pp. 1033-34.
129. Punjab Fortnightly Report for the Second half of July 1947 and First half of August 1947, *Home Political*, File No. 18/7/1947 and 18/8/1947.
130. *Ibid.*, July 7, 1947.
131. Kirpal Singh (ed.), *op.cit.*, pp. 185, 223, 247.
132. *Ibid.*, p. XXV.
133. Kirpal Singh, *Partition of Punjab*, Patiala, 1972, p. 87.
134. H.V. Hodson, *The Great Divide*, London, 1969, p. 418.
135. *Civil and Military Gazette*, Lahore, August 27, 1947.

Conclusion

The Punjab Provincial Muslim League, as it has become obvious from the present study, in the year 1935-36, was a disorganised, weak, narrowly-based, essentially an urban party with only middle class adherents to it. However, by the year 1946, the Provincial Muslim League became a mass-based instrument of political mobilization and realization of specific political goals. The League, during the most turbulent years in the history of the province, not only transformed its nature and character but also profoundly influenced and shaped the Provincial politics. This led to the establishment of a new nation-state, i.e. Pakistan, in the name of Islam. By all accounts, it was a remarkable achievements for very few political formations could achieve so much in so little period of time.

That the Muslim League in Punjab was weak and narrowly based, too got reflected in the results of the Provincial elections of 1936-37. Out of the 86 Muslim seats, the League obtained only two seats. The Muslim League was defeated because the Unionist Party had occupied a large political space so much so that it articulated even the partisan Muslim interests under a centralist secular umbrella organization. This marginalised the Muslim League since it had not much role left under such a dispensation. As a result, the Punjab Muslim League had little political stature and virtually no following nor any organizational structure. M.A.H. Isphani a close associate of Jinnah, remarked, 'In those days the League had not of course fifty coppers in its coffers. There was no office of the party—the president and the secretary, both honorary, carried their offices in their respective portmanteaus'.[1]

Moreover, the strong Unionist leadership of Fazl-i-Hussain was as tall as Jinnah's , if not taller than him, at least among the Muslims of Punjab. The Unionists under the leadership of Fazl-i-Hussain felt strong enough to rebuff Jinnah's efforts to rope in the Muslim Unionist leadership under the aegis of Muslim League. Fazl-i-Hussain and the Unionists, in fact, did not want to align with a communal party. Thus, Jinnah was told to keep his finger out of Punjab pie.[2]

The elections of 1937, thus, established the hegemony of the Unionists in the politics of Punjab. A disgusted Jinnah left Punjab swearing, 'I shall never come to Punjab again, it is such a hopeless place'.[3] It is indeed, remarkable, that only a decade later the very Jinnah and Muslim League not only became the master of Punjab but also achieved the goal of Pakistan. The Muslim League after the defeat of 1937, and faced with the prospect of being snuffed out politically, began to adopt new strategies, techniques and programmes. Jinnah, a shrewd politician, thought, that first the Muslim League ought to consolidate its position in all-India politics. Only then the Punjab Provincial Muslim League will be in a position to challenge the hegemony of the Unionist Party in the Provincial politics. To achieve this, Jinnah was even prepared, for the moment, to see the Punjab Muslim League to come under the complete control of the Unionist Party. This new strategy of Jinnah led to the signing of the Jinnah-Sikander Pact in October, 1937. Under this pact, the Muslim Unionist also became members of the Muslim League. Jinnah was accepted as the sole spokesman of Muslim India by the Unionist leadership and he was required not to interfere in the affairs of Punjab politics and government.

The Jinnah-Sikander Pact was, in fact, a sort of compromise that entailed advantages as well as disadvantages for the Unionist Party as well as to the Muslim League. Sikander Hayat Khan used this pact to assume complete control of the Punjab Muslim League whereas Jinnah utilized the pact to enhance the prestige of his party in the All-India politics. Besides, the far reaching consequences of the pact proved quite beneficial for the Muslim League. Punjab was an important Muslim majority province and Sir Sikander Hayat Khan was the tallest leader of the Muslims of Punjab. Thus, by joining the Muslim League and accepting Jinnah as sole spokesman of Muslim India, Sir Sikander and his Unionist Party enhanced the prestige of Jinnah and his Muslim League at the national level. Chaudhary Khaliquzzaman, one of the leaders of the League, has also asserted; No one can deny that without this action on the part of Sikander the Muslim League would have confined to the minority provinces alone, Sikander saved Muslim India by associating himself with the Muslim League'.[4]

The beginning of the Second World War, in September 1939, provided another opportunity to Jinnah to raise the influence of the Muslim League in the Indian politics by supporting the British Raj in its War efforts whereas the Congress was vehemently opposing the unconditional War efforts. The British Raj which was badly in need of Jinnah's support at this crucial hour, began to treat Jinnah on equal footing with Gandhi. Jinnah himself remarked, 'After the War was declared, the Viceroy naturally wanted help from the Muslim League. It was only then that he realised that the Muslim League was a power. For it will be remembered that upto the time of the declaration of the War, the Viceroy never thought of me but of Gandhi and Gandhi alone.'[5] This finally resulted in Raj's acceptance of Muslim League as the sole representative body of the Muslim India and Jinnah as its sole spokesman. This encouraged the League to pass the 'Pakistan Resolution' at Lahore in March, 1940.

It has become obvious from the preceding chapters, that how carefully and skilfully, Jinnah, once having gained unquestionable ascendancy in the Muslim politics at the national level, began to intervene in the politics of Punjab. Under Jinnah's inspiration, the Punjab Provincial Muslim League after the Pakistan Resolution began a relentless struggle against the hegemony of the Unionist Party and also started vigorous campaign for the cause of Muslim League and Pakistan. After the death of Sir Sikander Hayat Khan, in December 1942, the Unionist Party started losing political ground and faced erosion of its social base to Muslim League. This was due to League's strong religious appeal, its superior organizational abilities and the role played by the Punjab Muslim Students Federation. Thereafter, the Provincial League went from strength to strength.

The Provincial Muslim League, by early 1944, successfully challenged the dominance of the Unionist Party in the Provincial politics. It freed itself from the clutches of the Unionist Party and for the first time establish an independent Muslim League Assembly Party in the Provincial Legislative Assembly. It gave a tough time to the ruling benches in the Assembly. The Provincial League also made in roads into the countryside of the Punjab. The leaders and workers of the League undertook extensive tours of the countryside, made vigorous propaganda based on Islamic symbols and religious appeals, for the cause of Pakistan. The League also conducted public meetings and Conferences in rural and urban areas. These efforts raised the popularity of the League and its demand of Pakistan also became popular among the Punjabi Muslims. The landslide victory of the League in the Provincial elections of 1946 only reflected the new-found strength of the League in Punjab. Jinnah remarked:

> The Musalmans of Punjab have proved that the Punjab is the foundation stone of Pakistan. In spite of so many hurdles, 90 per cent success is a resounding victory, which the entire Muslim population can be proud of—it is the fatwa of the Muslims of Punjab that Muslim League is the only representative party of Muslims of India.[6]

Here, one witnesses a remarkable transformation of Muslim League from a narrowly based, essentially urban party to a mass based instrument of political mobilization in 1946, which is within a striking distance of achieving its grand goal of Pakistan. What brings about this turn around in the League's fortunes in such a short span of time has been the focus of this study. The foremost role in this turn around was played by a body called Punjab Muslim Students Federation. The Federation, between March 1940 to 1947 and particularly between July 1945 to March 1947, waged a relentless campaign for the cause of Muslim League and demand of Pakistan. They embarked on a highly organized, disciplined and dedicated campaign fanning out to the remotest corners of Muslim majority areas of the province. They made extensive use of religious symbols and Islamic appeals to crystallise a unified pan-national Muslim identity which, according to them, had a common destiny and a common goal i.e. Pakistan. They presented Pakistan as the panacea of all Muslim grievances, both perceived as well as genuine. The methods they employed for their purpose were straight forward and loaded with religion.

They made extensive use of religious platforms like Fridays prayers in mosques, evening prayers and public parading of the Holy Quran. The idea was to extract commitment for the cause of Pakistan. They worked in close collaboration with the local League cadres and even set up training schools to train volunteers for carrying out their propaganda. They evolved their own calender of anniversaries to give their campaign a sharper focus. Accordingly, they started observing 'Pakistan Day' and 'Iqbal Day' every year and holding Pakistan Conferences in major towns of the province. Lauding their role for the cause of Pakistan, Jinnah remarked, 'You have done wonderful work. I have not adequate words to praise all you have done and the sacrifices you have made. How sincerely and selflessly you have worked. I have no power to give you medals and shields or squares of land. But your reward is that you are serving the nation selflessly and sincerely.'[7]

Now, why the Muslim rural landed gentry, hitherto, the backbone of the Unionists in Punjab, defected to Muslim League. This was on two counts: one, the death of Sir Sikander Hayat Khan resulted in a leadership vacuum in the Unionist Party. There was no chrismatic personality left to hold the faction-ridden landed elites together. Two, this vacuum was filled by League with its higher agenda of Pakistan cloaked in a strong religious appeal that transcended the narrow confines of factions and personal interests. In other words, Muslim League presented them with a rallying point that was issue based (read Pakistan) rather than personality based.

At this juncture the desertions from Unionist Party to Muslim League were still few. However, what started of as a trickle became a deluge after the collapse of the Simla Conference where the Unionist leadership was seen as having lost considerable ground *vis-a-vis* the League. The Muslim League, till then, was never perceived as a serious contender for power by the landed elite whose natural instincts were to swim with the tide. This was a big factor in their *volte-face* after the Simla Conference when the tide turned in favour of the League. Characteristically, they dumped Unionist Party for the League.

Another equally important segment among the rural elite were the *Pirs* and *Sajjada-Nashins*. They were influential opinion makers and leaders in their own right in their areas. Their word carried greater weight because they derived their influence from matters spiritual rather than temporal. They had, by and large, supported Unionist Party because of the convergence of their interests with those of the Unionists. But they shifted their allegiance to Muslim League once it was on the ascendant in the province. David Gilmartin suggests they shifted their allegiance to Muslim League because they found its religious appeal closer to their liking.

However, the opinion of David Gilmartin appears only partly valid. This is because, for a vast majority of *Pirs* and *Sajjada-Nashins*, the League's brand of puritan pristine, Arab-inspired Islam went against their grain of localized, personality-based spirituality steeped in local customs, rituals and practices. In fact, the *Pirs* felt threatened by the League's brand of Islam which, they felt, stood to marginalise them in their own pocket boroughs. *Pirs'* agony was further accentuated when many of the League's office-bears *suo motto* appointed themselves as new *Pirs*. This usurpation was the proverbial last straw on the camel's back. The *Pirs* and *Sajjada-Nashins* could take no more and followed the time tested dectum of, 'If you cannot beat them, join them'. Since they could not beat the League, they joined its bandwagon.

Another important aspect is the impact of international events, particularly the Second World War, on the Provincial politics. The Raj, during the course of the Second World War, has been accused of deserting their loyal ally, the Unionists, by eminent historians like Ian Talbot. However, the present study shows that it was not willing desertion on the Raj's part. The Second World War resulted in a sea change in ground realities. The cosy, symbiotic Raj—Unionist relationship became a more complex, multi-dimensional Raj—Muslim League—Unionist interaction in the Punjab, with the Raj forced to do the tight ropewalking between its old loyalist, the Unionist, and the new found ally, the Muslim League.

The Raj, in its endeavour to checkmate the anti-War stance of Congress, had given Muslim League the *'Carte-blanche'*, on the Muslim question. Therefore, the Raj did not want to antagonize the League in the province (the Punjab) which was Central to its two nation theory, and in which it was, in any case, already on the up. It is true that the Raj still needed the Unionist in Punjab. But, now, the Raj needed the League more.

Furthermore, the fate of Punjab Muslim League was, inextricably, linked to the fortunes of Muslim League in the national politics. A decisive turn for the better for All India Muslim League occurred with the resignation of the Congress Ministries in October, 1939. The League seized this opportunity with both hands and observed it as a *Day of Deliverance.* The Congress, till then well-entrenched having decimated Muslim League in 1936 elections, left a political void. The League, in a political master stroke, rushed to fill this void by promising support to the Raj in its hour of need. This gave the League a leverage with the Raj it had never enjoyed before.

The League further pressed home its advantage when it got the Pakistan Resolution passed in 1940 in a province, which though central to its future scheme of things, was still not a happy hunting ground for it due to a strong Unionist presence. With the Pakistan Resolution the League gained both at the national as well as the Provincial level. By making the Unionists a party to this Resolution the League undermined their secular credentials. This marked the beginning of the end of the broad-based, inter-community social coalition that the Unionists represented in Punjab. This eventually led to the emasculation of Unionist Party and a concomitant ascendancy of the League.

At the national level, the League came to acquire a *de-facto* veto on the Muslim question. The Raj, for all practical purposes, recognized it as the sole representative body of Muslim India. The proposals of the Cripps Mission, though rejected both by the Congress and the League, gave an additional talking point to the League because its secession clause was the recognization of the scheme of Pakistan by implication. A disgusted Congress, after the failure of the Cripps Mission, started the Quit India Movement. The League, however, appealed to the Muslims not to participate in the Quit-India arguing that the Congress intended to establish a Hindu Raj. At this juncture the Raj looked to Jinnah for his support which he rendered. With the disappearance of the Congress from active politics for about three years, Jinnah seized the opportunity to consolidate his position and own the confidence of the Raj. The Gandhi-Jinnah negotiations of 1944 and the Simla Conference of 1945 further consolidated the position of the Muslim League.

The above mentioned points enabled the League to hit the 1946 campaign trail with an overt sectarian agenda. A vote for Muslim League is a vote for Pakistan and a vote for Pakistan is a vote for Islam, was the League's war cry. It positioned itself as the sole champion of Muslim interests and reaped a rich electoral harvest. It bagged seventy-five of 86 Muslim seats as opposed to two seats in 1936. It emerged as the single largest party in the Provincial Legislature. The Unionists, though much weakened with 18 seats, spoiled the party for the League. They formed the government with the help of Congress and Akalis to keep the League out. The League was infuriated. Now, it went for the jugular.

The League played the communal card to the hilt and confronted its adversaries head on. On one hand, it launched programmes like *Direct Action Day* which became an unending *Jehad* of sorts. This created fear in the minds of non-Muslim minorities and made the rapprochement impossible. This, in turn, led to final parting of the ways between the communities. On the other hand, the League sought to intimidate the much weakened Unionists into submission by launching agitations and demonstrations against them. The Unionist premier, Khizar Hayat Khan Tiwana, was targeted in particular. He was painted as the main road block in the attainment of Pakistan. Choicest Punjabi invectives were hurled at him. Finally, the Unionists succumbed to the pressure and resigned. The League succeeded in attaining its goal of Pakistan, even if it was truncated and moth-eaten.

Foot Notes

1. M.A. H. Isphani, *Qaid-e-Azam Jinnah As I knew Him*, p. 20.
2. Waheed Ahmad (ed.), *Letters of Mian Fazl-i-Hussain*, p. 428.
3. Azim Hussain, *op.cit.*, p. 311.
4. Chaudhary Khaliquzzaman, *op.cit.*, p. 290.
5. Jamal-ud-Din Ahmad (ed.), *Speeches and Writings of Mr. Jinnah*, Vol. I, p. 154.
6. Ikram Ali Malik, *op.cit.*, p. 590.
7. *Eastern Times*, Lahore, February 21, 1946.

Glossary

Ahrar	Literally, the free; Muslim political party founded in Punjab in 1931 by Mazhar Ali Khan and Maulana Ataullah Shah Bukhari.
Anjuman	Assembly, Society, Committee, Council.
Arain	A cultivator caste in Punjab.
Arya Samaj	A socio-religious reform movement among the Hindus which profoundly influenced the society of Punjab in the late nineteenth and early twentieth centuries.
Azad	Independent, Free.
Baraka	Charismatic power believed to flow from Sufi Saints to their disciples. This power could also be invested in their tombs and relics.
Barani	Unfertile land.
Biradari	Literally, brotherhood; Patrilineal kinship group.
Burqa	The practice of veiling women that has traditionally been more common to Muslims than non-Muslims in India.
Dargah	Tomb; Shrine of a Sufi Saint.
Din	Faith, the Islamic Religion.
Duniya	World.
Fatwa	A legal opinion delivered by a Muslim qualified to interpret Islamic law, namely, an alim or mufti.
Gaddar	A traitor.
Gurdwara	A Sikh temple.
Gurumukhi	Script of the Punjabi language.
Halal	An animal slaughtered as prescribed by Islamic Law.

Hartal	Strike.
Hindu Mahasabha	A political organisation based on Hindu revivalism.
Hukumat-i-Ilahi	The divine government.
Imam	Head in prayers.
Inquilab	Revolution.
Ittehad	Unity, Unionist.
Ittehad-i-Millat	Unity among a religious community (Islamic).
Jagir	Land assignment for the collection of land revenue and a person to whom the land was assigned was known as Jagirdar.
Jamait	Congregation, Collective body.
Jehad	The religious duty of Muslims to establish, if necessary by force, the sway of Islam over the non-Islamic world.
Jhatka	An animal slaughtered by having the head cut off in the Hindu manner.
Kafir	Unbeliever, non-Muslim.
Kalima	The bases of Quran.
Khadi	Hand-spun and hand-woven cloth.
Khaksar	Literally, humble, a para-military organisation led by Allama Mashriqi.
Khalsa	The pure, the Sikh community.
Khanqah	Hospice, alms-house of the early Sufi Saints.
Khans	Title used generally by the Pathans to refer to the landlords or tribal leaders.
Khatri	Hindu and Sikh commercial caste.
Khufristan	Region of Infidels.
Lambardar	Village headman.
Majlis	Assembly, meeting, gathering, party.
Malik	A title of respect used by certain Punjabi communities, for example the Tiwanas and the Noons.
Masheikh	Plural of Shaikh, used for the persons known for their piety.
Maulana	A title of respect reserved for Muslims reputed for their religious learning.
Maulvi	Muslim learned man.
Millat	Religious community (Muslim).
Mohalla	A ward or a street.

Momin	A cultivator caste in the Punjab.
Mussalman	A Muslim.
Murid	The disciple of a spiritual mentor or Pir.
Murdabad	Down with death (a slogan).
Naib Tehsildar	Officer-in-charge of a tehsil, a revenue and administrative sub-division of a district.
Nawab	A title of respect, power and authority used by some Muslim Chieftains.
Panth	The Religion, Sikhism.
Pir	Spiritual mentor or guide having a number of followers.
Piri-Muridi	The relationship of loyalty and obedience between a Pir and his disciple.
Qaum	Community based on religion, descent or nationality, a term used by the elite Indian Muslims in the late nineteenth and twentieth centuries to suggest their distinct religious, racial and social ancestry.
Quaid-i-Azam	A Great leader, a title bestowed upon Muhammad Ali Jinnah by his followers.
Raj	Kingdom, Rule or Sovereignty.
Sajjada Nashin	Literally one who sits on the prayer carpet, custonian of a sufi-shrine.
Safedposh	Rural semi-official, usually subordinate to a Zaildar.
Salar	A Commander.
Sardar	Chief of a tribe.
Satyagraha	Civil disobedience campaign.
Shaikh	Title of respect given to Sufis, caste title for some Punjabi Muslim non-agriculturists also used in some Punjabi communities as a general title of respect.
Shiromani Akali Dal	A political organization of the Sikhs.
Shariat	Islamic law, derived from the Quran and hadis.
Silsilah	Literally chain. Members of a Sufi order who are mystically linked to their Pir and his spiritual descendants.

Sufi	Muslim mystic, the word comes from the coarse woollen garment worn by the early Muslim mystic.
Taluqdar	Used for the landlord in the United Provinces who collected revenue from his own and other estates.
Tehsildar	Officer-in-charge of a tehsil, a revenue and administrative sub-division of a district.
Ulema	Class of Muslim learned in religious sciences.
Urs	Celebration of the death day of a Sufi Saint, major annual festival at many Sufi Shrines.
Zail	Administrative and revenue sub-division of a tehsil, each in the charge of a semi official known as zaildar.
Zamindar	Term is used loosely to refer to any landholder, large or small.
Zindabad	Long live, a slogan of victory.

Bibliography

PRIMARY SOURCES

Unpublished

National Archives of India, New Delhi
Fortnightly Reports of the Criminal Intelligence Department, Punjab.
Home Political Department Records.
Home (Public) Department Records.
Reform Office Records.
Nehru Memorial Museum and Library, New Delhi.
All India Congress Committee Papers.
Bhaulabhai Desai Papers
Gopi Chand Bhargava Papers
Linlithgow Papers
Mountbatten Papers
Sunder Singh Majithia Papers

Muslim League Sources

Unpublished

Syed Shamsul Hasan Collection. This Collection contains the correspondence of Punjab Provincial Muslim League with Mohammad Ali Jinnah during the years when Syed Shamsul Hasan was the Honorary Secretary of the All India Muslim League. I have very gratefully obtained the Photostat copies of these papers from Professor K.C. Yadav. The original Syed Shamshul Hasan Collection is in the possession of his son Khalid Shamshul Hasan of Karachi.

Published

Ahmad, Jamil-ud-Din (ed.), *Historic Documents of the Muslim Freedom Movement*, Lahore, 1970.

Ahmad, Jamil-ud-Din (ed.), *Speeches and Writings of Mr. Jinnah*, Vol. I, Lahore, 1960.

Allana, G. (ed.), *Pakistan Movement: Historic Documents*, Karachi, 1967.

Jafri, S.Q. Hussain, *Quaid-i-Azam's Correspondence with Punjab Muslim Leaders*, Lahore, 1977.

Mirza, Sarfaraz Hussain, *The Punjab Muslim Students Federation: An Annotated Document*, Lahore, 1978.

Pirzada, Syed Sharifuddin (ed.), *Foundation of Pakistan: All India Muslim League Documents, 1906-1947*, 2 Vols., Karachi, 1969-70.

Report of the Inquiry Committee Appointed by the All India Muslim League to Inquire into Muslim Grievances in Congress Provinces, Pirpur Report, November, 1938, Lucknow, 1938.

Sherwani, L.A. (ed.), *Pakistan in the Making: Documents and Readings*, Karachi, 1987.

Zaidi, Z.H. (ed.), *M.A. Jinnah-Isphani Correspondence 1936-1948*, Karachi, 1976.

Official Publications

Griffin, Lepel and Charles Massy, *Chiefs and Families of Note in the Punjab*, 2 Vols., Lahore, 1940.

India, *Census of India*, 1921, Vol. 15, Punjab, Part II, Lahore, 1923.

——, *Census of India*, 1931, Vol. 17, Punjab, Part-II, Lahore, 1933.

——, *Census of India*, 1941, Vol. 16, Punjab, Part-II, Lahore, 1943.

——, *Collected Works of Mahatma Gandhi*, Vol. LXXVII, New Delhi, 1975.

——, *Government of India Act*, 1935, Delhi, 1936.

——, *Report of the Indian Franchise Committee*, 1932, Calcutta, 1933.

——, *Return Showing the Results of Elections to the Central Legislative Assembly and the Provincial Legislatures in 1945-46*, New Delhi, 1948.

Mitra, N.N. (ed.), *The Indian Annual Register, 1936-1947*, Calcutta.

N. Mansergh, E.W.R. Lumby and Penderel Moon (eds.), *Constitutional Relations Between Britain and India: The Transfer of Power, 1942-1947*, Twelve Vols., London, 1970-83.

Punjab, *Administrative Report of the Canals in the Punjab*, 1928-29.

——, *Districts Gazetteers of Punjab*, Various Districts, Various Dates.

——, *Legislative Assembly Debates*, 1937-47.

——, *Legislative Council Debates*, 1923-36.

——, *Provincial Banking Enquiry Committee Report*, Lahore, 1929-30.

Punjab, *Report of the Punjab Provincial Banking Enquiry Committee*, Lahore, 1942.

——, *Report of the Working of Co-operative Societies in Punjab*, 1921.

——, *Report of the Operations of the Department of Land Records in Punjab*, 1939.

——, *Report on the External Land Trade of the Punjab*, 1907-08.

——, *Report on the Administration of Estates under the Charge of the Punjab Court of Wards*, Annual Series, 1911 and 1921.

——, *Settlement Reports of Punjab*, Various districts, various dates.

Newspapers

Civil and Military Gazette, Lahore
Eastern Times, Lahore
Harijan, Ahmedabad
The Dawn, Delhi
The Statesman, Delhi
The Tribune, Lahore.

SECONDARY SOURCES

Books

Afzal, M. Rafique, *Barkat Ali: His Life and Writings*, Lahore, 1969.

Ahmad, Syad Nur, *Mian Fazl-i-Hussain: A Review of His Life and Works*, Lahore, 1976.

Ahmad, Waheed (ed.), *Letters of Mian Fazl-i-Hussain 1924-1936*, Lahore, 1976.

Ahmad, Waheed (ed.), *Diary and Notes of Fazl-i-Hussain*, Lahore, 1977.

Ali, Imran, *Punjab Politics in the Decade before Partition*, Lahore, 1975.

Ambedkar, B.R., *Pakistan or the Partition of India*, Bombay, 1946.

Ansari, Sarah F.D., *Sufi Saints and State Power: The Pirs of Sind 1843-1947*, Cambridge, 1992.

Azad, Abul Kalam, *India Wins Freedom*, Bombay, 1960.

Aziz, K.K., *The Making of Pakistan: A Study of Nationalism*, London, 1957.

Bahadur, Lal, *The Muslim League: Its History, Activities and Achievement*, Agra, 1954.

Banerjee, A.C., *The Constitutional History of India*, Vol. III, Delhi, 1978.

Bolitho, Hector, *Jinnah: Creator of Pakistan*, London, 1954.

Batalvi, Ashiq Husain, *Iqbal Ke Akhari Do Saal* (Urdu), Lahore, 1978.

Brass, Paul, *Language, Religion and Politics in North India*, Cambridge, 1974.

Brown, Judith, *Gandhi and Civil Disobedience: The Mahatma in Indian Politics 1928-34*, Cambridge, 1977.

Calvert, Hubart, *The Wealth and the Welfare of the Punjab*, Lahore, 1936.

Chand, Duni, *The Ulster of India or An Analysis of the Punjab Problem*, Lahore, 1936.

Chand, Tara, *History of Freedom Movement in India*, Vol. IV, New Delhi, 1972.

Chandra, Bipan, *Nationalism and Colonialism in Modern India*, New Delhi, 1979.

Chandra, Bipan, *Communalism in Modern India*, New Delhi, 1984.

Chatterji, G.C., *The Punjab Past and Present*, Lahore, 1929.

Chatterji, Joya, *Bengal Divided: Hindu Communalism and Partition, 1932-1947*, Cambridge, 1995.

Chhabra, G.S., *Social and Economic History of the Punjab 1849-1901*, Jullundur, 1962.

Chopra, G.L., *Chiefs and Families of the Note in the Punjab*, Lahore, 1940.

Choudhry, Prem, *Punjab Politics: The Role of Sir Chhotu Ram*, New Delhi, 1984.

Collins, L. and Lapierre, D., *Mountbatten and the Partition of India*, Vol. I, New Delhi, 1982.

Coupland, Reginald, *Indian Politics 1936-1942—Report on the Constitutional Problem in India*, London, 1944.

Darling, Malcolm Lyall, *The Punjab Peasant in Prosperity and Debt*, London, 1925.

Das, M.N., *Partition and Independence of India: Inside Story of the Mountbatten Days*, New Delhi, 1982.

Datta, V.N., *Ideology of the Political Elite in Punjab 1900-1920*, Patiala, 1978.

Dixit, Prabha, *Communalism: A Struggle for Power*, Delhi, 1974.

Gandhi, Raj Mohan, *Understanding the Muslim Mind*, New Delhi, 1987.

Gilmartin, David, *Empire and Islam: Punjab and the Making of Pakistan*, California, 1988.

Gopal, Madan, *Sir Chhotu Ram: Political Biography*, Delhi; 1977.

Gopal, S., *Jawaharlal Nehru: A Biography*, Vol. I, 1889-1947, Delhi, 1976.

Gopal, S. (ed.), *Selected Works of Jawaharlal Nehru*, Vol. III, New Delhi, 1977.

Gupta, H.R., *History of the Punjab*, New Delhi, 1973.

Hardy, Peter, *The Muslims of British India*, Cambridge, 1972.

Hasan, Mushirul, *Nationalism and Communal Politics in India*, New Delhi, 1979.

Hasan, Mushirul (ed.), *India's Partition: Process, Strategy and Mobilization*, Delhi, 1993.

Hodson, H.V., *The Great Divide: Britain, India and Pakistan*, London, 1969.

Hussain, Azim, *Mian Fazl-i-Hussain: A Political Biography*, London, 1966.

Ikram, S.M., *Modern Muslim India and the Birth of Pakistan*, Lahore, 1970.

Isphani, M.A.H., *Quaid-e-Azam Jinnah as I knew Him*, Karachi, 1966.

Jalal, Ayesha, *The Sole Spokesman: Jinnah, the Muslim League and the Demand for Pakistan*, Cambridge, 1985.

Jones, Kenneth W., *Arya Dharm: Hindu Consciousness in the 19th Century Punjab*, Delhi, 1976.

Josh, Bhagwan, *Communist Movement in the Punjab*, Delhi, 1979.

Khaliquzzaman, Choudhary, *Pathway to Pakistan*, Lahore, 1961.

Kumar, Ravinder, *The Making of a Nation: Essays in Indian History and Politics*, New Delhi, 1989.

Low, D.A. (ed.), *Congress and the Raj: Facets of the Indian Struggle 1917-1947*, London, 1977.

Malhotra, S.L., *Gandhi: An Experiment with Communal Politics*, Chandigarh, 1975.

Malhotra, S.L., *From Civil Disobedience to Quit India*, Chandigarh, 1979.

Malik, Iftikhar Haider, *Sikander Hayat Khan 1892-1942: A Political Biography*, Islamabad, 1985.

Malik, Ikram Ali, *History of the Punjab 1799-1947*, Lahore, 1970.

Mathur, Y.B., *Muslims and Changing India*, New Delhi, 1972.

Mehrotra, S.R., *Towards India's Freedom and Partition*, New Delhi, 1979.

Mehta, A. and Patwardhan, A., *The Communal Triangle in India*, Allahabad, 1942.

Menon, V.P., *The Transfer of Power in India*, Bombay, 1957.

Metcalf, Thomas R., *The Aftermath of the Revolt*, Princeton, 1965.

Mittal, S.C., *Freedom Movement in the Punjab 1905-1929*, New Delhi, 1977.

Mirza, Sarafaraz Hussain, *The Punjab Muslim Students Federation 1937-47*, Islamabad, 1991.

Moon, Penderel, *Divide and Quit*, London, 1961.

Moon, Penderel (ed.), *Wavell: The Viceroy's Journal*, Oxford, 1973.

Moore, R.J., *Churchil, Cripps and India 1939-1945*, Oxford, 1979.

Moore, R.J., *Escape from Empire: The Attlee Government and the Indian Problem*, Oxford, 1983.

Mujeeb, M., *The Indian Muslims*, London, 1967.

Nath, Amar, *The Development of the Local Self Government in the Punjab 1849-1900*, Lahore, 1929.

Nair, Lajpat Rai, *Sikander Hayat Khan: The Soldier Statesman of the Punjab*, Lahore.

Nehru, Jawaharlal, *An Autobiography*, New Delhi, 1962.

Noon, Firoz Khan, *From Memory*, Lahore, 1966.

Noman, M., *Muslim India: The Rise and Growth of the All India Muslim League*, Allahabad, 1942.

Page, David, *Prelude to Partition: The Indian Muslims and Imperial System of Control 1920-32*, Oxford, 1982.

Pandey, B.N. (ed.), *Leadership in South Asia*, New Delhi, 1977.

Panikkar, K.N. (ed.), *Communalism in India: History Politics and Culture*, Delhi, 1991.

Philips, C.H. (ed.), *The Evolution of India and Pakistan 1858-1947; Select Documents*, London, 1962.

Philips, C. H. and Wainwright M.D. (ed.), *The Partition of India: Policies and Perspectives, 1935-47*, London, 1970.

Prasad, Bimal, *Pathway to India's Partition*, Vol. 1: *The Foundation of Muslim Nationalism*, New Delhi, 1999.

Prasad, Bimal, *Pathway to India's Partition*, Vol. 2: *A Nation Within A Nation*, New Delhi, 2000.

Punjab Provincial Muslim League, *Manifesto of the Punjab Provincial Muslim League*, Lahore, 1944.

Punjab Unionist Party, *Aims and Objectives of the Punjab Unionist Party (Urdu)*, Lahore, 1936.

Puri, Nina, *Political Elite and Society in the Punjab*, Delhi, 1987.

Qureshi, I.H., *The Struggle For Pakistan*, Karachi, 1965.

Rai, Satya M., *Partition of the Punjab*, Bombay, 1975.

Rai, Satya M., *Legislative Politics and the Freedom Movement in Punjab 1849-1947*, New Delhi, 1984.

Rizvi, Gowher, *Linlithgow and India: A Study of the British Policy and the Political Impasse in India 1936-1943*, London, 1978.

Robinson, Francis, *Separatism among Indian Muslims: The Politics of the United Provinces Muslims 1860-1923*, Cambridge, 1974.

Saini, B.S., *The Social and Economic History of the Punjab 1901-39*, Delhi, 1975.

Sayeed, K.B., *Pakistan: The Formative Phase 1875-1948*, London, 1968.

Shah, Sayed Wiqar Ali, *Ethinicity, Islam and Nationalism: Muslim Politics in the North-West Frontier Province 1937-1947*, Oxford, 1999.

Shaikh, Farzana, *Community and Consensus in Islam : Muslim Representation in Colonial India, 1860-1947*, Cambridge, 1989.

Sikander Hayat Khan, *Outline of a Scheme of Indian Federation*, Lahore, 1939.

Singh, Anita Inder, *The Origins of the Partition of India 1936-1947*, New Delhi, 1987.

Singh, Durlab, *The Valiant Fighter: A Biographical Sketch of Master Tara Singh*, Lahore, 1940.

Singh, Fauja, *A Brief Account of the Freedom Movement in Punjab*, Delhi, 1972.

Singh, Ganda, *History of the Gurdwara Shahidganj*, Lahore, 1935.

Singh, Khushwant, *A History of the Sikhs*, 2 Vols., Princeton, 1966.

Singh, Kirpal, *Partition of the Punjab*, Patiala, 1972.

Singh, Kirpal (ed.), *Select Documents on Partition of Punjab 1947: India and Pakistan*, New Delhi, 1991.

Singh, Mohinder, *The Akali Movement*, Delhi, 1978.

Sitaramayya, Patabhi, *History of the Indian National Congress*, Vols. 1 and 2, Bombay, 1947.

Smith, W.C., *The Muslim League*, Lahore, 1945.

Smith, W.C., *Modern Islam in India*, Lahore, 1945.

Talbot, Ian, *The Punjab and the Raj 1849-1947*, New Delhi, 1988.

Talbot, Ian, *Provincial Politics and the Pakistan Movement: The Growth of the Muslim League in North-West and North-East India, 1937-1947*, Delhi, 1988.

Talbot, Ian, *Khizar Tiwana: The Punjab Unionist Party and the Partition of India*, Richmond, 1996.

Tanwar, Raghuvender, *Politics of Sharing Power: The Punjab Unionist Party 1923-1947*, New Delhi, 1999.

Tika Ram, *Sir Chhotu Ram: An Apostle of Hindu-Muslim Unity*, Lahore, 1946.

Thorborn, S.S., *The Punjab in Peace and War*, London, 1904.

Thorborn, S.S., *Musalmans and Moneylenders in the Punjab*, Delhi, 1923.

Tuteja, K.L., *Sikh Politics 1920-1940*, Kurukshetra, 1984.

Ullah, A., *The Co-operative Movement in the Punjab*, London, 1937.

Verma, D.C., *Sir Chhotu Ram: Life and Times*, New Delhi, 1981.

Wolpert, Stanley, *Jinnah of Pakistan*, Oxford, 1985.

Yadav, K.C., *Elections in Punjab 1920-1947*, Tokyo, 1981.

Zaidi, M.A. (ed.), *Evolution of Muslim Political Thought in India*, New Delhi, 1978.

Zaman, Mukhtar, *Students' Role in the Pakistan Movements*, Karachi, 1978.

Unpublished Ph.D. Thesis

Dhingra, Jayoti—*The Congress and the Partition of India, 1940-47*, Kurukshetra University, Kurukshetra, 1991.

Tanwar, Raghuvender—*The Unionist Party in Punjab 1923-1947*, Kurukshetra University, Kurukshetra, 1989.

Articles

Ali, Imran, 'Relations Between the Muslim League and the Punjab National Unionist Party 1935-1947', *The Journal of South Asia,* VII, II, 1980, pp. 47-55.

Bajaj, Y.P., 'Unionist Politics and the General Elections of 1936-37: An Analysis', *Punjab History Congress Proceedings,* Patiala, 1986, pp. 331-52.

Barrier, N.G., 'The Punjab Government and Communal Politics, 1870-1908', *Journal of Asian Studies,* 27, 3, 1958, pp. 180-205.

Baxter, Craig, 'Union or Partition: Some Aspects of Politics in Punjab 1936-1945', *Pakistan: The Long View,* ed. by L. Ziring, Duke, 1970, pp. 40-69.

Baxter, Craig, 'The People's Party *v.s.* the Punjab Feudalists,' *Journal of Asian and African Studies,* VIII, 4, 1990, pp. 166-89.

Choudhury, Prem, 'The Congress Triumph in South-East Punjab: Elections of 1946,' *Studies in History,* 2.2, 1980, pp. 81-110.

Churchil, Edward D., 'Muslim Societies of the Punjab 1860-1890', *The Punjab Past and Present,* April, 1974, pp. 117-36.

Datta, V.N., 'Interpreting Partition', General Presidential Address, *Indian History Congress Proceedings,* 1996, pp. 4-24.

Gilmartin, David, 'Religious Leadership and the Pakistan Movement in the Punjab', *Modern Asian Studies,* 13, 3, 1979, pp. 485-517.

Gupta, R.S., 'The British Raj and the Communal Question: Sept. 1939—Jan. 1940', *Indian History Congress Proceedings,* 1973, Vol. II, pp. 56-69.

Heegar, G.A., 'The Growth of the Congress Movement in the Punjab 1920-49', *Journal of the Asian Studies,* 32, 1, 1972, pp. 43-64.

Malik, Iftikhar H., 'Identify Formation and Muslim Party Politics in the Punjab, 1897-1936: A Retrospective Analysis', *Modern Asian Studies,* 29, 2, 1995, pp. 293-323.

Mehrotra, S.R., 'Reflections on Indian Nationalism', *First Deva Singh Memorial Lecture,* November 1997.

Moore, R.J., 'Jinnah and the Pakistan Demand', *Modern Asian Studies,* 17, 4, 1983, pp. 529-61.

Oren, Stephen, 'The Sikhs, Congress and the Unionists in British Punjab, 1937-45,' *Modern Asian Studies,* 8, 3, 1974, pp. 397-418.

Pandey, Deepak, 'Congress-Muslim League Relations 1937-39,' *Modern Asian Studies*, 12, 4, 1978, pp. 629-54.

Talbot, I.A., 'The 1946 Punjab Elections,' *Modern Asian Studies*, 19, 1, 1980, pp. 65-91.

Talbot, Ian, 'The Growth of the Muslim League in the Punjab 1937-46', *Journal of Commonwealth and Comparative Politics*, 13, 1, 1982.

Talbot, I.A., 'Deserted Collaborators: The Political Background to the Rise and Fall of the Punjab Unionist Party, 1923-1947', *The Journal of Imperial and Commonwealth History*, October, 1982, pp. 73-93.

Talbot, I.A., 'The Role of the Crowd in the Muslim League Struggle for Pakistan', *The Journal of Imperial and Commonwealth History*, 21, 2, 1993, pp. 315-30.

Tanwar, Raghuvender, 'Origin of the Punjab National Unionist Party: Feudal Elite and Legislative Politics,' *Journal of the Pakistan Historical Society*, April, 1995, pp. 153-63.

Tuteja, K.L., 'Hindu Consciousness, Communalism and the Congress in Pre-Partition Punjab,' Presidential Address, Modern Indian History, *Indian History Congress*, Bangalore, 1997.

Willmer, David, 'Women as Participants in the Pakistan Movement: Modernization and the Promise of a Moral State', *Modern Asian Studies*, 30, 3, 1996, pp. 573-90.

Yadav, K.C., 'The Partition of India: A Study of the Muslim Politics in Punjab, 1849-1947,' *The Punjab Past and Present*, April, 1983, pp. 105-44.

Index

Q

R

S

T

U